THE ART OF TECHNIQUE

THE ART OF TECHNIQUE

An Aesthetic Approach to Film and Video Production

John S. Douglass

Glenn P. Harnden

School of Communication
The American University

Allyn and Bacon
Boston • London • Toronto • Sydney • Tokyo • Singapore

Vice President, Humanities: Joseph Opiela
Editorial Assistant: Susannah Davidson
Marketing Manager: Karon Bowers
Editorial-Production Administrator: Donna Simons
Editorial-Production Service: Ruttle, Shaw & Wetherill, Inc.
Composition and Prepress Buyer: Linda Cox
Manufacturing Buyer: Aloka Rathnam
Cover Administrator: Suzanne Harbison

Coláiste
Mhuire Gan Smál
Luimneach

	791·4301
	DOU
	17000864

Library of Congress Cataloging-in-Publication Data

Douglass, John S.
  The art of technique : an aesthetic approach to film and video
production / John S. Douglass, Glenn P. Harnden.
    p. cm.
  Includes index.
  ISBN 0-205-14248-6
  1. Motion pictures—Aesthetics. 2. Cinematography. 3. Motion
pictures—Production and direction. 4. Video recordings—Production
and direction. I. Harnden, Glenn P. II. Title
PN1995.D68 1996
791.43′01—dc20   95-24513
                                                                         CIP

Printed in the United States of America

10 9 8 7 6 5 4 3 2 1   00 99 98 97 96 95

*This book
is dedicated to
John Huston, Thom Noble, Roman Polanski,
Martin Scorsese, Ridley Scott, Robert Towne, Peter Weir, Vilmos Zsigmond
and other film and video artists
whose work has
enriched and enthralled us,
to our students,
who have taught us at least as much as we
have taught them,
and to
Jinx, Ghada,
Eric, Lina, James, and Earle.*

CONTENTS

PREFACE

The reason we think you are reading this book is that, somehow, film, video, or television has touched your imagination and now you want to know how to create the wonderful experiences these media can induce. You want to use these forms of visual communication and personal expression to speak to others, to invoke emotions, and to construct persuasive visions of reality.

Just as art students learn by studying the masters, film and video students can learn by studying the works of great film and video artists. The reader will find that the references to films and television series in the index are fairly extensive and emphasizes more current productions rather than older classics. This is to specifically encourage the reader to go to these works and study them. Videotape makes it easy to examine the craft of writers, directors, cinematographers, and editors and to discover techniques that communicate and create beautiful, interesting, and moving moments on the screen. Videotapes and laserdiscs cannot reproduce the effect of large screen productions, but they are readily available and make repeated viewing possible. They enable students to examine productions closely, using the pause, slow-motion, rewind, and fast-forward scan controls. Clearly these media are invaluable texts for students of production.

We believe some contemporary works, *Witness, Raging Bull, Chinatown,* and *Thelma & Louise,* for example, are classics and will become so recognized as time passes. More pertinent to our purposes, however, is that these works illustrate modern techniques that form the basis of contemporary production practice. We refer to the techniques used in these and other works as examples of what the reader can accomplish, even with a low budget.

In film, video, and television production, it is helpful to recognize the difference between technical proficiency and technique. Technical proficiency is the body of skills that provides the foundation for effective work in film and video production. We learn technical production competence in the same way a painter discovers how to handle the brush and palette knife, or learns the basics of color, composition, and perspective.

The importance of technical proficiency with film, video, and television equipment must not be underestimated. But, when we apply technical methods without plan or purpose, they become mere contrivances, and we lose their potential as a means of expression. Technique is the application of the technical methods of production for coherent, expressive purposes. We intend for this book to encourage students to go beyond technical proficiency toward the thoughtful application of technique for the articulation and interpretation of content.

Many fine books are available to provide film and video students with useful information on the technical aspects of production. Some texts are broadly inclusive and survey basic methods from preproduction through postproduction. Other, usually more advanced, texts explore just one production area, such as lighting, cinematography, audio production, or editing. Some texts deal with film production exclusively. Others are "how-to" books for students of video production. The content of these books ranges from technical explanations, such as how to operate cameras, measure light, select microphones, and build SMPTE editing decision lists, to more conceptual discussions, such as shooting and editing for continuity, executing camera angles and framing, casting and rehearsing talent, and juxtaposing sound and picture.

In addition, there are several good texts that guide students through the process of writing nonfiction and theatrical scripts. Some of these emphasize script formats and formula plot construction, whereas others emphasize the creative process and the basics of good storytelling. Many encourage students to think about how they treat subjects, develop themes, and create interesting narratives, but few of them go on to suggest how the tools of production can realize these intentions.

We believe this book can be useful to screenwriting students as well as to students of production. A script is not the end of the process, only the beginning. The screenwriter's work is the first creative step, which serves as a guide towards the final product, the work on the screen. This book deals with formulating and interpreting subject and theme and with realizing the intentions of the script through the production process. It takes up such concerns as finding and developing ideas for the screen, creating portraiture, building narrative structure, and using symbols. Such topics are a major concern to screenwriters as well as to producers and directors.

This text supplements technical instruction with methods for purposefully using the media as a coherent means of expression. What we have tried to present is a discussion of production techniques as a thoughtful series of creative decisions that effectively interpret scenes, subjects, and themes. Our goal is for students of production who read this book to learn how to coordinate these decisions to produce the kinds of works that can engage us, arouse our feelings, and transport us into the worlds portrayed on the screen.

We thank A. B. Cooper, Jr., who read every page of the preliminary draft and offered detailed comments that were consistently helpful. In addition, we thank Courtney Froemming for her thoughtful comments on the second draft; Kelly Murphy, who helped in gathering stills for use in this text; Peter Kent, Andrew Long, Miho Nasu, and Steve Rosa, who read portions of our drafts and made helpful suggestions; and April Cantor and Nate Clapp for their willingness to appear as subjects in our photographic illustrations. We would also like to thank the following reviewers of the text for their helpful comments and suggestions: Allan Barber, Temple University; Dominique Caristi, Missouri Southern State College; J. Robert Craig, Central Michigan University; Stephen Mims, University of Texas at Austin; Dennis Pack, Winona State University; Michael Schoonmaker, Syracuse University; Dave Viera, California State University, Long Beach; and Patricia R. Zimmerman, Ithaca College.

1

INTERPRETATION AND TREATMENT

Interpretation

Gertrude Stein's rose may be a rose, but ten different artists painting a rose will render it in ten different ways. The subject is the same, but the treatment is different.

The 1931 version of *The Front Page,* directed by Lewis Milestone, with Adolph Menjou as the editor battling with reporter Pat O'Brien, was adapted from the stageplay by Ben Hecht and Charles MacArthur. In 1940, Howard Hawks remade it as *His Girl Friday,* starring Cary Grant as the editor and Rosalind Russell in the gender-switched role as reporter, but it was essentially the same story. Ben Hecht even co-wrote the screenplay. Billy Wilder remade it in 1974, going back to the original title and re-switching the reporter's gender to star Jack Lemmon with Walter Matthau. In 1988, director Ted Kotcheff made the re-re-re-make as *Switching Channels* with Burt Reynolds and re-switched the gender to let Kathleen Turner play the role now changed to a TV reporter.[1]

Why were so many versions of *The Front Page* made? Although the basic story is the same in each version, the different treatments, or interpretations, allow the directors to explore different themes: interpersonal relationships, character issues, social struggles, financial interests versus personal integrity, the value to women of a professional career versus being a homemaker, and so on. In each case, the treatment is unique.

Treatment of the Subject

The term "treatment" as it pertains to a film, video, or television production refers to how the process and techniques of production will contribute to the interpretation of a given subject, idea, or script. Treatment has to do with interpreting the subject, exploring an idea, or using production as a vehicle to explore themes. It also means getting an audience to think about or experience something in a new way.

In selling products—from Coke and Pepsi to candidates for public office—each new campaign treats the product differently than the previous one. The product or subject doesn't change; the treatment does. It reinterprets the product for the audience. It casts it in a new light with hopes that the audience will reconsider and become stimulated to buy something that has become too familiar. It's not the product that sells the product, it's the advertising agency's angle, device, or treatment of the product.

In theater, the script is a text not to be trifled with the way it is in film, but stage actors, directors, and scene designers still look on it as something to be interpreted. Given the same lines, Kenneth Branagh's *Henry V* is quite different from Sir Laurence Olivier's interpretation of the same play.

There is a tradition of restaging the action of a play in a different period to give the production new dimension, to get the audience to rethink the drama. If we put a different spin on a piece, different aspects become more relevant as they are made more prominent. *Richard III,* performed in stark, black Nazi-esque costuming, plays up the parallels of Richard to a Hitler-type despot. *West Side Story* reinterpreted *Romeo and Juliet* in the context of contemporary gang rivalry, first as a Broadway musical and then again as a film. *The Tempest* had its story line and characters cast into the future in the classic 1956 science fiction film *Forbidden Planet.* Perhaps the reason for the enduring success of Shakespeare's works is that the plays are almost like Rorschach ink blots. They allow production companies to discover, reinterpret, and reveal different themes with each production.

Books are often treated differently when they are made into films. Although many suffer in the transition, an excellent example of a successful treatment is Francis Ford Coppola's *Apocalypse Now,* based on Joseph Conrad's *Heart of Darkness.*[2] Coppola's treatment is interesting. He restaged the story from colonial Africa to wartime Vietnam and drastically changed the interpretation of the characters and the story itself. However, he preserved the theme of the painful trek into the dark side of human character.

It is not a production's story, plot, information, or facts that make it unique; it is how we interpret them. Once we have decided on a subject for a production, we have only begun. The critical endeavor still before us is to create a coherent and meaningful interpretation of the subject. Formulating an interpretation of the subject involves determining purpose, discovering theme, employing technique, and exercising imagination and originality.

Determining Purpose

Identifying the purpose of a production usually begins by identifying the intended audience. Journalists and essayists always consciously address their audiences. Poets and novelists sometimes forget or ignore this concern and may address themselves. Film, video, and television productions usually are made to convey thoughts, ideas, emotions, and experiences to an audience.

Let's see how purpose can affect the treatment of a subject in a production. Suppose we have an opportunity to do a film or video on the subject of fox hunting. The project might be on contract for a client, or it might even be that a fox hunt is a scene within a larger theatrical or documentary production.

The subject of fox hunting is fertile. The activity involves many elements which we can show, emphasize, or disregard. We may, for example, decide not to reveal how hunting dogs are trained, but go to considerable length to display the horse-riding ability involved. We may take some time to detail the habits of the fox. The tone of our piece can be exuberant, seriously dramatic, comic, even horrific. Depending on our purposes, we can present fox hunting in nearly endless variations.

What are our purposes? If we are doing an educational or public relations piece for the American Horse Council, the scenes of fox hunting we create will probably look very different from the scenes we might create for the Defenders of Wildlife. One version will be an ode to grace, strength, and discipline; the other, a dark lament of mayhem and murder. The American Horse Council may want to educate an audience in the historical background and medieval traditions of fox hunting. The Defenders of Wildlife probably want to discourage the sport to save the fox.

Perhaps another client might want to use the scene in a commercial as a colorful backdrop for its fall line of clothes. Maybe a local television station would like a documentary piece on horse and dog trainers, both skilled veterans and young apprentices. Their slant might be on those who have chosen a rural way of life over the routines of city and suburbs.

Maybe this is our own idea. Driving through the countryside, we saw a fox hunt, became interested, and decided to do a short piece for our portfolio. Perhaps this is a scene in a dramatic production. We want to provide a striking context for a hostile confrontation between adversaries for a young woman's attentions. Maybe we want to provide a comic setting for a social-climbing urbanite with genteel pretenses and a total lack of equestrian aptitude.

We may have many different purposes for doing a piece about fox hunting. Whatever our purposes, they will affect our interpretation of the scene and our treatment of it.

Discovering Theme

This is where our creativity begins. This is where we examine our attitude toward the subject, study the material, and analyze our knowledge of the audience to determine themes that will resonate between the production and audience. Theme allows us to focus our attention (and ultimately the audience's) on certain aspects of the subject while excluding others. To the extent that we can discover our theme *before* we go into production and use it to determine our treatment of the subject, we will use time and often limited resources effectively.

Shooting without a clue, the scatter-gun approach, forces us to discover what our production is about while editing. We then must use those scenes and shots that support our theme as best we can. This unfocused approach to production is expensive and risky because we will end up discarding much of what have we shot. It affects the quality of the production because the coordination of techniques to support a single theme wasn't planned. At best, there's serendipity. At worst, there's reshooting. In the middle is mediocrity.

For the moment, let's assume we are doing the fox hunting piece for the American Horse Council. They like our suggestion to emphasize the history and antique traditions of the sport. For this purpose, one theme we probably will highlight is the ritual quality of pageantry and traditions inherent in the sport. Riding boots, flared breeches, red jackets, hunting horns, titles, ceremony, formalities—all become material to support this theme within our historic rendition of fox hunting.

To convey the theme of pageantry, we might choose to execute shots of our hunters on their horses from a low angle. The low angle would accentuate height and dignity, but the angle should not be so low as to cause the hunters to loom monstrously. We might use shorter-than-normal focal lengths. This would exaggerate size. Again, the focal length shouldn't be so extreme or the camera placed so close that it would distort faces, figures, and even the horses' heads. We could work with longer focal lengths to capture quick actions and flood the frame with bright color and motion. We might use a long lens to compose close-up portraits—a profile, perhaps, as the huntsman raises the horn to his lips. Our strategy might be to seek out compositions in both wide and close framings that exhibit formal, balanced patterns and repeated regularity. In editing, we would emphasize an orderly pace and perhaps select appropriate English horn music for the sound track.

How different this piece would be if our purpose were to discourage the sport and we chose to develop a theme of insensitive cruelty. Our material might include laughing faces, exchanges of social pleasantries, and contrasting shots of thundering hooves, dark shadows, tumult, and disorder. For techniques, we might employ extreme angles, distorting lenses, unstable compositions with disjointed patterns, and drab or disturbing colors. Wide, bucolic point-of-view shots from the rider's level above the horse might be intercut with closely shot, fast-paced, ground-level tracking shots from the quarry's perspective. Editing would emphasize erratic rhythms and violent juxtapositions, and the music might contrast harpsichord with a noisy blare of brass and percussion.

The techniques we use—the shots we take, the angles and framing we select, the lens focal lengths we use, the pacing and rhythms and juxtapositions we edit, the sound tracks we compose and build—all depend on the theme we wish to support to serve the purpose of the production. Treatment, then, is the interpretation of a subject through techniques selected according to the purposes we have for a presentation.

Employing Technique

Techniques render and interpret subjects, giving them significance. Technique is inextricably integrated with content. In the fine arts—painting, for example—techniques of mixing and applying color with brush or pallet knife are intrinsically intertwined with the interpretation of the subject and how it is to be presented on canvas. The tools of presentation in any media are the tools of interpretation.

The techniques of film and video are the tools we use to build our interpretation of the subject. Technique is a way to make the content of a presentation have meaning. Technical facility is useless without a well-conceived subject. However, even the most interesting or important subject can be made boring and pointless if the director does not know how to present it. Ultimately, technique serves theme and becomes merged with content.

Exercising Imagination and Originality

The final facet of treatment goes beyond execution and moves the production more into an area of visual artistry and design. This enables us to create productions that are powerful visual experiences that provide memorable images for an audience.

Intelligently conceived visuals are often integral to subject and theme. As shown in Figure 1.1, John Seale's shot of the tractor trailer truck stuck on a country road behind the Amish horse and buggy in the opening of *Witness*

FIGURE 1.1
Intelligently shot visuals, such as John Seale's shot of the tractor trailer truck stuck on the country road behind the Amish buggy in the opening scene of *Witness,* are often integral to subject and theme.

"WITNESS" Copyright © 1995 by Paramount Pictures. All Rights Reserved. Courtesy of Paramount Pictures.

supports the conrasting worlds in which the story takes place. The starkly composed shot by Gordon Willis of Woody Allen with Mariel Hemingway in the apartment living room in *Manhattan* sets the tone of their relationship. Nicolas Roeg's sensuous camera work playing over the limbs of the trees in *Walkabout* serves as a visual metaphor for the lovemaking going on beneath the boughs.

Sometimes these scenes simply amplify the visual text: the beautiful night-time shots of Monument Valley by Adrian Biddle in *Thelma & Louise;* Gregg Toland's starkly silhouetted reporters in the projection room of *Citizen Kane;* Freddie Young's spider web shot in *Ryan's Daughter;* Vilmos Zsigmond's other-worldly mountaintop shot at the beginning of the hunting scene in *The Deer Hunter.*

Sometimes memorable shots occur by accidents of nature or by being ready at that right moment when something happens. Dumb luck. Much more often, however, such fine images are a result of previsualization. This comes about through a clear understanding of the purpose and theme of our production, and through careful planning, often storyboarding angles and actions, and then taking the time to get the shots. Too often, productions are behind, the crew is rushed, and we have barely enough time to execute the photography with any sense of craft and purposeful technique. But, as good and professional as this work can be, it's that little bit extra that earns the Emmys and Oscars.

Virtual Reality

Treating Reality in Documentary

In film and video, we commonly make a distinction between documentary and theatrical genres. Documentary productions present fact; theatrical productions present fiction. Because we think of documentary as presenting "real" subjects, we can easily misunderstand the processes of documentary production and believe that the documentary genre uses no techniques and provides no interpretation of subject. Nothing could be further from the truth.

The simple fact is that most of the world is interpreted to us. Media producers—writers, editors, filmmakers, videographers, and so on—present subjects to us with the intent of making the content understandable, interesting, and significant. Usually there is the further intent of attributing to the subject recognizable qualities—handsomeness, beauty, credibility, ugliness, dangerousness, and so on.

The mass media convey most of what we know about the world to us. Books, television, movies, newspapers, radio, and magazines bring us a world far greater and richer than is available to us through direct experience. We are familiar with many people, for example, only through the media: Socrates, Napoleon, Thomas Jefferson, D. W. Griffith, Richard Nixon, Norman Mailer, Dan

Rather, and David Letterman. Few of us have ever met the famous people we know, living or dead. Yet, these well-known individuals are so familiar to us that it is easy to forget that our knowledge of them is constructed of images and impressions presented through the media. For most of us they are products of manufactured presentations. They are a part of a "mediated" reality, to use a term popular among some media theorists.

All film and video images are artifacts created by intelligent people who cannot avoid imparting relative importance to subjects merely by exercising selectivity in what they shoot. It is impossible not to interpret subjects when presenting them through media devices. Even the most neutral presentation of a locked-down security camera interprets a scene through camera height and direction, lens focal length, image resolution and size, and so on. That *any* presentation through media is an artifact, an interpreting construction, is unavoidable. On any location, simply the choices of where to place the camera, where to point the camera, what lenses to use, and what to include in the frame—all can be arbitrary and meaningless, or a series of production decisions based on subject, theme, and treatment.

Differences in subject affect the way we deal with a documentary setting. We would shoot a classroom quite differently, for example, depending on whether our subject was the teacher or a student. Even after we have defined the subject, we can apply significantly different treatments to the subject depending on our purposes.

Intention

In documentary and theatrical production, when we conceive a topic and think about our purposes, we then translate our intentions into a script. The intentions of the script become the intentions of the production.

The Written Treatment

Often writers make a written treatment of an idea or story before developing it into a script as a way to work out story and character ideas. Writers also write treatments to help define and refine their intentions, which are sometimes not obvious in the initial stages of conception.

Written treatments describe the action of the production in the *present tense* as if the writer were describing the show exactly as it unfolds on the screen. The writer tells us only what we see and hear. Although a treatment may summarize action and the points being made by narration or through dialogue, it should not describe inner motivation beyond what the viewer could discern from watching the production.

Word choice is essential to convey mood and pacing, as well as to suggest shots and points of view. The writer rarely mentions specific shots. However, when the treatment is read, the reader should begin to "see" shots. Obviously it helps to see the shots in our mind as we write the treatment so we can convey our visualization. In other words, we could have the following descriptive passage:

> *The huntsman blows his horn and the riders take off across the fields behind the pack of hounds.*

This certainly describes the action in the story, but as we begin to *see* this action in terms of shots in our own mind, we might describe the action as follows:

> *The huntsman sounds the call. With a snap of quirt and jab of spur, the horses leap forward. Hounds, eager to be free, streak across the field. The riders lean to the withers. Grim exaltation burns in their eyes.*

In this last example, we can see an MS (medium shot) of the huntsman blowing his horn. We then cut to a CU (close-up) of a quirt snapping a horse's neck and another CU of a boot kicking back into a horse's flank. An MS of the hounds pans with them as they lunge forward and holds as they take off across the field. This cuts to a long-lensed tracking MS of a determined rider with several other riders compressed into the background of the shot.

A well-written treatment telegraphs to the reader a visual image of each of the story's important scenes. Occasionally a bit of dialogue in a treatment not only helps give the flavor of the intended project, but also helps define the characterization. It is a good idea to work out the visualization of the production in the treatment and be concerned about dialogue or narration during the scripting phase. This helps avoid productions that lack action and visual interest.

A treatment can range in length from a short synopsis to a full-blown short story approaching the length of the finished script. For the sake of developing story detail and evolving characters beyond stereotypes, we usually encourage beginning students to err on the side of lengthiness rather than brevity.

Interpreting the Script

In narrative production, the subject is in the script or story. As the producer or director,[3] we try to identify what touches, excites, amuses, or interests us in the story. Through deciding purpose and defining themes, we discover our intentions.

The writer initiates and first expresses the intentions of a production. Producers and directors form their own intentions for a production, based on their reaction to the writer's material and what they hope will be the ultimate reaction of the audience. Often the intentions of a production can be quite different from the writer's original intentions. The script is like the rough-hewn piece of wood before being put on the lathe. It has shape and form and we can perceive its ultimate use, but what this piece of wood will look like still depends on the craft and vision of the person at the lathe.

Producers or directors look for that spark that attracts them to a project. They look for how a project resonates within themselves. This is perhaps something akin to a theme or a concept or a perception about the human condition they wish to express using this script as a vehicle. They hone and develop that aspect of the production in all its facets. Their intention becomes the purpose for the production as a whole and for individual scenes and sequences, as well as the key to the motivation of the characters.

Once the intention is defined, the role of the producer or director is to convey this vision of the production—the treatment of the production—to the photographer, scene designer, and talent. Within the context of this general vision, those involved in the production will contribute their interpretation, technique, and artistry.

The goal of most productions is not to regurgitate the hackneyed images of previous productions, but to strive to create something new. There has long been a competition to make a more unique chase scene, for example. For years, the chase scene over the hills of San Francisco in *Bullitt* was acknowledged as one of film's all-time best. In 1971, director William Friedkin took a credible shot at the title in his film *The French Connection*. Since then, we have seen directors trying for the definitive chase sequence using kids on dirt bikes, helicopters, or even sixteen-wheeler trucks.

Expression through technique as it contributes to interpretation is what makes production satisfying. Treatment enables us to push the envelope, go beyond what others have done, take audiences and characters to new places. We can, of course, use cliché and stereotype treatments to make lap dogs look cuddly, playing children look cute and effervescent, graveyards look sad and grim, poor people look pathetic, farmers look folksy, Italian restaurants look romantic, steel workers look tough, mountain rivers look pure and liberating, and so on. However, treatment also allows us to impart qualities *not commonly associated* with a subject. We then can go far beyond cliché and develop original and truly interesting variations.

How could we present a lovable looking dog so that it is fearsome and terrifying (*Cujo*)? How could we show threatening, scary children (*Village of the Damned*), or a scene of children playing that creates an ominous sense of doom (*Terminator 2*)? What about a rollicking graveyard scene (*The Addams Family*), an evil-corrupted mountain river (*Deliverance*)? A home into a prison (*Misery*)? A murderous television producer into a winner (*The Player*)?

Treatment gives meaning to action. Take the simple, everyday action of washing the dishes, for example. As directors, how might we treat the scene of a couple doing dishes if: (1) the man and woman involved are having an argument and getting more and more angry or (2) the man and woman involved have recently met, are strongly attracted to each other, and are telegraphing their erotic desires.

It is easy to see how we can instruct our talent to act differently in each of these scenarios. We can apply different treatments to the scenes using distinctive combinations of technique. For example, we could light the fighting scene harshly, the romantic scene softly. We can use short focal lengths for the fight scene to create depth of field and distort features. We could use longer focal lengths on the romantic scene to make the depth of field shallow, softening the focus on the background. In terms of composition, we could contrive rounded, bubbly, sparkling frames for the romantic scene, whereas for the fight scene we could compose angular, hard-edged frames with dingy or disturbing colors.

Almost all directors regularly confront scenes of normal activities of daily living. These scenes provide vehicles through which to interpret emotion and meaning. Unlike literature, film and video do not lend themselves easily to interior monologues. A literary line such as, "She knew she would never understand how he felt," is impossible to render on the screen. There is nothing that can be shot.

Film and video render inner states of mind only through outer manifestations of action or through voice-over. On the screen, we can only show what we can shoot. Occasionally a practiced director can execute an interior monologue that does not seem too contrived—the voice-over narrations in *Apocalypse Now, Little Big Man,* and *Dances with Wolves* come to mind. In each of these instances, the voice-over device is introduced early and used sparingly throughout. Often, however, such devices can be self-conscious and break the illusion of reality that the director is striving to create.

Alternatively, directors and scriptwriters will express emotions and meaning through the day-to-day actions in which characters find themselves. It is the treatment of these actions that makes them significant. Consider, for example, the scene in *Kramer vs. Kramer* in which Ted (Dustin Hoffman) copes for the first time with the necessities of the kitchen and breakfast after he and his wife, Joanna (Meryl Streep) have separated. (See Figure 1.2.) As his son looks on with concern, Ted attempts to fry eggs. At the same time, he tries to make coffee with one of those diabolical espresso coffee makers that use a screened plunger to force the grounds to the bottom of a glass carafe. Making coffee becomes a wonderful vehicle with which to express Ted's anxiety and ineptitude. The scene of scorched eggs and burned fingers ends with Ted erupting coffee all over the kitchen. This is a powerful example of using everyday action to give outward manifestation to an inner state of mind.

Personal Style

The artistic choices we note as we employ the techniques of film and video, the ideas, visions, and themes we choose to explore as we interpret our subject, begin to define our unique styles as creators of film, video, and television. It

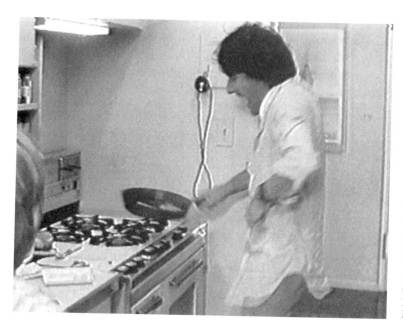

FIGURE 1.2
In *Kramer vs. Kramer,*
Ted (Dustin Hoffman)
coping with breakfast
is a powerful example
of using everyday
action to give outward
manifestation to an
inner state of mind.

begins with the selection of the subject or idea for the production. It concludes in the significance and meaning of the work we create.

We come, then, to the central thesis of this book. After choosing the subject, we must consider our treatment, which is the *use of technique to express ideas.* Technique is not just technical skill and hardware proficiency. Technique is not just a way to execute concepts conceived separately and independently from the medium. Technique provides the terms with which we express our ideas. It is the method for the expression of thought and meaning. It is not separate from subject. Technique both serves the intelligent presentation of subject and is integral to the very rendering and interpretation of subject.

In the creative process, any subject is incomplete and undefined without technique that is organized in coherent treatment. How technique serves content—interprets content—is the subject of this book. It is the method of *treatment.*

Exercise

Read the following four scenes. Analyze each separately, making notes on purpose and theme. In producing these scenes, what techniques would you use? Do any of them spark your creativity? Produce one or more of the scenes (or make up your own where the subject is the same, but the treatment varies.)

INT.-KITCHEN-NIGHT

The door opens and FRED enters. He's of medium height, thirty-ish, and not bad looking. He crosses to the refrigerator and starts to open the door when his eyes hit the note held in place by a magnetized noteholder. He snatches it from the door and reads: *I'm sorry, Fred, I've thought it over and I still love Enrico. By the time your read this, I'll be gone.*

He pauses, looks around, then, forgetting the refrigerator, exits the kitchen . . .

INT.-LIVING ROOM-NIGHT

. . . enters the living room and slowly sits in the arm chair by the fireplace. He picks up a magazine and begins to turn the pages.

INT.-KITCHEN-NIGHT

The door opens and FRED enters. He's of medium height, thirty-ish, and not bad looking. He crosses to the refrigerator and starts to open the door when his eyes hit the note held in place by a magnetized noteholder. He snatches it from the door and reads: *We did it! We won! Ed McMahon called and we're multimillionaires! I've gone for champagne! Trudy.*

He pauses, looks around, then, forgetting the refrigerator, exits the kitchen . . .

INT.-LIVING ROOM-NIGHT

. . . enters the living room and slowly sits in the arm chair by the fireplace. He picks up a magazine and begins to turn the pages.

INT.-KITCHEN-NIGHT

The door opens and FRED enters. He's of medium height, thirty-ish, and not bad looking. He crosses to the refrigerator and starts to open the door when his eyes hit the note held in place by a magnetized noteholder. He snatches it from the door and reads: *Congratulations on surviving so long. But you haven't won until you've spent the entire night in Poltergeist Palace! We are watching.*

He pauses, looks around, then, forgetting the refrigerator, exits the kitchen . . .

INT.-LIVING ROOM-NIGHT

. . . enters the living room and slowly sits in the arm chair by the fireplace. He picks up a magazine and begins to turn the pages.

INT.-KITCHEN-NIGHT

The door opens and FRED enters. He's of medium height, thirty-ish, and not bad looking. He crosses to the refrigerator and starts to open the door when his eyes hit the note held in place by a magnetized noteholder. He snatches it from the door and reads: *You are surrounded. Give up the girl and walk out with your hands up. You have ten minutes.*

He pauses, looks around, then, forgetting the refrigerator, exits the kitchen...

INT.-LIVING ROOM-NIGHT
...enters the living room and slowly sits in the arm chair by the fireplace. He picks up a magazine and begins to turn the pages.

Notes

1. Some remakes or reinterpretations are very instructive and we recommend them to you. Of the ones listed here, you might want to look at the original *The Front Page* and *His Girl Friday.* Others worth comparing are the two versions of *Cape Fear, The Magnificent Seven* with *The Seven Samurai,* and *Dangerous Liaisons* (the 1988 version directed by Stephen Frears) with *Valmont.*

2. *Hearts of Darkness* by Eleanor Coppola chronicles her husband Francis Ford Coppola's efforts to treat the Conrad story and is not only an excellent documentary, but one of the best movies on movie making.

3. The role of a producer in television as the individual with ultimate responsibility and creative control over the production approximates the role of a director in feature film production. The producer in feature film production is more associated with the business aspects of the project, and the director in television is more associated with coordinating the craftspersons on the production to execute the vision of the producer.

2

IDEAS

The Storytellers

As makers of film, video, and television, we are the storytellers. Storytelling may be the most important civilizing factor of our species. Stories are the glue of cultural heritage, passing on traditions, histories, and social mores. Stories give meaning and purpose to our lives and help us define heroism, leadership, responsibility, love—all the ideals that guide our actions. Stories define our enemies and bury them when they are defeated. Stories interpret religion, give succor to the downtrodden, and carry secrets to the besieged. All societies have both revered and reviled the storyteller. Considering the media of today, not much has changed.

Typically storytellers in ancient societies would be the repository of the events and deeds of the clan or tribe. They would regale young and old, recounting tales heard hundreds of times for generation after generation. As tribes grew into kingdoms and kingdoms into nations, the storyteller carried news of far-off events and deeds to the various pockets of civilization in the form of ballads, chronicles, epic sagas, plays, and the like. From these traditions came the Bible; *Beowulf;* the fables of Aesop; the stories of Geoffrey Chaucer and the Grimm brothers; the stories about Anansi, Br'er Rabbit, and Paul Bunyan; and the marvelous tales of storytellers in our own age, from Damon Runyon and William Faulkner to Alfred Hitchcock, George Lucas, and Steven Spielberg.

Conflict and Mood

The storyteller's gift is to discern conflict in events, and among and within characters, and to relate these conflicts meaningfully and with feeling. The drama, the excitement, and the voice of the storyteller, rising, falling, changing pace, and weaving the actions into a fabric of emotions that envelopes, involves, and electrifies us—these are the basic elements of story. Within this context, the good storyteller can reveal truths of the human condition, convey social or political consciousness, teach values, and, through allegory, preach religion—all while entertaining an audience.

When analyzing the seminal forms of conflict, we quickly realize that there aren't too many possibilities. Most stories rely on a mere handful of basic predicaments because there are only so many ways in which a character can become involved in conflict. Take a film like *Jurassic Park*. It has story elements of "Jack and the Beanstalk" and "Hansel and Gretel," especially the scene where the children return to the main pavilion and discover all the food. Many of our basic stories derive from forms we've known since childhood.

Jack the Giant Killer

One prominent basic story is some variation on the conflict of individual cunning, intelligence, and perseverance against brute strength or power. This is the basis for David and Goliath as well as *Peter Pan, High Noon, Scent of a Woman,* the Bill and Ted films, all of the James Bond stories, many horror films, and movies such as *Kagemusha* and *Dirty Harry*. In nontheatrical production, this kind of story takes the form of exposés of government, industry, and other powerful interests in conflict with the interests of communities or individuals. We find these in the reports on *20/20* and *60 Minutes,* and in documentaries such as Michael Moore's *Roger and Me*. (For the sake of convenience, when we refer to nontheatrical, we mean those that are not narrative such as industrial or government-sponsored informational or motivational productions, educational or anthropological productions, or television documentaries.)

Prince and the Pauper

Another story variation is based on the conflicts arising out of how the other side lives, often showing the exotic, the remote, or obscure in ways parallel to our own. In effect, this is a version of the weak defeating the strong by uncloaking and revealing the high and mighty to be the same as we are. Obviously this is a "Prince and the Pauper" type of story. It is similar to stories like *Cyrano de Bergerac, Citizen Kane,* and *The Philadelphia Story;* television shows like *Green Acres* and *Dallas;* and most supermarket tabloids. Reversing this—making us like them, or the meek inheriting the wealth—is the rags-to-riches "Cinderella" type of story. A few of the many examples that come to mind are *Born Yesterday, The Beverly Hillbillies, Fresh Prince of Bel Air,* and *Pretty Woman*.

Clash of the Titans

Similar to the weak versus strong is the clash of the titans. In these, two opposing forces are more nearly equal in strength, power, and cunning, but generally, good triumphs over evil. This encompasses many myths and legends describing battles of elemental forces, historical accounts, and stories based on history such as Shakespeare's *Henry V* and Eisenstein's *Alexander Nevsky*. Many modern stories fit this type, such as the *Star Wars* films or the *Star Trek* series where the Federation starship "Enterprise" battles the Klingons, Romulans, and other alien forces. This type of dramatic conflict gives interest to news coverage of the President versus Congress, Democrats versus Republicans, cops versus criminals, the public versus their elected representatives. It also involves stories of one strong individual in conflict with another, like *Dracula; Miracle on 34th Street; Prizzi's Honor; Driving Miss Daisy;* the Godzilla, Rambo, or Terminator movies; and, during the political campaign season, candidates conflicting with each other.

The Peacemaker

Often "good" is defined as protecting or saving the weak. These are stories about peacemakers like *Shane, The Seven Samurai,* many westerns, and almost any of the many Robin Hood or Tarzan stories. Peacemakers are not necessarily always representatives of law and order. Clint Eastwood's *The Unforgiven* is a peacemaker story in which the peacemaker is a "man of notoriously vicious and intemperate disposition." Peacemaker stories are usually exciting because peace is established only after much bloodcurdling mayhem.

Triumph of Courage

Often "bad" is not an adversary but an adversity such as disease, disaster, famine, flood, a great white whale, or the darker side of our own human nature. The stories are presented as triumphs of human fortitude, the individual as survivor. These stories are as old as the story of Noah and the epic of Gilgamesh and are the foundation of Shakespeare's *The Tempest,* and films like *The Gold Rush, The Poseidon Adventure, Death of a Salesman, Terms of Endearment,* or *Repulsion.*

Tempting Fate

A basic story structure rooted in mythology is one in which a group or an individual challenges divine order. It's a clash of the titans where the concept of free will battles the rules of the universe. Aspects of this are found in the biblical stories of Adam and Eve, Cain and Abel, and Lot's wife. Perhaps the most famous of the Greek plays, Sophocles' *Oedipus Rex,* and Shakespeare's *Julius Caesar* are stories of a man's violation of acceptable behavior. Films such as *The Seventh Seal, Easy Rider,* and *The Mosquito Coast* explore this idea as well as the series of films engendered by Mary Shelley's *Frankenstein.* Generally, in these stories, the hero loses or is forced to recant.

Role Reversals

Role reversal stories are a marvelous way to exploit social conflicts. Shakespeare exploited the possibilities in *Twelfth Night.* More recently, Steve Martin played the son of black sharecroppers in *The Jerk,* and Jack Lemmon and Tony Curtis joined an all-girl band in *Some Like It Hot.*

During the 1940s, when it must have seemed like role reversal to most audiences, a variety of women played typically male roles in films such as *His Girl Friday.* We get a sense of this in Penny Marshall's more recent *A League of Their Own.*

Fish Out of Water

The fish out of water story is a variation on role reversal except that it typically puts the character in situations or timeframes that evoke the social conflict rather than switching the character with another person. Mark Twain's *A Connecticut Yankee in King Arthur's Court* is a marvelous example. All the *Back to the Future* films fall into this category, as well as *Big,* the television series *A Hitchhiker's Guide to the Universe,* and *Sister Act.*

Many of the earlier comedy films placed their heroes or comedy teams in a variety of settings such the Hope and Crosby "Road" pictures or Laurel and Hardy's *A Chump at Oxford, The Devil's Brother* (eighteenth-century Italy), and *Bonnie Scotland* (with British troops in India). The heroes didn't really change, but the settings did. Several science fiction films and stories fit into this category, including *King Kong,* Jules Verne's *Journey to the Center of the Earth,* and the film *Westworld.*

It is probably true that, to some extent, any film that presents an exotic location or historical period appeals to the audience. It allows *them* to explore a different vista as "fish" themselves.

Strange Bedfellows

Strange bedfellow stories are those that play on the extremes of character conflict. Perhaps the most famous of these is the film and later television series *The Odd Couple. Twins,* pairing Arnold Schwarzenegger with Danny DeVito as genetic brothers, is another delightful example. Most comedy teams are paired based on this convention, from Stan Laurel and Oliver Hardy to Lucille Ball and Vivien Vance. Not just comedy, but everything from the light drama of Spencer Tracy and Katharine Hepburn to mysteries like the *Thin Man* series of films relies heavily on the contrast in two major characters. Two other excellent examples are *The African Queen* and *Rain Man.*

Buddy Pictures and Love Stories

Stories about relationships are often an extension of the strange bedfellows type of story, except that the focus is not so much on characters' differences, but on their coming together as friends or lovers. Many stories fit this grouping. There are the buddy pictures like *Becket, Butch Cassidy and the Sundance Kid, Arthur, 48 Hrs., Lethal Weapon, Thelma & Louise,* and *The Goodbye Girl.* Romance stories abound with examples such as *Romeo and Juliet, A Man and a Woman, Love Story,* and *Elvira Madigan,* or where the love theme is turned to social satire and commentary as in *Shampoo* or *Valmont.*

Ship of Fools

In the ship of fools type of story, the conflict comes from a group of well-defined and quite different characters thrust together in the story. *Return of the Secaucus Seven, The Big Chill, Grand Canyon,* and *Deliverance* are some examples. Most of these stories bring contrasting characters together for such purposes as creating conflict, developing character, and establishing interesting relationships.

The Quest

The quest story, usually involving a trial of the spirit, is another basic form. Mythology tells of the trials of Hercules; the Bible relates the story of the Exodus. Homer gave us *The Odyssey.* Chaucer gave us *The Canterbury Tales.* And, of course, there are the King Arthur legends. *Pinocchio* is a quest story as are *Huckleberry Finn, Stagecoach, Little Big Man, The Treasure of the Sierra Madre, Das Boot, Apocalypse Now, Chinatown,* and most mystery stories and whodunits in which a puzzle must be solved.

Portraiture

Films can also be about individuals. Frequently an individual has such strength of character or has made such an enormous contribution to our world that we can concoct a story around that person's life. Conflicts are those with which the individual struggled that made them great. Shakespeare treated *Macbeth, King Lear, Richard III,* and *Othello* with a great deal of portraiture. Cinema has a long tradition of portraiture from Eisenstein's *Ivan the Terrible, Part I,* to the variety of film portraits of actors, inventors, sports figures, war heroes, and politicians. This type of story lends itself to nonfictional biographies such as *Lust for Life,* the story of Vincent Van Gogh; *Annie Get Your Gun,* Irving Berlin's musical based on the life of Annie Oakley; or the made-for-TV production of *The Jesse Owens Story.* However, there have been some excellent semifictional portraits as well, for example, *Auntie Mame, Annie Hall,* and *The Autobiography of Miss Jane Pittman.*

Portraiture is often at the base of good documentary and nontheatrical production. The nonnarrative or documentary approach may also follow a segment of the person's life as that person confronts adversity or adversaries. However, another approach to portraiture is to start with what the audience may already know about the individual and move into what makes the person both human and unique. The audience wants to know what makes this person tick. Here the production may choose to free itself from rigid chronology, which often is part and parcel of narrative production. In cases in which the subject is process, portraiture adds interest and depth to the production.

We can also apply the idea of portraiture to places or events. Fred Wiseman's *The Store* about Neiman Marcus, *High School* about the Philadelphia public school system, or *Primate* about the Yerkes Primate Center all use the techniques or treatment of portraiture applied to a place, stripping away facades and letting reality show through.

Often these basic story lines or plot patterns are combined. Because quest stories tend to be episodic, we might combine one with a conflict between a weak but wily protagonist and a strong and powerful adversary. *Terminator* is in this vein, whereas *Terminator 2* is more of a clash of titans model, with the boy, John Connor (Edward Furlong), and his Terminator (Arnold Schwarzenegger) proving to be strange bedfellows. Sometimes, as in *The Gods Must Be Crazy,* portraiture dominates story conflict altogether.

The basis of a story is conflict. People—or more often, a particular person who wants something, needs something, or has a goal to achieve—is in conflict with another person, the system, the odds, the gods, the enemy without, or the enemy within.

Stories

Story ideas are everywhere. People are always in conflict. What makes a particularly good story, however, has to do with how significant the conflict is both to the person involved in the story and to our audience. Significance to an audience is partly a function of how well we can touch our audience with true emotion—fear, surprise, anxiety, laughter, sympathy, or empathy. If the piece is funny, for instance, the conflict may not have to be very significant. Often, shows like *Roseanne* or *Seinfeld* will take a small problem or everyday conflict and work it for its humorous aspects. Generally, though, the conflict has to have importance to the person and cause some significant, perhaps irreversible change.

Our ability to turn events and individuals into stories depends on our ability to see the impact of events and actions on individuals. In fact, because emotions drive actions more often than rational thought does, it's more than just being able to see the impact. We must *feel* the impact by projecting ourselves into these scenes and experiencing them as they parallel our own lives. The death of a pet, an embarrassing moment at school, or with a date, love, lust, fear of the unknown, lack of confidence, and frustrations with parents, with stupidity, and with the system are all part of the continuum of emotional experiences on which we can call.

Your Experiences

The best source of story ideas is your own self. They come from your own interests, from what you respond to, from your experiences, and from your knowledge.

What are you majoring in? What's the subject matter of the books you like to read? Magazine articles? What sorts of news stories do you tend to follow? Do you read space and science books? Do you enjoy *Scientific American* and *Omni,* read sci-fi? If so, it's pretty obvious that the sciences interest you, even if you didn't do well in them in school. Interest is what really counts. Often an interest is better than an expertise in a subject. Stick to what interests you. How are you going to make an interesting production, if you really don't care? Start by listing your general interests: topics, people, places, events, themes, stories, and so on. As you discover new interests, add them to your list.

It's not too soon to begin carving out an area of production expertise or to begin developing a type or style of production you want to pursue. Whatever your interests are, there are probably groups of people with similar interests—community groups, political organizations, trade organizations, or even associations that hold regular meetings or conventions. If you are not a professional in a particular field, you may not be able to join specific professional organizations. However, most organizations publish journals and specialized publications that may be available through a subscription or at the library.

Beyond specific areas of interest, it helps to have a general awareness of our times. There is no substitute for being broadly educated, well read, and well informed. Film and video producers make their living presenting and interpreting subjects. Knowledge is their stock in trade. Most media producers are curious by nature and enjoy learning about the world around them. They have wide-ranging interests and are generally knowledgeable in the arts, sciences, humanities, and current affairs. Many producers, writers, directors, and actors are familiar with their culture and consider themselves active players in it. It's not by accident that people involved in film and television are vocal on a variety of issues and causes. Even in the feature film and entertainment television industries, producers regularly try to ride the crest of popular culture. They always seem to be looking for innovative ways to approach issues in the current cultural dialogue.

Professionals try to stay informed about international, national, regional, and local events. Legislators, responding to changing social needs, pass legislation leading to new programs and new areas of support and research. Shifts in the economy alter trends in industry, manufacturing, and services in the private sector. At the most practical level of making a living in the film and video business, it pays to keep abreast of these public and commercial activities. New social programs and new products require both investigation and dissemination to the public of information, which will take the form of news features, documentary segments, and contracted public information productions.

By staying knowledgeable about current work and research in the areas that interest you, you will begin to see which individuals, organizations, and government agencies have similar interests. This may help locate financing, sympathetic participants, or likely production companies to support your project. Both the private and the public sector regularly produce public information productions, public service announcements, or sponsored programming on subjects you may care about. They may also be a source of funding for projects you would like to make.

When these projects become available, there is usually some kind of bidding process for the job. The more aware you are of what is going on in the field, the better you can bid an approach that is a unique and effective idea based on an informed understanding. It will be up to date, cut to the heart of important issues, provide insight, and be provocative.

Often social or scientific research grants require some kind of documentation and reporting at the end of the grant. Look for foundations that support research in an area in which you are interested, and for universities, individuals, or organizations that do the research. Many researchers don't think of film or video as documentation or reporting, but maybe they can be convinced of it and at least a part of a production you want to make can be paid for out of their grant.

Other Sources for Story Ideas

A good source of stories outside your own experiences is the newspaper. Many made-for-TV movies come from stories in the *New York Times, Los Angeles Times,* or the *Wall Street Journal.* Others come from magazines, novels, and nonfiction works. These are stories that grab some producer's imagination. In the newspaper account, the producer sees conflict, struggle, human interest, or values—perhaps an inspiring example of the indomitable spirit of an individual struggling through a conflict with someone or something. An example of a particularly strong TV movie was *The Burning Bed*. This was a story of a woman whose husband habitually beat her and her ultimate revenge by setting him on fire. Many TV movies are Jack the giant killer stories based on the true-life struggles of real individuals.

A good idea is to keep a clipping file of stories in the paper that catch your interest or imagination. Years may go by before you ever refer to them, but often these are the seeds of terrific tales.

If you do see a story that captures your imagination, obviously it's possible to approach the person in the story. You can conduct an interview, get more information, and create a script or production based on the person's experiences. Be aware that involving an actual person's "story" means you must obtain the rights to it. These can be optioned for a time for a small percentage of their full value. If the other person is willing, the rest can be paid contingent on the sale of the script or production. If the idea is hot enough, but a producer doesn't want *your* script nor *you* to produce it, the producer may still buy the rights from you at a handsome profit for both you and the original owner. If this is your plan, first check with the individual whose story you want to see if the rights are available and negotiable. Then seek out an attorney to help you draft a simple agreement between you and the individual.

Often, however, the idea that captured your attention in the story can be easily translated to another situation, character, or period. You can preserve the element that attracted you to the story without the specifics that might conjure the dark clouds of law suits.

Stories for Episodic Television

Creating a production for an existing cast and story arena, as in an existing television series where characters and format are locked, still presents the problem of coming up with a story. When we are creating something for an existing cast and established sets or locations, we don't want to suggest too many changes or additions. We want to serve that cast and use some combination of the basic conflict situations in a way that has contemporary appeal.

Portraiture may not seem an obvious approach, but reversing the process of constructing a portrait may be helpful in identifying a unique treatment. If we can identify the core of the character, what is at the character's heart, and then remove it, perhaps we will find interesting character behavior. Look at the center of the character. What makes him or her tick? Knock it out, take it away, and what would the character do?

In *Murphy Brown,* what is Murphy without "FYI"? In the first seasons, she was a middle-aged, former alcoholic who dated occasionally, but lived alone. In the last season she was with the show, Diane English created the baby, giving Murphy a new center. This altered Murphy and the show forever. Even on a smaller scale, if for a short period your character couldn't do something the character normally does in the story, what would he or she do?

Another approach is to reverse the buddy story structure. Push the relationships to the edge, stretch them, and then let them come back. What is Seinfeld's attitude toward George? What would he be willing to do or give up for George? Inventing circumstances that test characters and relationships is always a rewarding way to find stories.

Inspiration

Ideas or observations can just come out of the blue, in a moment of inspiration. Sometimes, for example, overheard bits of conversation or brief scenes in real life that we witness will momentarily catch our attention and trigger our imagination. Always keep pen and paper nearby to jot down your ideas. Good ideas often beget other good ideas, and suddenly we find ourselves on a creative roll.

These moments may be infrequent and often the logic of how one idea hooks to the next may get lost in the excitement of the creative moment. It is possible that the idea will remain intact against the onslaught of conversation, music, sleep, or daily activities, but more than likely it will diminish or get lost altogether. *Write ideas down,* even if it means turning on the light in those last precious moments before drifting off to sleep. Keep them in a notebook or idea file or apply them to the project at hand. Inspiration is a jewel that should not be lost.

Lack of Inspiration

Writers call it "writer's block," but anyone can hit a snag in creating a story, making decisions about approach, or working out treatment. The key to success in all production phases, including writing, is organization and a disciplined approach.

If you think you are a night person, you might be wrong. Try getting up early in the morning and work before the day has had a chance to have much impact on you. It's important to start writing even if you don't know what to write. Summarize your ideas for the project, what you know about the subject. Write down problems and possible solutions. If confusion or feeling lost is one of your problems, write that down, too. Often the act of putting these in front of yourself makes them easier to sort out.

Make an outline. Create a road map. Make a plan of what has to be done, by whom and by when. List everything you know that will go into the production. Write down what the audience already knows and what they need to know before the ending. Or, work backwards. Don't discard notes or scraps of ideas. Keep all the garbage. Somewhere in there might be the word, scene, name, or sentence that will serve as a point of departure for a new path.

Sometimes we know too much about the subject or the "real" actions of a person get in our way as we are developing the character. In these cases, we may begin to lose perspective on the core idea or core conflict for the project. We should always be able to go back to the original idea that attracted us to the project. Did any visual images come with that idea? Any action? Is perhaps a scene or a mood associated with the idea? If so, start over from there. Try to think of different openings, different types of conflict. Change the point of view to another character or individual. Look again at the purpose of the production. How would you explain it in twenty-five words or less?

It's not unusual to have an idea that, at first, seems trite and overdone. With so much exposure to media programming, we may find that our first ideas are often simply replications of productions we've already seen. It's important to go beyond this stage and brainstorm the idea, thinking up possibilities and asking questions that can lead to genuine originality. For most of us, most of the time, real creativity is not so much a matter of spontaneous intuition. It takes persistence and not being satisfied with an idea at first blush. Pursuing it makes it singular and exceptional. The idea may have been done before, but how you treat it can make it fresh.

Sometimes the problem is that we don't know enough about the problem, story, or character and need to research it further. Seldom do we know enough about a subject to undertake a production without at least some research. Research immerses us in the subject, enabling us not simply to know but to understand the subject. Information becomes the key that sets us on the path to conceiving a distinctive treatment. Whether a client or producer presents us with an idea or whether it's our own, chances are it will need some research.

Research

Story Research

The goal of story research is to help discover treatment or augment an already planned treatment. Once we know our treatment of the subject, we will have some guide about how to proceed, what to look for, and what to include. Before we have determined the treatment, our research is at best preliminary.

Story research generally involves research into character, events, environment, and period. Researching a period not only involves determining what costumes, props, and sets are appropriate, but also how people reacted to events of the day and related to one another. A period production requires significantly more research in terms of both depth and quantity than would a modern-day piece. Some of this is discussed later in Chapter 7.

Location Research

If we are doing a narrative project, nothing beats visiting the location where the events will take place in the production. It gives reality to the spatial relations necessary for logical action. In addition, as William Kelley, former lecturer at USC and co-writer of *Witness* and numerous television productions, exhorts his students, "You *must* tread the ground."[1] It gives us a feel for the place that we can't envision or imagine. It puts us in the shoes of our characters.

Research should provide texture and depth for stories. Researching contemporary stories may mean visiting a police station, going on a ride-along, and perhaps talking with a judge or prosecutor about the process of arrest and trial. We may need to visit a newsroom, coal mine, or auto plant. We shouldn't trust our knowledge of these places or events to film or television productions we have seen because these productions probably did what our production will probably do—omit nonessential parts of the process, condense the activities of several people into a role for one, or restructure and truncate process for the sake of time, plot development, and theme. *We* must do the research and make these decisions ourselves. The last person who treated this subject may have altogether omitted what to us may be critical to our production's authenticity.

Library Research

Depending on the nature of the project, library research may be necessary to help learn about characters, events, or historic periods. We may need to look up such details as the ranks of officers in the military for a given nation or a given period, the appropriate weapons, the style of dress, and transportation routes and schedules. This research may suggest interesting story ramifications on a character's ability to act. Verisimilitude is essential in narrative productions, and the details of the locale, events, and period may make the difference in believability in the perceived reality of our production.

Sometimes, references to big events don't bring realism because they seem forced ("Gee, did you hear that the Hindenberg just burned in New Jersey yesterday?"). Little touches like humor, songs, or lesser events—like the trolley accident in *Avalon*—do more to bring home the period or time for us in a credible way. These details can be gleaned by looking at newspapers and magazines of the period and trying to understand what was important to the people then, not what we remember as important.

Interviewing

Part of research is interviewing knowledgeable sources. When it appears that the person's interview will be used in the production, we may want to conduct a second interview. The first interview will be a preliminary, research interview, whereas the second interview will be on-camera or on the voice track of the production.

Interviews are very important because published material usually will be, by nature of publication, somewhat dated. Talking to people involved in the subject of our production brings us closer to the edge of the ongoing debate in that field, whatever it might be. Interviews may be important for developing narrative projects and are usually essential when creating a documentary.

Prepare for research interviews. Don't come at the subject too naively. Use the interviewee's time wisely, especially if you want to come back for a second interview. Show respect, even if you disagree with the person's views. Do your homework. Don't ask questions that the person already answered elsewhere—in books, articles, films, or tapes; ask questions *based* on having read or seen them. When setting up the interview, it's sometimes appropriate to ask the subject to recommend preparatory material you could read in advance.

In research, we want to learn the basic questions of who, what, where, when, how, and why. Get some perspective on the situation. In the interview, we want to fill in the gaps. We want to not only build our perspective, but also develop the perspective of the interviewee. ("What do you feel is the biggest problem you are facing now?" "If you could solve one problem, what would it be?") Try to get into this person's world so you can then share it with your audience. *Listen* to what interests and excites this interviewee. Find out which questions lead to engaging material and which lead to dead ends. If during the interview the level of expertise or the area of experience goes way beyond your frame of reference, it helps to ask how the resource person would explain the subject or process to a group of interested, but uninitiated listeners such as a group of students.

Ultimately, remember that it's not who the person is or what is said, but how we use it in the production that will be important. If we anticipate using the person in the production, we must evaluate speaking ability as well as looks, demeanor, and presence. Does this person speak in short, declarative statements or in a run-on fashion with little "um's" between sentences? If so, editing will be difficult. Are we dealing with a monotone voice or one with some color? Are excitement and involvement conveyed through the person's voice?

Every interview is a juggling act. We should have in mind what the balance will be between the information being conveyed and the portraiture of the person being interviewed. Some interviews are all character and portraiture. We conduct other interviews because a person is an expert on the information being conveyed. Most interviews fall somewhere in between. The way we ask our questions and the format we choose for the interview are affected by the balance chosen between information and portraiture.

For example, if we want to emphasize information, we may ask questions that elicit simple answers and choose to include our questions in the interview. This format lends itself to a concise presentation of information. On the other hand, if portraiture is the main goal, we may ask questions that require full answers ("Tell me what happened after you discovered you were adopted?") This enables a format in which we can edit out our questions so that no interviewer stands between the character and the audience.

In addition, we need to conduct interviews with two parts of the brain. One part should keep in mind the themes we want to develop, the research and information we already know, the areas of interest we anticipate, while evaluating the articulation of statements for editing. The other part of the brain must *listen* to the interviewee, participate in an exchange, respond to significant statements, and follow up on unexpected revelations. Even when using a recorder, it is a good idea to have a pad of paper to take notes and keep the interview on track.

It is important to distinguish between interviews being made for background information for a narrative or documentary and interviews potentially to be used as program material. Naturally we need interviews for possible program material to be technically clean, with close, noiseless miking technique; minimum location noise; and no stepping on the interviewee's responses. Interviews conducted for program material also must fit within planned formats. We may conduct one type of interview to emphasize the expertise or personality of one person. We may conduct a totally different type of interview to elicit a point of view and edit it against another interview representing an opposing point of view. A third type of interview format combines responses from several people, usually emphasizing short, snappy comments and a mix of different ages, races, sexes, and cultures.

Synthesizing Research

The danger in research is in becoming a convert, forgetting *our* purpose and adopting the purposes of the subject. We run the risk of becoming so involved we lose our professional distance. If we become too well informed before an interview, the interviewee will talk to us as a colleague, not as someone who is being informed.

In narrative production, it is always dangerous to create a character who overtly knows the theme of the production because the character will begin to talk and talk, and it becomes impossible to move the story forward. The same is true in nontheatrical production when *we* know too much. Visualization becomes secondary to a narrator who talks incessantly. We should avoid the temptation to simply espouse our own opinions. The power of the visual media is in showing a version of reality, not in talking about it.

After completing the research, the major creative effort is still ahead of us. Effective productions are not illustrated lectures nor are they encapsulations of research in long voice tracks with accompanying pictures. They are reconceived as visual presentations grounded in the knowledge gained through research.

The processes and strengths of research are, therefore, to synthesize it. Match what you read and learn through interviewing with your own experience. Don't underestimate your own insight into the subject nor the insight of an audience.

Visualization

The most important tasks of a visual storyteller are to visualize and *de*verbalize stories. Having more than likely grown up being taught that the verbal skills of reading and writing are the mark of education and that television and movies were merely entertainment, it is understandable that many of us have honed our verbal skills more than our visual ones. Or, at least we trust them more.

Visualization might come out of either subject or treatment. If the subject is visual—an exciting chase, a poignant love scene, a stunning piece of nature photography—our only concern is not letting it get ruined by overblown dialogue or wall-to-wall narration. Let the visuals tell their story. Don't point out the obvious. Let the audience think and reflect. Don't sell them short. Our treatment of the subject should also guide us as to visualization. This was discussed in the example of the fox hunt in Chapter 1.

Motif and Symbols

The subject may suggest a visual treatment to you in terms of motif. As you think about your characters or subject, what visuals come to mind? What characteristics? Do you want to show strength? If so, bold colors, straight lines, images of trees, or block-like buildings may come to mind. Do you want to show anxiety? If so, irregularly paced shots, canted angles, unbalanced compositions, or an unclear point-of-view shot may come to mind.

In thinking of visualization, it's probably a good idea to avoid trying to think of symbolic visuals because broadly acknowledged symbols such as crosses, bars, flags, graves, blood, the ocean, Madonna figures, eternal flames, zodiac signs, swastikas, and so on are so overused that they will likely seem hackneyed to an audience. The best place to look for visualization is within yourself. Create your own symbols and establish their meaning through your storytelling. What has meaning for you?

Visualization is essential. As you plan the production, try to *see* through the whole project. Visualize the finished product. How does it look? How will it affect an audience? What will they think? How will they react to the production? Do you have long blocks of narration over shots with no movement? Are there long passages with the audience looking at someone talking on the phone, directly to the audience on camera, to another character? Are your dialogue scenes more than three to five pages of your script? If so, perhaps too much time is being spent in developing internal character conflict or in presenting characters with conflicting points of view. Try showing the action that is motivated by the conflict. Perhaps more outside events could provide sources of conflict. Talent should do things, show things, and share experiences with us, not just talk to us. The film *My Dinner with Andre* is an instructive anomaly. As interesting, insightful, and sometimes humorous as it is, this film may be ultimately unsatisfying to some viewers due to its lack of visualization.

Always, somewhere in the back of our minds, during the process of choosing or developing an idea and deciding our treatment of it, we should be visualizing the action. Remember that film, video, and television are excellent at showing events, scenes, people, and human interactions—stories told visually. Visual media productions are not bound by time or location. When our initial idea is an issue or abstraction—the roles of women, the plight of the poor, racial disharmony, and so on—we have not yet arrived at an idea for our production. When we want to explore interpersonal relationships in a family or between a couple and our vision is of them talking or even yelling in a room, then maybe it's television, but not feature film material. When we want to examine an individual's innermost feelings, motivations, and insights, we may be on the track of portraiture or characterization. But, without external events and actions, the piece will be radio. We must translate our concerns and interests into concrete, photographable scenes and situations. We must capture and convey the abstract through the specific.

Not every idea or story is a movie or television show. Some subjects are best left to the print media. Some ideas may best be slide shows or even a series of charts with live presenters. Some concepts are best explored in song. If the subject is internal, verbal, or just not very visual, it may need to be expressed in a different way. But, if it has conflict, action, beauty, events, and circumstances that can be shown to an audience, we are probably on the right track. Moving pictures have to move.

Exercise 1

Write a treatment (third-person, present tense description/synopsis of the story action) for a short film, video, or television production based on a story in the newspaper.

Exercise 2

Interview one or more people on a specific subject of your choice. It may be human interest or informational. Research your topic before the interview. Plan the final production before you begin the interview. Decide whether or not to include your questions in the final edited interview. Work for a coherent flow of ideas or development of a theme.

Notes

1. William Kelley, Master Screenwriters' Conference, Atlantic Beach, NC, 1991.

3

POINT OF VIEW

The Points of View

Point of view is one of the most interesting and basic narrative devices available to the storyteller. For any storyteller, a fundamental consideration in crafting a tale is deciding from whose point(s) of view to tell the story. All else—chronologies, plots, characters, themes, and interpretations—flows from this decision. Consider how differently the story would be told if the first words of Melville's *Moby Dick* were not "Call me Ishmael," but, "I am Ahab."

The term "point of view" has several definitions. First, within film and video, the term "point of view" (POV) has a special meaning. POV refers to a camera shot taken as if seen through the eyes of a character.

Second, point of view refers to the perspective of the storyteller. Is this an eyewitness account of an incident or an expression of the storyteller's thoughts and theories, or is this a recounting of events from a detached point of view? This is referred to in literature as "person."

The third meaning of the term "point of view" is actually the source of the phrase itself. Point of view refers to the interests, attitudes, and beliefs associated with a character's or group's particular *perspective*.

POV Shots

POV shots are commonplace in theatrical productions. They can be used as brief insert shots of a scene following a reaction shot, or even as long-moving camera shots. The moving POV shot is particularly effective in horror and monster movies (McTiernan's *Predator*, Coppola's *Bram Stoker's Dracula*) to build suspense. The effect is that we are looking through the eyes of a predator at some potential victim. It is very unsettling. Because of its effectiveness in building expectation in the audience, this type of POV shot usually precedes the showing of the actual creature and is often the first indication that an unknown predator is nearby.

POV shots momentarily shift the storytelling to a first-person account from a character's point of view. The Raymond Chandler mystery *Lady in the Lake,* directed by and starring Robert Montgomery, used the camera exclusively to show the lead character's POV in an attempt to tell the story visually from a first-person point of view. Marlowe, the hero, appeared only in shots that included a mirror. Sometimes the hero's hands would move out from below the frame as if we, the audience, were his eyes. The film proved very artificial and contrived.

Today many amusement park rides such as Universal's "Back to the Future" feature wide-screen point-of-view camera work in combination with electronic devices that move these small theaters to give the audience the impression of being a character involved in the action on the screen. The promise of virtual reality games is that they too will create a sense of participating in the arenas of action through computer-generated graphics or scenes that respond to the participant's actions and movement. These can be quite convincing experiences for a short time. A television or movie audience, however, cannot be put inside the visual experience of a character for very long and continue to find it credible. The audience is firmly rooted in its role outside the action as a viewer of the events on the screen. Oddly enough, although first-person point of view is a common and effective device when applied to sound in film and video productions, as with a first-person narrator, it fails when used for too long in the visualization. This illustrates a fundamental difference in word-based literary narrative versus image-based visual media.

The POV shot is a camera and editing device. We discuss it at some length in Chapter 8, so we will not discuss it further here.

Perspective of the Storyteller

Decisions about what point of view the video or filmmaker should adopt toward the presentation of a particular production is often related to the level of very real involvement the producer has had in the events being communicated. However, individual involvement or even just the impression of involvement is still a creative choice that the producer makes. The voice or person in which the production is cast also relates to the level of verisimilitude the producer wants to create for the audience. Presenting the "truth" about events is probably most credible as a first-person, eyewitness account. However, as the voice shifts from first person to third, the audience becomes less distanced and more willing to suspend disbelief and become emotionally involved in the events being portrayed.

First Person

Direct, personal expression is possible in film and video production. These productions are a direct communication of thought and ideas to the audience using the images and sound capabilities of the media as the creator's voice. The actions of a character or subject are not described from a detached point of view nor is the camera used to involve the audience in the creator's point of view. It is as pure a personal expression as music, art, or sculpture. Frank Mouris created *Frank Film,* a kaleidoscopic collage of pictures clipped from magazines, and animated these into an amusing, yet introspective autobiographical film. In the experimental film classic *Dog Star Man,* Stan Brakhage attempts to reproduce the first-person vision of the world as seen through the eyes of an infant. Several artists such as Nam June Paik and Vitto Acconci use video to express themselves.

Documentary often uses the story device of the quest to give a first-person account of the documentarian. In the Academy Award winning documentary *Kon-Tiki,* Thor Heyerdahl chronicled his incredible raft trip from Peru to Tahiti. Bruce Brown involved audiences in his global search for the perfect wave in his engaging and amusing *Endless Summer.* Most of these are fascinating accounts by visual storytellers. Some, like the beautifully photographed works of Jacques-Yves Cousteau, the National Geographic productions, or the nature documentaries on the Discovery or Learning Channels, have become familiar television programming.

The quest by documentarians is often for some social, moral, or political cause (point of view as attitude). In *Roger and Me,* filmmaker Michael Moore was ostensibly searching for General Motors Chairman of the Board Roger Smith. However, he used the documentary form to express his views about the changing nature of the Flint, Michigan, community.

Extended first-person perspective (rather than occasional POV shots) is most easily established through voice-over narration. While the camera shows the character involved in the action from the standard, third-person point of view, the character's voice-over provides the audience with a first-person commentary.

The voiced narrative in the first person gives us a character's thoughts and provides opportunities for characterization and commentary. Arthur Penn's *Little Big Man* is an example of this, as are Kevin Costner's *Dances with Wolves,* Warren Beatty's *Reds,* and Milos Forman's *Amadeus,* to name a few.

The literary convention that has carried over into narrative film is of a character relating the story, as in the opening of the *Star Trek* television series. This type of first person is particularly characteristic of the *film noir* genre. The hero, often a hard-boiled detective, speaks as a voice-over narrator telling his or her story (*Romancing the Stone, The Maltese Falcon,* and *Body Heat.*)

First-person narrative can shift the balance from visuals and dialogue, to commentary and contemplative language. For adaptations of literature with beautiful language this can help preserve some of the tone and value of the original work. Robert Redford's *A River Runs Through It* is an example.

In nontheatrical productions, narrators have only a third-person point of view about the events of the production. Narrators may speak in generalities about concepts, historical events, exposition, and backstory, but it is usually not appropriate for narrators to do more than speculate on the motivations of individuals unless there is an obvious means for the narrator to be aware of what a character is thinking.

Audiences also may be unwilling to believe a narrator who is speaking in the third person about subjects for which this person has no obvious credentials. A solution is simply to shift from a third-person narrator to a different first-person narrator. The individual with first-hand knowledge can provide in-depth information or provide a perspective that requires special experience or expertise. First-person narrative is an ideal technique, then, for characters or personalities speaking about issues or events with which they are intimately involved. Shifting from a third-person narrator to a first-person account also breaks the monotony of a single voice speaking for the duration of a production.

Second Person

Second person, addressing "you," is not generally incorporated in a treatment, screenplay, or shooting script because the "you" in these documents would be the director, talent, or production crew. However, second-person point of view is inherent in many productions, but the "you" being addressed is the audience.

Some productions adopt the second-person point of view in the voice of the narrator or on-camera personality directly addressing the viewers. Instructional productions such as videos to improve your soccer, golf, or waistline are certainly second person, directed at *you* the audience. The production is a direct address with the silent, but hopefully active, participant. Training films and videos, closed-circuit television for internal corporate or government use, and interactive educational media fall into this area. With or without someone on-screen addressing the viewer, the message is personal to each member of the audience. This is how *you* do such-and-such. This is of concern to *you* and *you* and *you.*

Advertising messages are sometimes second person. The client or sponsor's spokesperson is talking directly to *you* as a consumer and telling you to buy something. In public service announcements, they are informing *you* about something; in political ads, they are telling *you* to do something—vote for them. These productions can express their points of view without having someone on-camera addressing the "you" in front of the television.

In *cinéma vérité*, or "direct cinema" documentary, the camera creates a point of view for the audience that is somewhere between first and second person. The camera is a participant instead of remaining an invisible observer. The subjects of the documentary acknowledge its presence and sometimes address the camera directly. When the photographer of the documentary is not established as a character in the scene, the audience feels that the direct address being made to the camera speaks directly to them in a second-person point of view.

Third Person

Most productions are created in the third person. The actions of characters and people on the screen are rendered from an observer's point of view, but this point of view *is not omniscient.* In literature, the omniscient point of view allows the reader to enter the mind and hear the conscious thought of a character. This is not possible in film, video, or television productions created with pure third-person points of view, without first-person voice-over narrations. Instead we witness the actions of characters. We do not know their thoughts directly, as we would in an interior monologue. We discern and decipher what is in their minds through action and dialogue.

Scriptwriters occasionally break from this detached point of view in a script to convey a mood or tone of a scene or to reveal a character's thoughts to the director or talent. This is done only when it might help an actor interpret the style or pacing of a production or motivation that might be misunderstood, as in the following passage from *Chinatown:*

> *He waits. The Men seem to have passed him by. But there is another SOUND now—an echoing growing sound. It puzzles Gittes. He starts to lift his head to catch the direction.*[1]

In pointing out that Gittes is "puzzled," scriptwriter Robert Towne departs from merely describing the action to suggesting how the actor might react to the noise he hears. Towne is actually speaking to Nicholson and Polanski, telling them what is on the character's mind. Also, the writer occasionally will suggest how to deliver lines in a parenthetical note to the actor or in the dialogue block. This is done when the talent might misinterpret a line due to possible ambiguity in motivation or when action is to occur during the delivery of the line.

GITTES
(a little surprised, he laughs)
What do you mean, 'why?' Nobody's here, that's all.

EVELYN
(handing Gittes his drink)
I gave everybody the night off.[2]

Presentation in the third person is common in nonnarrative and narrative productions. Many documentaries we see provide a look at other cultures, places, or persons. The detached perspective we associate with third person is evident in many of these, including the best, such as Disney's *The Living Desert* (directed by James Algar). Documentaries created in the third person can be highly involving. An excellent example is Les Blank's *Burden of Dreams,* which chronicles the making of Werner Herzog's *Fitzcarraldo.* This third-person documentary is an engrossing depiction of the difficulties Herzog and his company faced filming in the Peruvian Amazon. (See Figure 3.1.) Eleanor Coppola, Francis Ford Coppola's wife, is the storyteller in *Hearts of Darkness,* which documents in third person the amazing production of Coppola's *Apocalypse Now. The War Room* by D. A. Pennebaker and Chris Hughes is a fascinating look at the people behind the struggle for power during the Clinton campaign. In each of these, a first-person account would have been quite logical a choice to create believability, yet the third-person account makes them far more involving.

Character Point of View

A narrative does not even have to be confined to a single storyteller or point of view. The narrative can be told and interpreted to us second, or even third hand, through the perspectives of intervening narrators. Storytellers can tell stories of storytellers telling stories.

Literary narratives can be told with many variations in the point(s) of view, but at any given moment, it is usually obvious who is telling the story. In literature, relating events through the points of view of various characters has evolved into a highly refined technique that provides powerful opportunities for characterization and commentary.

In film and video, on the other hand, point of view as perspective tends to be much more limited in variation. Point of view is not usually obvious to the audience because the objective camera almost always presents the subject from a third-person point of view. The camera is, however, often associated with the perspective of one character in the story or at least one character in a given scene. Welles's *Citizen Kane,* for example, begins the narrative in the omni-

FIGURE 3.1
Les Blank's *Burden of Dreams* is an engrossing third-person documentary that chronicles the making of Werner Herzog's *Fitzcarraldo* in the Peruvian Amazon.

Maureen Gosling, Photographer. Courtesy of Les Blank-Flower Films.

scient third person showing the death of Charles Foster Kane. It then shifts perspective to a newsreel account of the life of Kane, which includes first-person commentary. The balance then alternates between third person as we follow the newsreel journalist, Mr. Thompson, and the first-person accounts of Kane's life pieced together as Thompson attempts to discover the meaning of the word "Rosebud." However, in these first-person accounts, because the camera favors Kane, we associate much of the film as being from his perspective.

In *Amadeus,* Milos Forman chooses a jealous but admiring contemporary, Salieri, to tell the story of Mozart from his point of view. We would assume that characters in dramas, like people in nontheatrical productions, have only first-person knowledge about their own affairs and third-person knowledge about the affairs of others. Mysteriously, however, Salieri is able to reveal events he never could have known. Because the camera associates with Mozart's point of view in these scenes, we forget the convention that Salieri is ostensibly telling the story.

The difference in the use of point of view between film and literature lies in the media being used—the printed word versus voice and visuals. Literary narrative can easily establish first-person as well as third-person narrative. However, with the exception of the POV shot, the camera records the actions of characters in the third person. This does not change, even when using a first-person voice-over narrator.

Film audiences share the point of view of the leading character. Obviously portraits and character-driven productions like the Indiana Jones films or the Seinfeld television shows are stories told from the perspective of Indiana Jones (Harrison Ford) or Jerry Seinfeld. The stories are about the events that happen to them. They appear in nearly every scene of the main plot, or A-story, and the important events of the story are those that affect them. Their actions drive the story forward. It is as if we are at their elbow.

The lead in the story provides the focus for the audience. If we like the leading character and care what happens to him or her, we will become involved in the events of the story. We become involved in drama through a character and generally, although not always, this is the lead. In nontheatrical productions and news, we often focus on the personality of the on-camera moderator, reporter, or host of the show. Many journalists are involved in producing shows like *20/20, 60 Minutes,* and the *Today Show,* yet the show's personalities present the stories on air.

Sharing the point of view with the lead may not seem as obvious in ensemble productions. However, even in ensemble work, one character is usually dominant for most of the production. The show *Northern Exposure,* for instance, was, for many episodes, about a young New Yorker, Joel Fleishman. Fleishman arranged for the state of Alaska to pay for his medical school and now has to work in the remote boondocks of Cicily, Alaska. *Northern Exposure* was not always Fleishman's story each week, but, in general, his was the point of view we see on the show. The same was true of *Cheers.* It was Sam's show. *Night Court* was Harry's show. *M*A*S*H* was Hawkeye's.

Character point of view is a critical consideration. It is one of the most important decisions we make in defining the project. And, it's not always an obvious decision. Notice how the tone of *Northern Exposure* changed when Fleishman left and the show's point of view had to be shifted. It was no longer a fish-out-of-water story. It lost the inherent conflict that Fleishman's alien New York–ness brings to the Alaskan landscape. In *Cheers,* what if the point of view were shifted to Carla? How would *M*A*S*H* be different if the shows were Klinger's? In each case, the very nature of the conflict in the dramas would shift. If it didn't, the lead would be merely an observer of events, not a participant in them. Imagine *Superman* from the point of view of Lois Lane. Someone else, Superman, would always be resolving the conflict for the main character. Or worse, coming to tell her about events that occurred off-screen while she was sitting at work at the *Daily Planet.*

The lead needs to be involved in the central conflict of the story. The lead needs to be active and be the one to whom the events of the narrative happen. Don't let your characters be observers of the events in their own stories. Get them to take charge of their story and move the events, not watch them. Creative people are often observers of the passing scene. Writers, directors, and actors constantly study others for ideas and inspiration. We tend to be voyeurs. We gather story ideas and bits and pieces of character wherever we are and from whomever we are with. The danger is in modeling our leading characters in our own image, as someone who watches others in the ensemble move the story forward by their actions. Decide whose story it is and make that character essential to the action.

The character who is the lead in a narrative obviously has a point of view (attitude) toward the story events. This is discussed in Chapter 6. For now, consider that the character should be unique and have an attitude toward the events of the plot. In a portrait documentary, it is the person's point of view that often makes them significant and interesting enough to do the portrait in the first place. Whatever the character's point of view, it should be consistent.

Once we make the decision, we should stick with it. It is worth pointing out one truly notable exception to this: Akira Kurosawa's 1950 classic film *Rashomon.* The film used the varying points of view of four people to relate the events of a rape. It studies truth: how point of view influences our perceptions of reality. It also shows how sharing the lead's point of view affects the audience's understanding of a story. In this film, the lead shifted among four different storytellers. Similarly, in *King Rat,* George Segal plays the lead, and the point of view is associated with his character as opposed to Tom Courtenay's. Segal is given top billing and the camera work clearly associates the audience with him as the good guy. Only at the end of the film do we realize that the conventions of point of view have warped our perceptions.

In documentary as in narrative, the choice of person—whether to tell the story about one's own experiences or those of others—is a decision affecting the impact of the story. The best choice is the one that tells the story in the most compelling way.

Attitude

In Chapter 1, we discussed how theme and treatment derive from our purpose, and we used a production about fox hunting as an example. Each hypothetical sponsor brought a specific point of view and set of attitudes, which ultimately shaped the interpretation of the subject. Similarly, consider how different a production about timber logging might be if it were sponsored by a lumber company as opposed to an environmental group. Each group would bring very different points of view, and by this we mean the concerns and opinions that would mold the film.

We regularly see various film and video productions that present the same subjects from differing points of view (attitudes). The point of view in *Norma Rae,* for example, is very sympathetic toward unions, whereas in *On the Waterfront,* it is quite critical. On the other hand, the point of view in *On the Waterfront* casts the Catholic Church in a generally positive light, whereas *Aguirre: The Wrath of God* and *The Mission* show the Church as an instrument of destruction. *9 to 5* and *Thelma & Louise* portray men, in their relationships with women, as stupid and abusive or, at best, ineffectual, but *Klute* and *Witness* show men as sympathetic and effective partners. *Casablanca* depicts the French colonial presence in North Africa as benign, but it appears inhumanly brutal in *The Battle of Algiers.* These are all differing renditions of subject that result from varying points of view, that is, varying opinions, attitudes, and beliefs.

The purpose of many productions is to persuade an audience to adopt a predetermined opinion or attitude about a certain subject. This is obviously true of product advertising and propaganda. We usually think of propaganda as primarily political, but most so-called public information pieces done for corporations, nonprofit associations, and various special-interest groups are forms of propaganda.

We involve ourselves in propaganda whenever we undertake a fiction or nonfiction production with the major purpose of convincing our audience of a particular set of principles, beliefs, or opinions. The propaganda intent behind many documentaries is often obvious. This includes the productions we see on such subjects as the homeless, the environment, health care, drug addiction, urban violence, and so on. These are still propaganda, even though we support the points of view. Even nature documentaries carry the propaganda message: if we don't take action, the natural beauty we are witnessing will soon disappear. Although Bill Moyers provides insight and underscores values that many people appreciate, much of what he does (*Listening to America,* for example) is, in the end, propaganda.

There is a danger when producing shows primarily for propaganda of letting the production become too strident and polemic. Often, in productions motivated by the intent of persuasion, we find the strengths of the visual media—scenes, actions and interactions, human experience, characterization, story, powerful imagery, and sound—abandoned in favor of abstract argument and forced, rhetorical cinematography and editing. The audience withdraws its attention from involvement in the events on the screen and they become all too aware of the producer's intent. Few of us like being preached at, and many of these works are too transparent in their motives to hold an audience's attention or be convincing.

However, during World War II, audiences filled with patriotic conviction, flocked to films filled with not so subtle messages. Even the cartoons of the day encouraged enlistment and preached support for the war effort. Some of these, like Chaplin's *The Great Dictator,* Howard Hawks's *Sergeant York,* Herman Shumlin's filmed adaptation of Lillian Hellman's *Watch on the Rhine,* or Michael Curtiz's *Casablanca* transcended dogmatic demagoguery. They achieved this by using strong, dramatic story lines to carry the message. Others were effective due to the high level of their craft. Two examples are Michael Curtiz's *Yankee Doodle Dandy,* and George Sydney's fun, if dated, *Anchors Aweigh,* which includes the wonderful dance between Gene Kelly and Jerry from the Tom and Jerry cartoon series.

Several documentaries produced during that time were quite remarkable. Some examples are the joint production by the U.S. Navy and Twentieth Century Fox, *The Fighting Lady,* the British *Desert Victory,* and the Australian News and Information Bureau's *Kokoda Front Line.* Two stunning examples are Leni Riefenstahl's documentary *Triumph of the Will,* made in 1935 to propagandize Hitler's Nuremberg rallies and her film *Olympia* on the 1936 Berlin Olympics. Both blatantly glorified the Nazi regime. Riefenstahl's point of view (attitudes) notwithstanding, we study her works today for her ability to manipulate images. Her films created meaning through the masterful use of suggestive imagery. The most well-known example is her famous diving sequence in *Olympia,* where she shot the high divers from below and cut the footage together to give the impression of flying Aryan supermen.

Although documentary has a long tradition predating Riefenstahl of manipulating images to convey a message, the conventional expectation for documentary somehow to present reality has survived. Audiences continue to believe that most documentaries present a true, if perhaps a one-sided picture. Most documentarians, however, know that how they treat their subject—how they shoot it, what questions they ask, what they include in the editing—provides them with an array of colorings to put on their palette and use to paint their view of reality for the audience. Thus, with less obvious artifice, documentarians use technique instead of blatant argument to express their points of view.

Documentarian Frederick Wiseman, for instance, has used the images captured by his cameras to express his point of view (observations and opinions) regarding social situations ranging from the use of animals in laboratory experiments in his film *Primate* to the abuses of the Philadelphia public school system in *High School.* His works, however, have no sermonizing narrators nor any blatant and contrived contrasts in juxtaposed images. His films go to great pains to show all sides and let all parties express *their* points of view. Wiseman apparently believes that given enough rope, bureaucrats and officials will hang themselves. And, hang themselves they do in his films.

A remarkable documentary, *The Thin Blue Line* by Errol Morris, presented the filmmaker's point of view (opinion) regarding the innocence of a man accused of murdering a Dallas police officer. Morris made many aesthetic choices to support his point of view, including the clothes worn by his interviewees and the camera framings to create positive and negative images. The film's presentation was so strong that the case was reopened and the accused man ultimately exonerated.

Docudramas trade on the reputation of documentaries for presenting "truth." Although many are well researched and present as unbiased a point of view as time and budget will allow, as with documentaries, they can only represent a version of "truth." More often than not, they provide a forum for filmmakers or videographers to present their points of view (opinions) to an audience. The director Costa-Gavras, for instance, has aired strong, sociopolitical points of view in films such as *Z* and *Missing.*

The question of "truth" versus the documentarian's point of view in the gray area of docudrama is an area of ongoing controversy. Because the believability of the medium is so beguiling to audiences, critics have expressed concern that media producers manipulate our perception of history through these productions. Productions dealing with recent history such as Oliver Stone's *JFK* fall prey to this criticism. Critics were not only troubled about the historical accuracy of the film, they were also seriously concerned with impact of Stone's advocating a conspiracy theory related to John F. Kennedy's death. Although screenwriter Paddy Chayefsky and director Sidney Lumet raised the specter of an industrial cabal-type conspiracy in *Network,* it wasn't nearly as threatening as the theory advocated by Stone. (See Figure 3.2.) Works of fiction don't pretend to be based on fact. Point of view expressed in docudrama is more realistic and therefore more subject to scrutiny and criticism.

The adage in Hollywood has long been "If you want to send a message, call Western Union." Yet, from the earliest days of filmmaking, filmmakers such as Eisenstein and Griffith with strong points of view have used the screen to carry social and political messages to audiences in narrative films such as *Potemkin* and *Intolerance.* The best writers and directors still use storytelling techniques to promote their points of view. In 1930, director Lewis Milestone adapted Erich Maria Remarque's stunning pacifist work, *All Quiet on the Western Front,* as an antiwar statement even as Germany was rebuilding its war machine. Directors like Frank Capra followed this tradition with films like *Meet John Doe* and *Mr. Smith Goes to Washington.* Films such as these are like the works of Aesop or Dickens's *A Christmas Carol*—the story is primarily a vehicle for the message.

On some level, almost all productions have a message of some kind. It is the reason that most of us are in this business, to express our points of view (beliefs, concerns, and opinions). Communicating messages is the *raison d'être* behind storytelling. Even the most entertainment-oriented prime-time televi-

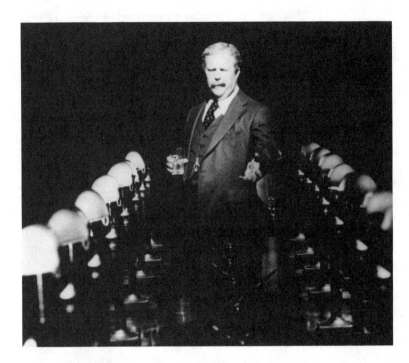

FIGURE 3.2
Screenwriter Paddy
Chayefsky and director
Sidney Lumet raised
the specter of an
industrial cabal-type
conspiracy in *Network*.

sion program has some kind of message. Usually TV's messages have to do with ego-assuaging themes, reassuring the audience members that they are not alone with their foibles and frustrations. Sometimes shows like *Saturday Night Live, Murphy Brown,* or *In Living Color* have moral or social messages. Shows with a strong political message have not done well on television in the United States. *That Was The Week That Was,* a political satire in the 1970s, was very popular, but has not been duplicated except in *Saturday Night Live's* "Weekend Update" feature. Religious points of view also have not fared very well on network television. Occasionally Hallmark or a Movie of the Week will take on a religious subject, but it is invariably safe and close to the mainstream. Religious and political points of view are too hot for most networks or distributors to gamble on.

Sometimes the message doesn't jump off the screen and hit you in the face. In 1952, Fred Zinnemann lashed out at McCarthyism with *High Noon* merely by showing Will Kane (Gary Cooper) having the courage to stand up alone for what he thought was right. Director George Stevens was shocked by the brutal reality of death he had seen in World War II. In *Shane,* he attempted to make murder horrific by staging his gunfights in the mud and amplifying gunshots by shooting into metal trash cans.

The message in most films, however, is not political but more often than not deals with the human truths of everyday life. We could interpret the film *Rain Man* as making a political statement, but its strongest message is about being "your brother's keeper." *Witness* makes the pitch that the source of a community's strength lies in the land and, more importantly perhaps, that the source of an individual's safety and security lies in one's community.

Point of view (opinion) is ultimately the message of the creator. It leads to treatment. In Chapter 1, we discussed the different treatments of the play *The Front Page* in several films. The subject was the same, the story was the same, but the treatments were different. However, in looking at Raoul Walsh's 1941 production *They Died with Their Boots On* and Arthur Penn's 1970 production *Little Big Man,* both of which involve accounts of the battle of Little Big Horn and the events preceding it, we find the point of view of each film diametrically opposed. In *They Died with Their Boots On,* Custer (Errol Flynn) was a flamboyant, self-sacrificing hero who bought time for the army to regroup and successfully attack the Indians. In *Little Big Man,* Custer (Richard Mulligan) is oblivious to the humanity of the Indians—a jingoistic butcher senselessly killing women and children. The point of view expressed by Walsh during the dark days of World War II was of a great, heroic, self-sacrificing leader. Penn's film, released during the dark days of the war in Vietnam, depicts militaristic callousness, bloodlust, and massacre.

Point of view is more than perspective, more than just the person and vantage point from which the story is told. It is also the bias, conviction, and attitude enfolded and expressed, either deliberately or inadvertently, in a production. It's a question of how those who have creative control over the production—client, scriptwriter, director, and producer—exercise that control. It's how much those who have strong creative influence in the production—talent, set designer, photographer, editor, and music arranger—influence it. And finally, there is the question of how obvious or how subtle the point of view should be. Should it be bold or nearly subliminal?

The Audience's Point of View

In our arrogance as media producers, we sometimes forget our audience's point of view. The audience is not merely a voyeur. They are active participants in the production. Films, videos, and television are merely conduits from the creators, the programmers, and the producers to the audience. It is no more a production without someone watching than is a conversation without someone listening. (If a tree falls in a forest and it isn't on television . . .)

Audiences care about characters, become involved in problems, and share experiences. They become involved at a gut level, visceral and emotional. The media speaks to our beings, our souls, extending our experiences beyond ourselves and occasionally adding to our accumulation of knowledge by speaking to our intellect.

Being an audience is a pleasurable experience, and most of us seek it out. We become captivated by the flickering light and shadows on the cave wall, by the rituals performed by firelight. We willingly suspend our disbelief that what we are seeing is a created reality. And, we respond involuntarily to the events as if we were there—with fear to horrific images, with laughter to comedic events, with pumping adrenalin to the excitement of the chase.

Defining the Audience

As with any two-way communication, it's important to identify the audience's point of view, its prior experience and attitude. In narrative production, we attempt to immediately establish the type, style, and genre of a production so that the audience can respond with their point of view. As an audience, we know how to prepare ourselves to respond to comedies, action dramas, talk shows, or soap operas. We even know what kind of show we can expect from a specific director, or the sort of production to anticipate if a certain actor is associated with it. The opening scene sets the stage for the audience that has perhaps already been prepared by the theater's marquee, a blurb in *TV Guide,* or a promo on a previous show. We are ready and waiting eagerly for the production to deliver, for promises to be fulfilled.

In information or documentary production, often the audience is more easily defined than the very general, theatrical designations of G, PG, PG-13, R, NC-17, and X, or the television designations of probable viewing audience by time of day. Often this audience has a particular point of view, attitude, and some background knowledge. Because the audience is not "general," it may become very impatient with a production that tries to reinvent the wheel, point out the obvious, or pass off simplistic arguments.

The goal of informational and instructional productions is to impart an experience or body of knowledge. Consequently it is essential to consider what the audience's point of view about the subject is at the beginning in order for it to be where we want it to be at the end. Even in narrative productions where the writer or director has a particular message or point of view to get across to the audience, it is important to know the audience's attitude and point of view. Without this, we run the danger of pontificating, talking down to the audience or shooting over its heads to such a degree that they miss the point altogether.

In informational, instructional, and some documentary productions, it's sometimes helpful to think of the audience as the leading character of the film or tape. The audience is "introduced" in the opening teaser, addressed at an appropriate level, and involved in something they care about. We define the learning goal or experience for the audience. We raise a question that challenges members of the audience in much the same way that characters and events challenge the leading character in a drama. We should then keep in mind what they are thinking in response to what the production is illustrating, allowing them to participate emotionally and intellectually in the one-sided dialogue. While they answer one question, we raise another. Throughout the production, we confront their preconceived notions and attitudes with new ideas, concepts, and experiences. By the end, they are new and different people.

Their point of view has shifted slightly, their attitude changed somewhat, their experiences broadened a bit, and their realm of knowledge increased.

As we define the project, we simultaneously determine the production's point of view. This begins with our reasons for selecting the subject. It continues as we develop the treatment, select the cast, editor, music arranger, choose camera angles, and sound elements. These can be deliberate and conscious decisions or random choices that could result in losing control of the project's point of view.

Exercise

Take one of the story ideas you came up with in Chapter 2 and re-conceive the idea from a different person's or different character's point of view. If possible, shoot the scene two or more times from each point of view.

If the scene you created earlier isn't appropriate, create a new one: boy meets girl or girl meets boy, buying your first car or selling a car to a first-time buyer, or waiting on a table of rude customers or trying to get service in a crowded restaurant.

Notes

1. Towne, Robert. "Chinatown," third draft, October 9, 1973, p. 50.

2. Towne, p. 101.

4

STORY STRUCTURES

The Rules of the Game

We all know structure. We've grown up with it. Dramatic structure and its conventions are as familiar as bedtime stories. Children who grow up on a diet of old movies know that if Errol Flynn and Olivia De Havilland hate each other when they meet in the opening moments of *Captain Blood* or *Robin Hood,* they will be madly in love by the end. They know that the hero will always be in the most danger; that, as in *Hook,* the hero, Peter Pan (Robin Williams), might have an army of sidekicks who can easily overwhelm a shipload of nasty pirates, but the hero always has to fight the archvillain singlehandedly. And, everyone knows that no matter how tough the opposition or sticky the situation, the hero will survive it. These are the rules of the game.

Adults know that rules are meant to be broken, but that they *usually* aren't. The rules of structure and conventions are like the rules of perspective in art, harmony in music, or grammar and spelling in language. Once conquered, they can be abandoned or at least trifled with for interesting effect. But, most of what we see and most of what we produce recognize that the audience understands and anticipates these rules of structure. When we change the rules, we need to prepare the audience or they will feel cheated or confused.

Movies are a kind of game between the audience and the movie maker. The word "entertainment" derives from the Latin *inter* plus *tenere,* "to hold between." Losing the audience, failing to hold them, can be the consequence of creating new rules or not recognizing those with which they are familiar.

Dramatic conventions and structures apply to nontheatrical films and documentaries as well as to narrative theatrical and prime time television productions. This is not to say that nontheatricals have to have stories and heroes just like prime time. They usually don't. But at the elemental level, everything is story. Story means dramatic structure.

Beginning, Middle, and End

The basic elements of dramatic structure found in most productions are a beginning, a middle, and an end. This sounds so basic that it is often ignored or not taken seriously. A show starts at the beginning, it goes on for a while in the middle, and it stops at the end—big deal. Wrong! Each of the three elements is developed and each has its own characteristics. Normally the beginning is about one-quarter the length of a production. The middle section is about half the production or even a little longer. Partly in recognition of audience fanny fatigue and partly because the pace of events should be picking up, the end is usually a little shorter than a full quarter of the length. Even without curtains, most film, video, and television dramas break down into these three distinct sections or acts. The basic three-act structure is the setup, the struggle, and finally the realization.

The Beginning

It is critical in the beginning of a production to start moving the story forward. There is no story until it starts. Preliminary background information is not story, it is *backstory,* the events that happen before the narrative starts. Backstory may need to be revealed later in the story, but not at the beginning. A good rule to remember is not to tell the audience anything it doesn't *need* to know and don't tell them *until* they need to know it. In the beginning, we establish what the hero wants—the goal. In nonfiction, we establish the goals for the audience experiencing the production. In any case, the most important task is to get the story going. Filling in the backstory can take place in the middle, when the audience is involved and cares enough to know more.

We state the rules of the game in the beginning. We present the hero and other major participants, the locale[1] in which the game will be played, the problem or premise, and the theme. In *The African Queen,* Rose (Katharine Hepburn), a spinster sister to a missionary (Robert Morley), and Charlie (Humphrey Bogart), a rough and tumble loner who carries supplies to the outposts, are quickly established as the major participants. The locale is an African missionary outpost at the outbreak of World War II. The problem is that these two unlikely accomplices must escape together. Although escaping might be sufficient, they set the further goal of destroying the *Louisa,* a German gunboat, which poses a threat to river traffic in that part of Africa.

The beginning also sets up themes and devices that the characters will use later in the drama. When James Bond gets all those nifty weapons, we expect to see him use them during the middle or in the end of the film. Not just weapons, but characters, relationships, personality traits—anything that is essential to the latter part of a production—need to be introduced at the beginning so they will not seem arbitrarily invented merely to solve a problem. Wile E. Coyote can produce anything he thinks will help him catch the elusive Road Runner from behind his back or from an Acme shipping crate just before he plans to use it, but audiences will find it cheap for real characters to find easy solutions to problems just as the need arises. If a character is going to need something, set it up in the beginning.

Conventions and stylistic devices that will be used during the production must also be established in the beginning. This might include music, moving camera, voice-over narration, or breaking the fourth wall and addressing the camera directly. In the beginning, let the audience know where the story is going. The solution to a problem at the end is inherent in the problem as it is defined in the beginning.

Foreshadowing of events is an important guide for the audience. Especially at first, when the audience is seeking to discover the rules we are playing by, they will believe that nothing is unintentional. Everything is pertinent. Audiences construe every line and every action as having bearing and importance on the balance of the production to come. If it doesn't, we aren't playing by the rules.

The Middle

The middle is the struggle to achieve the solution to the problem defined, discovered, or created in the beginning. This has to be accomplished in the face of *further* complications. Act two, or the middle of our production, is usually the longest part. For the sake of convenience, it can be roughly divided into two sections.

In the first part, the story must clearly take a new direction. Often this is compelled by actions or events beyond the hero or heroine's control. In *Driving Miss Daisy*, Daisy Werthan (Jessica Tandy) suspects that Hoke (Morgan Freeman) is eating food from her pantry and, to get rid of him, accuses him of stealing. In *Romancing the Stone*, Joan Wilder (Kathleen Turner) is fleeing the personal army of a Colombian drug lord. In *The Fugitive*, Dr. Kimball (Harrison Ford) is no longer headed for prison, but is escaping recapture. Any details of plot or backstory that the audience still needs to know should come out in this section.

Events should also clearly add momentum to the hero's predicament. In *The African Queen*, Rose and Charlie face rapids, a German fortress along the shore, and the maze of the river itself. They reach a turning point at the midpoint of act two, when they have escaped their first dangerous encounter with the Germans, survived a raging torrent, and have at last fallen in love. In the aftermath of these events, Charlie is no longer reluctant and complaining about their proposed task of blowing up the *Louisa* and he takes command, with Rose admitting to having some qualms, if only to bolster Charlie's attitude.

At the turning point, the hero takes some action to move events in a different direction. In *Driving Miss Daisy*, Daisy, alone in her car at night while Hoke is relieving himself at the side of the road, realizes she needs him and calls out to him. In *Romancing the Stone*, Joan Wilder (Kathleen Turner), now teamed up with Jack Colton (Michael Douglas), decides to go after the jewel to give her the leverage to rescue her sister. The original goal of rescuing her sister hasn't changed, but now she is taking charge of the events that drive the story forward. In *The Fugitive,* Kimball, after a particularly spectacular escape, decides *he* must locate the one-armed man to resolve his predicament. During the last part of the middle section of *The African Queen,* Rose and Charlie discover the better qualities in themselves and each other as they approach the destiny they have chosen, the sinking of the *Louisa.* The middle should increase the stakes for the character and show some growth. The middle can't just play out the problems set up in the beginning. There have to be surprises; otherwise, the audience knows what will happen and lose interest.

The End

The end is the climax, the resolving of the problem in a way satisfactory to the audience. It usually involves some growth either in the characters, the audience, or both. Often we discover that the initial problem is not the *real* problem to be solved in the end. Or, the hero can resolve the problem in a way that could not have been achieved without the growth that occurs throughout the middle. In the end section of *The African Queen,* Rose and Charlie satisfactorily resolve the story problem they set out to resolve in the opening. They also resolve her problem of being a single woman and his of being a loner. This, after all, was their *real* problem.

Rising Action

As the word "structure" suggests, drama builds. What we call action in drama is the movement of the story forward, not the busy activities of the cast. Action constitutes those events and exploits of the characters that move the story forward. Dramatic action is like an athletic contest. Every play, every action, moves the game toward the conclusion. Activities off the field do not affect the progress of the game. Events that happened before the referee's whistle blew to start the game may have interest for the play-by-play or color commentator, but they have no direct bearing on the outcome of the game.

As time progresses toward the conclusion, the contest usually grows more fierce, the opponents tougher, the field muddier, the refs blinder, and, as tension mounts, the audience grows wilder and more affected by the outcome. The better contests are close. Some of the great moments come when the teams are evenly matched, the game comes down to the wire, and our team, through some spectacular play, snatches victory from the jaws of defeat.

Sports can be *very* dramatic. In team sports, the action drives the game forward in a series of plays, each ending with a change in fortune for one side or the other. In dramatic structure, the action propels the production to the climax in a series of scenes, each ending in a crisis ranging from a perplexing problem to a total disaster for the protagonist.

The Inciting Incident

There needs to be an incident or event to start the action of the story. In real life, people may wake up in the morning and *decide* to change their lives, but in real life, other people aren't usually watching as spectators trying to make sense out of the events they see on the screen. Our story shouldn't go on too long before an inciting event occurs because action doesn't start until the event takes place. We need to understand what is motivating the characters early, what has hooked the hero into the story, and what is at stake for them. The incident should be important, imperative. The actions that follow need to seem reasonable. If the hero truly cares and we truly care about the hero, we as an audience, will get hooked into the story.

The Crisis

Stories can be viewed as a series of crises leading to a climax or final crisis. Most people like their lives uncomplicated—free of family conflict, unwanted responsibility, false accusations, threatening legal complications, attacking villains, monsters, vampires, and menacing alien warlords. But, these are what make drama. There has to be a crisis that complicates the life of the protagonist in a way that sorely affects them. Nonnarrative productions confront the audience with information, a situation, or event that touches them or has some obvious impact on them. Both the audience or the protagonist must make a commitment to resolve the problem. The hero, or audience, then grows through a series of events on the way to resolving the problem or achieving the goal so that life can get back to normal.

The path increases in difficulty and intensity. Action advances the plot from point to point in this series of crises. The word "crisis" may seem too strong, but a crisis is really a decision point, a turning point. Having encountered new obstacles or discovered new information, the protagonist responds, adjusts, and somehow changes course. The drama alters the direction in which the story appeared to be heading at the beginning of the scene. These moments of changing direction in the story narrative are the *plot points*. At each plot point, there is an important crisis. The protagonist suffers a reversal of fortune, or the story takes a turn in a new and not too predictable direction.

Each scene in the opening section of our production should introduce new characters, move the story forward, or propel the hero into action. We walk a fine line—keeping story information simple and concise so we don't slow story development, but giving the audience enough information so that characters are well rounded and story logic seems believable. Remember the guideline of limiting the exposition in the opening of the production to just what the audience *needs* to know. By the midpoint of the beginning of the first act, we need to know the conflict of the drama and the hero's goal. The protagonist needs to make a commitment to resolve the plot problem. We need to have seen the character traits that compel the protagonist's triumph in the end. After we hook the audience into the show, about halfway through the beginning, then we can slow down a little and provide some exposition.

The Point of No Return

At some point, also usually about halfway through the beginning, the protagonist has made a commitment. It is still possible to go back, run away, or somehow reverse the events and get out. Although the protagonist makes a commitment to solve the problem or achieve the goal, there is usually a way out, a way to reverse events and run away.

In the middle of the production, however, the hero reaches a point of no return. At this point, the protagonist *decides* to go forward, knowing, at least in some general way, the irreversible consequences of this decision. This is different from committing to solve the problem. For example, we could commit to going swimming, but up until that final moment at the end of the diving board, we can still turn around and walk away. Once we *decide* to jump and do jump, there is no turning back. Because of gravity's irresistible force, ending up in the water is inevitable. Once the protagonist decides to go on, from there to the climax, there is no quitting—no matter how impossible the task appears to be.

The Climax

From the introduction of the first problem in the story, the climax becomes inevitable. In tragedy, the climax occurs just after the opportunity for success appears to be the greatest. In comedy, it happens when failure seems assured and then there is a reversal in fortunes. In *The African Queen,* it happens after Charlie and Rose realize they are hopelessly lost, have given up, and are prepared to die. In *Taxi Driver,* it comes after Travis Bickle (Robert De Niro) returns to the house to kill the pimp.

When the protagonist reaches the ultimate confrontation at the climax, the forces are nearly equal, the options are equally tough, and everything is riding on the protagonist's actions and decisions. This is the plot point when the tension is the highest, when the conflict is the greatest and may ultimately involve a clash of wills or values as well as the final battle between the good guys and the bad guys. The resolution of the climax returns life to normal, but not quite. People have changed and the world is a little different. In nontheatrical productions, if we are successful, the audience has been changed in some way.

The reversal at the climax often comes as a surprise. However, it involves some event or action set in motion in the beginning. It is a realization. The hero, or audience in nonnarrative productions, through the struggle of the middle, may now realize what the real problem is and that the means for resolving it are at hand. Or, in tragedy, the hero is overtaken by the events set in motion in the beginning.

The original inciting incident spins off the twin forces that will compete throughout the drama until their resolution at the climax. As the crisis occurs or the problem is presented, the seeds for its solutions are also sewn.

We can see these twin threads as Charlie and Rose escape aboard the *African Queen.* The boat is more than a means of escape, it becomes the instrument for destroying the *Louisa.* In tragedy, the inciting moment may seem a positive action while the seeds of destruction are overlooked. In the film *The Commitments,* Jimmy (Robert Arkins) first sees Deco (Andrew Strong) singing up a storm but also blind drunk and annoying the band and guests at a wedding.

When Deco first meets with the band members, he grabs Jimmy's sister and, as the story builds, he escalates his abusive ways. His singing is so terrific, however, that the group is willing to put up with his obnoxious behavior. But in the end, when the group appears to be on the verge of success, it's that behavior that destroys them. These are the twin threads of the story that keep the viewer entertained, "held between." The dynamic that keeps the audience entertained by nontheatrical productions can be the thesis of the production, the way things should be. This can be in conflict with the antithesis, the problem—social, environmental, and so on—that is being depicted. The course of the production produces synthesis at the climax such as a solution or a call to action.

A-Story and B-Story (Plots and Subplots)

The main story spine, or story line, is usually called the plot or, in television, the A-story. A-stories are generally driven by the narrative action and the events that move the story forward. Subplots, or B-stories, are usually related to the plot, or A-story, at least thematically. They may involve the secondary characters who are connected to the A-story through the hero. Often you will see the main plot and the subplot connect at the end. When constructing a production, it is generally a good idea to work out the main plot line, or the story spine, first and then see how the subplots work.

Subplots are very important storytelling devices. They can provide balancing or alternative points of view toward the themes of the A-story. They can allow us to draw characters in more than one dimension and show the impact of the main story on other aspects of their lives. Subplots enable us to develop and reflect themes in the main plot. They provide variation in pacing and point of view so that our story can be orchestrated with greater flexibility. They provide depth.

Other Formats

Although most productions we watch or create follow the pattern laid out in this chapter, it's worth noting that not all structures employ the same proportion of beginning, middle, and end. We should be aware of other approaches to structuring that don't rely on resolving a big plot problem.

Skits

Some short productions—about three to five minutes long, like the exercises suggested throughout this text—can be categorized as skits. Skits usually spend little or no time on the beginning and ending aspects of the story. They rely heavily on the audience's trained media perceptions and recognition of stereotypes to establish the setup very quickly. Most of the skit is middle. The character or characters are placed in a familiar situation and given a recognizable character trait. They will not undergo any development or change, but will just run out the many permutations of the joke or premise established in the setup. The end is usually quick and has a twist or some unexpected action.

A Day in the Life

Other structures are particularly useful in organizing material in nontheatrical or documentary productions. One of these is "A Day in the Life," or some variation of this such as "Throughout Time." As you might guess, the production will follow a "typical" day in the life of a platypus, a politician or personality, a pig iron factory, Patagonia, Pittsburgh—almost anything. It still has a beginning, middle, and end, but the spine is constructed purely on the timeline elected for the production. Sequences and events hook onto it, but don't drive it. The piece is usually episodic in nature, with interest deriving from the uniqueness, originality, conflict of ideas, or lifestyle within each vignette.

Portraiture

Portraiture may have a clearly defined beginning, middle, and end, but it also may tend to be more episodic. Portraiture is like peeling off the layers of an onion to discover the unique center of the individual. There is mystery in the outcome. We are fascinated with other people and what makes them tick. This is the glue that keeps the audience in their seats, not solving a problem or watching a character achieve a goal.

A Special Place

Similar to portraiture, another type of production explores a unique place. Often, vignettes of this type focus on portraiture and human interaction. An excellent example of this is Frederick Wiseman's documentary work, such as *High School.* Obviously National Geographic and Discovery Channel types of productions often fall into this category. Even some features are ultimately portraits of place—Peter Weir's *Year of Living Dangerously,* for example.

Constructing the Structure

In constructing a narrative, the beginning is easy. We create a problem for a character or an audience. There is an old French proverb about storytelling, that goes something like this: A character wakes up in the morning and walks out the front door and finds a tree. The tree is the problem. What to do with it? The character decides to deal with it. Maybe the character has always wanted to be taller anyway and so decides to climb the tree.

In the script for a half-hour TV show, this is about page 5 or two minutes into the drama. In feature film, it is somewhere between page 3 and page 10—early in the story. By the end of act one, the character gets to the top and realizes it's impossible to get down. The beginning section ends with a clearly defined problem and the character committed to resolving it.

The middle, or act two, is tougher. Remember, it will comprise half or even more of the production as a whole. While the character is up in the tree, someone throws stones at our hero, or a storm comes along. But, something happens to complicate the problem. Act two should introduce at least one more complication, and we need to see initial growth in the character. Make it tough. Force growth. It can't be as easy as the character thought it was going to be when the commitment was made in act one.

The turning point, or the middle of act two, finds the character's making the irrevocable decision to solve the tree problem in spite of the stones being hurled: "As God is my witness, I'm going to get out of this tree!" Then it gets harder. The character tries harder. Night falls. The storm comes. Enemies attack. Family support withers. We believe the character won't make it back down the tree. Failure seems certain.

Then, in act three, we solve the problem. In act three, the shortest act, all we have to do is get the character out of the tree. The easy way is for someone to talk the character down, but that is usually not the creative way; that is not the visual or physical way and seldom are words really convincing. Seeing is believing. We don't believe half of what we hear, so to convince the audience, we have to see the events that motivate the character to get out of the tree. Something we set up in the opening scenes will save the character in the end. The character had ordered a load of hay, which never came, but it finally arrives and our hero jumps down in the wagon to safety.

The solution should be organic to the story and the character, some facet of a relationship, an event set in motion earlier, a character trait that pays off. If the solution comes from outside the story—a meteor falls from space—in a way the audience could never have anticipated, we violate the rules the same as if we had an ace up our sleeve or loaded dice. People have been shot for less. No cheap endings such as the character waking up and it was all a dream, or they merely misunderstood what they overheard. Throughout the course of the story the character should have learned how to solve the problem.

Hamlet had to ultimately kill his stepfather, King Claudius. He couldn't wake up and realize he didn't have to do it. He couldn't discover he misunderstood what the ghost of his real father had said. He couldn't have the problem solved for him by a tree falling on Claudius. *He* had to do it. Maybe the solution is only temporary or it works in a twisted way, but the character learns something and achieves something.

Structuring an Idea

Let's structure a story. The first step in structuring is to find the germ of the idea that appeals to us. We should be able to state it simply in a couple of sentences or a very short paragraph. This is called the *log line*. At its shortest, it could be the title. Samuel Goldwyn paid fifty thousand dollars for the title for the film, *The Cowboy and the Lady*. No script. No treatment. Just the title.[2]

Log Lines: The **TV** Guide *Version*
Often the log line is compared to the *TV Guide* description of a television show or movie. Actually, one that is a little more developed may be more useful to us. The point is that it needs to be short and concise. But, it also ought to sug-

gest what is unique about the story—what might intrigue an audience more than the thousand or so other versions of the same story.

What is it that interests us about a particular idea? Sometimes we have to dig to realize exactly why we want to produce the production we have in mind. What attracts us to the subject? What is it that fascinates us? What strikes the emotional chords or harmonics? Why does this character, man or woman, place or event interest us? How does the situation or conflict allow us to explore this person? How are we stretching or taking these characters to a unique place in the human condition? Our log line should clearly express whatever we find interesting or unique in the story, the character, or our approach.

When creating the log line, we describe what interests us in terms of the central or inherent conflict. What is the duality, the polarity, the nexus of conflict? How is this manifest? How do we see it?

- *Hamlet*:   A teenaged prince in medieval Denmark confronts adult responsibility and his own emerging emotions of filial and sexual love when his father's ghost demands that young Hamlet avenge his murder and kill Claudius.

- *The Civil War*:   A television series that presents the war between the states with intimacy and timely relevance through a series of personal accounts of the events that transformed people's lives.

- *Phantom of the Opera*:   A vengeful, hideously disfigured composer prowls the bowels of the Paris Opera House appearing only when his love for an attractive young singer can be stifled no longer.

If we were doing log lines for the children's story "The Three Little Pigs," they might vary according to the tone of the piece we anticipate producing:

- Three pigs learn the value of balancing work and play and manage to keep the wolf from the door, or

- Practical Pig demonstrates the advantages of brick construction and saves his family and the town from the evil wolf, or

- An "Ugly Duckling" story about Practical Pig, cruelly rejected for his compulsive behavior, even by his own brothers, who proves his mania for masonry is the only salvation for the Pig family.

Our treatment should be reflected in the log line along with the core idea of our story, mentioning how the major events, as we plan to present them, affect the main characters.

Beats: The Story Steps

Stories move along by *story beats*—the major events of the story. These are often the "reversals" of our story. Reversals are the points at which the story turns, but not in the sense that the story actually reverses direction. Rather, it moves in a different direction much as we would if we hit a detour and had to try another path to continue making progress. Think of it as a reversal of fortunes for the protagonist or a change in the mind of the audience—places where they go "Ah ha!" or "Oh no!" and sometimes even laugh aloud.

Story beats are the points of conflict, the big decisions our characters make. If we are describing a TV show or movie to a friend, story beats are the major actions and events we relate in describing how the story unfolds. First this happened, then that happened, and then . . .

Laying out our story by beats is the most important step we take to give our narrative coherence. It solves story structure problems at the beginning and allows us to improve and embellish the story as we write, rather than trying to structure it while solving the problems. First, expand the log line to a short synopsis. Then, break down the synopsis into the events that move the story forward. Remember that this is visual storytelling. The audience should *see* the story unfold, not have someone *tell* them what is going on. Visuals are not just photographed activities on the screen. Much as storytellers use their hands to help shape their stories visually, we use images, symbols, and icons to help convey the significance of character, places, and events.

Continuing with the Three Little Pigs example, images of famine, drought, and desperate desolation that would embolden the hungry wolf come to mind. Images of a fattened, trivializing aristocracy—in pre-revolution France or Russia, for example—come to mind. Images of cocky, challenging, in-your-face kids filled with youthful bravado come to mind. In terms of symbols, the building materials they choose speak of their points of view (attitudes) and personalities. In some versions, the two indolent brothers given names are drawn from their characteristic activities: Fifer Pig, who plays a flute, and Fiddler Pig, who plays a fiddle. Practical Pig just likes bricks. Then we have to decide whose story it is. Practical Pig is the one who resolves the problem of the main plot more than his brothers, so we will adopt his point of view for our story.

With images beginning to take form and point of view decided, we begin the story synopsis:

> *This is going to be about Practical Pig and his two brothers, Fifer Pig and Fiddler Pig, who build inferior homes, while his stands against the attack of the wolf. In the end, the wolf and pigs will match wits and the pigs will win.*

As we expand the story into the synopsis, we can already see it falling into a distinct beginning, middle, and end: building the houses, the attack on the three houses by the wolf, and the final confrontation between wolf and pig. Generally we work out our main plot, or A-story, first and then worry about the subplots. For the example we are developing from the log line, the B-story will be:

> *Fifer and Fiddler, two fun-loving pigs, deride their brother Practical for his parental attitude, but learn his loyalty to family stems from true filial affection. At the same time, Practical learns to loosen up a little.*

The beginning will be the two younger pigs letting their older brother take on a role of responsibility for them while they flute and fiddle. The middle will be their ridiculing his conscientious hard work and their bravado about hypothetical wolves. In the end, they appreciate his seriousness and he begins to share in some of their fun.

Now we are ready to define the beats and build sequences. The first story beat must be the incident or event that incites the action. In the story book version, the pigs just decide out of the blue to build houses. We should be prepared to answer the questions: Why now? Why not yesterday? Why not tomorrow? We need an inciting incident to start the action moving, to nail down why it is imperative for the story to happen *now*. Whatever the event we contrive, it should logically propel the story forward.

We could choose a weather forecast or someone coming into the town telling the pigs a wolf was sighted, but neither of these lead to the heart of how the story will ultimately be resolved, with new-found trust and cooperation among the brothers. A better way then might be to create a mother pig who is sending the three brothers out on their own for the first time. She could tell them they need to build houses: "It is a harsh world out there." Her warning establishes the problem and is the first story beat.

Inciting action is not something to be taken lightly. Once we have committed to a story beginning, it's hard to go back and think about starting the story anew from a different point of view or timeframe. If we started the story earlier, for instance, with the little pigs being born, what would happen to our story? It would become structurally unbalanced with too much time spent on the pigs growing up and leaving home and too little time spent on the attack of the houses and the final matching wits of pig and wolf. It would be a different story, probably about separation and severing the silver cord with the home sty instead of about self-reliance.

What about the old montage-of-them-growing-up trick? This kind of montage carries very little information for the time it takes. It's a series of snap shots that we flip through. It provides explanation and exposition and may help set mood or tone. But we sit back as an audience and view it without becoming involved in the drama of the moment.

Generally, unless we are undertaking an epic like *The Color Purple, Empire of the Sun, The Last Emperor,* or *Gone with the Wind,* films and television shows tend to deal with a short timeframe—the cusp of change. Condensing time, or putting the clock on the action, heightens the tension in the drama. It's no accident that many narratives like *48 Hours, High Noon,* and *The Longest Day* define a specific period for the action.

What about starting after the pigs' houses are already built? The pigs are at their various homes and the wolf attacks in the opening scene? Sure, that could be a grabber, but we forego the opportunities for Practical Pig to say, "I told you so," or not, depending on what kind of porker we are portraying. In other words, we are giving up the chance to develop a B-story about the relationship between the brothers. Chances are, it is this B-story about relationships that we find the most interesting and revealing and not the good pig versus bad wolf A-story.

Start with the wolf attack and then flash back? Okay, that gives us an exciting opening, but it also creates other problems. First, it robs us of the opportunities to build tension to this event. We may be willing to sacrifice it for an opening "gotcha," but we give away a big scene. Do we really want to? Will it make the middle section too flat? Second, it is important to realize that sequences don't have to be chronological or linear, but with each jump in time the audience needs to stay with us. Generally the audience is willing to make the time leap when the jump is fairly short and the leap is forward in time. When the leap is over several months or years or backward in time, we need to spend some screen time reorienting the audience. Sometime this strategy is the solution to a special problem, but generally if we keep our story linear and confined to as narrow a timeframe as possible, we will get the audience involved in the events of the story, the characters, and their problems without having to risk distancing, or worse, confusing our audience.

Convoluted, interior, psychological structures that use flashbacks and force juxtapositions of scenes and perceptions in literary narrative (Faulkner's *The Sound and the Fury,* for example, or Joyce's *Ulysses*) usually do not work well in visual narrative. They often seem contrived, distracting, and confusing. There are some exceptions, for example, *Incident at Owl Creek Bridge, Little Big Man,* and *Petulia,* in which the flashback device does work well. Most visual narratives, however, take a straight line from beginning to end.

We should start our narrative at the last possible moment before the story begins. If we start too early, we labor the backstory and bore our audience to tears. If we start too late, we will have to find ways of going back to catch up. What is the first important action of the story and what is the last moment we can approach it? Let's say our inciting action is mother pig advising the three brothers to build shelters. We don't want a long scene showing them having their last farewell slop together and then finally, at the end of the meal, mother warning them about the cruel world. As we fade in, we want the meal to be concluding. Perhaps there is some brotherly bickering going on. Then, as they are wiping their chinny-chin-chins, Mother delivers her warning.

Now, if all three pigs built houses out of brick, there would be no story. So, the next beat is Fifer and Fiddler Pig running off to have fun. The third beat shows our hero Practical, who is fairly uptight about doing things the right way and starchily self-righteous about frivolity. This beat sets up some good fraternal conflict for the B-story about brotherly love. For the sake of irony, we could end the beginning part of our story with a fourth beat: rain pouring down, night falling, and Fifer and Fiddler dry in their homes, while poor Practical is out in the storm spending a miserable night because his brick house is unfinished.

The middle of the story introduces us to the wolf. He is our second act complication, being part of the "harsh world" as predicted by Mother pig, but far worse than the pigs are really prepared for. Before he enters, however, there are three story beats. The first has the two brothers, rested and chipper, visiting their brother, not to help, but to chide him for never having any fun in his life. In the next, Practical raises the specter of a wolf in the forest. And, finally, they respond by laughing and singing their "Who's Afraid of the Big Bad Wolf?" song. These three beats raise the ante in their relationships and dig Fiddler and Fifer deeper into the hole they will have to crawl out of when they ask Practical for refuge. In the production, this may appear to be just one scene of Fifer and Fiddler confronting Practical. Obviously, however, in telling the story, three distinct and important events happen in this scene, so there are three beats.

At this point, everything in the story so far could be reversed. Fifer and Fiddler could change their minds and go build better homes. They could help their brother and all get along better. All that is possible. Once the wolf is on the scene, however, none of that is possible. The pigs have reached the point of no return and events must play out the way they have been set up. Fifer and Fiddler have dug themselves down to the bottom of the pit with their devil-may-care behavior, and now they need to climb back out.

So the turning point of the drama comes when the protagonist reaches this point of no return and decides, or is forced by events, to go on. In *Gone with the Wind,* for example, it's when Scarlett (Vivien Leigh) says, "I'll never go hungry again."

In drama and in comedy, the beats now should begin to happen faster. The action heats up. If we want to, we can even put a chase scene in at the end of this section of the story when we really feel the wolf will get the two frivolous little pigs but their brother saves them at the last moment.

The first beat of the rising action is the huffing, puffing, and blowing down of the straw house. In the Disney version, the next beat shows the wolf attempting to fool the pigs by dressing himself in sheepskins and asking them to take him in. This doesn't fool them, and we see some growth by Fifer and Fiddler. And, if we assumed the wolf was trying to pull the wool over their eyes because he was incapable of blowing down a stick house, our estimate of the wolf's prowess was sadly inadequate. In the next beat, the wolf rises to the challenge and the house of sticks is blown away. This can be followed by a chase scene beat and the narrow escape of Fifer and Fiddler Pig to their brother's brick home where he saves them by taking them in.

At this point, our story could end happily, but not satisfactorily, with a reconciliation of the brothers. The audience has to feel that our hero has been truly challenged. For Practical Pig to have merely been right is not enough. In *The African Queen,* it is not enough for Rose and Charlie to negotiate the river and escape the Germans. The Germans have killed Rose's brother and torched the mission. The *Louisa* must be sunk. We need to see the final duel between good and evil. Practical Pig needs to be tested. We made this decision when we assigned him the point of view of the production. It's his story—he has to compel the events that lead to the conclusion. Our hero or the villain has to see this thing through to the end. For the pigs, it's not satisfactory to leave a loose wolf wandering the neighborhood. For the wolf, his pride has been hurt and pride is one of the sins, the final one in fact, which goes just before the fall. Here, it's the villain who decides to continue and carry the battle beyond the level of force to a new level—one of wits.

In the first beat of the end section, the wolf attempts and fails to blow down the house of bricks. Fifer and Fiddler admit Practical was right and apologize. He accepts their apology. We and the pigs think it's over as they celebrate their victory.

Then, as in *Alien* when the monster is discovered hiding out in the space shuttle after Ripley and the audience think the danger has passed, and as in most good suspense dramas with a "gotcha" at the end, while the pigs are seemingly lulled into complacency, the next beat of the drama takes place. The wolf, noting that the flaw in their brick fortress is their flue, scampers up onto the roof and jumps down the chimney. It is a good twist. The surprise ending beat to the story is that the pigs have put a pot on the fire in which to catch the wolf. This reinforces their growth while also solving the A-story wolf problem. It's guaranteed to keep the audience worried to the last moment of the drama. The final beat, or the *dénouement,* completes the resolution of the B-story line dealing with fraternal relationships when Practical joins his brothers in song and dance. He's learned something as well. A very satisfactory story.

A good idea at this point is to chart out the story beats and make certain we have achieved a good balance in terms of our beginning, middle, and end. Remember, the beginning is about one-quarter of the story, in this case, four beats. The middle is about half or a little more, and our outline shows seven beats. The end is a final quarter or a little less—we have four beats. The beats we have identified for the Three Little Pigs are summarized in Table 4.1.

The next step in organizing the story is to make notes, expanding down the page below a column headed by the beat description. After fleshing it out a little, we are ready to prepare a script or treatment or otherwise put together our production.

Writers who come out of a short story, essay, or English composition approach of starting at page one and running to the end may find it difficult to break old habits and try creating stories in this fashion. However, structuring first helps prevent a natural inclination to be linear. We've all heard people say, "All I need is a good opening sentence or paragraph and then out it pours." What pours out may be good stuff. They may have always gotten good grades doing this and see no need to try another method. Big mistake. Art is expression and raw creation, but it is also manipulation and refinement. The blob of clay thrown on the potter's wheel is not art until it is manipulated into a vase or bowl. Selecting the right stone or piece of wood or mixing the right colors is important, but until these materials are carved or put on canvas, they are nothing by themselves. Some contend that art can be created by the random unconscious, and others say that an infinite number of monkeys at typewriters will eventually re-create all the works of Shakespeare. Both arguments are

TABLE 4.1   Beat Chart for the Three Little Pigs

Beginning

- Mother pig tells her three sons to build houses because of the harsh environment.
- Fifer and Fiddler Pig build straw and stick houses and run off to have fun.
- Practical self-righteously builds his house of brick and berates his brothers for their frivolous behavior.
- Rain and night. Fifer and Fiddler are snug in their homes; Practical is out in the cold.

Middle

- Brothers heckle Practical for his all-work-and-no-play attitude.
- Practical warns about wolf.
- Brothers say they're not afraid.
- Wolf attacks Fifer's house of straw and blows it down.
- Wolf pretends to be a little lost lamb.
- Wolf blows down Fiddler's house of sticks.
- Chase scene. Just in the nick of time, Practical lets them in and they are saved.

End

- Wolf fails to blow down house of bricks. Practical congratulates himself.
- Wolf climbs roof and comes down chimney.
- Pot of hot water awaits and wolf is killed (or shoots back up the chimney, depending on the rating).
- Pigs reconcile differences, and Practical begins to sing and dance with his brothers.

probably true, but the film and television business is ultimately a business and time is money. So create, then manipulate.

Structuring the Production

A Real-Time Medium

Film, video, and television productions are projected onto the screen with relentless forward motion. Film clicks through the projector at 24 frames per second, and television tubes are scanned at the rate of 30 frames per second. On the other hand, individuals vary their speed when reading. When we read a book, we can pause to digest a salient point, slow to savor a moment, dig in for difficult material, or gloss over easy information. If we forget a character's name or a particularly difficult term or convoluted concept, we can go back and look at it again.

Because of film and television's relentless advance through real time, our productions must:

- Provide pauses for important points to sink in, for the consequences of a reversal to be realized, for difficult or new information to be synthesized.
- Create expectation for important information so the audience will recognize its importance when they get to it.
- Vary the pacing of scenes and sequences to heighten excitement, increase tension, or allow audiences to pause to enjoy the moment.
- Provide reminders of names or reinforce terms we don't want the audience to forget.

Pauses

Providing pauses is easy. They happen naturally at the end of sentences, paragraphs, or blocks of dialogue and narration. If we put important points just before any of these pauses—while our talent breathes or moves or we move the camera or cut to another scene—the audience has a brief moment to reflect on the implications of what has just developed. When writing sentences for characters or narrators, put the important point at or near the end of a line of dialogue or narration. That brief pause when the talent hits the period and takes a breath allows for the word to sink in. Thus, in the line, "Nothing else matters, I love Mary," the character's admission of his affection for Mary is the most important point. Reversing the line, "I love Mary, nothing else matters," tells the audience that "something else" *is* going to be important. (Audiences understand that negatives and positives are often interchangeable!)

When we build dialogue bites or blocks of narration so that the most important point is at the end, the slightly longer pause before the next speaker or block of narration allows slightly more time for the point to sink in. Building bites or blocks in this way also makes dialogue or narration flow better when the next line relates to the last one. "I'm going to meet my mother in Panama" should generate a response about the impending trip. The audience thinks "Panama" is the most important word in the sentence. "I'm going to Panama to meet my mother" should more logically lead to a conversation about Mom.

Building productions in this way not only makes them enormously comprehensible and easy to follow, it also gives them a drive as actions and events, ever increasing in power and importance, confront the viewer.

Creating Expectation

The audience looks for clues that set up characters, events, props, or plot points as important. It's like handing out a program or providing the roster of players at a ball game. It ensures that important details don't slip by unnoticed. Or, if we *are* trying to slip one by the audience, like burying a clue in a mystery drama, it allows us to do so in a way that the audience doesn't feel cheated. At the end, they'll remember, "Ah yes, that *was* mentioned. I just didn't think it was important." They'll think it was their fault and not our cleverness that kept them from figuring it all out.

Several techniques are commonly used for setting up an expectation for an audience. Obviously characters or narrators can point details out and create expectation for subsequent action or even the next shot. A line like, "Tomorrow we'll visit Murphy and get to the bottom of this," obviously sets up the expectation for a scene with Murphy. A character's quick look off-screen sets up the audience's expectation for a cut to a shot of the object or person the character looked at.

The camera can also create expectancy in the audience. A point-of-view camera shot moving slowly toward a door, window, or cave opening is a familiar shot in action dramas. In the horror genre, the shot of the unaware character appearing to hear or sense something and quickly glancing to the side is often followed by a cut to the character's point of view revealing that nothing was there. It's a fun game of "made you look" between the filmmaker and the audience.

Another technique for establishing expectation is the use of "threes." High school mathematics teaches that having two points on a graph allows us to predict a third point with some anticipated accuracy. Discovering that the third point is about where we had predicted it would be reinforces our projection. Now it has become truth. Using threes and remembering that the most important statement should come last, we can establish a variety of things. For a mystery, consider the following lines:

"It sure is dark. . . . This old house give me the creeps. . . . I think I heard something in the basement!"

Putting the most important point at the end of the sentence and the most important sentence at the end of the three lines allows the audience to have every expectation that something malevolent is in the basement and that it will be extremely important to the story and characters. It is essential that each iteration increase in importance or power over the preceding one. The first mention is a hint or suggestion; the second, a clear statement; and the third, an affirmation of truth that compels action or a decision.

The exception to this is burying clues. The audience expects to hear the most important point at the end of a sentence and the most important sentence at the end of a line of dialogue. If we have a clue to a mystery or other type of information we want the audience to hear but not attach too much importance to, we can bury it mid-sentence in the middle of a line of dialogue. The audience will then easily believe that the characters in the scene might miss the importance of the clue. It's even possible that many in the audience will miss it themselves and yet still remember when they finally recognize its importance that they did in fact hear the word in dialogue.

Using threes can help convey thoughts and motivations in character development or relationships, as in the following dialogue segment:

"It was really a shock to run into Sonia tonight. . . . After not seeing her for all these years, we picked up right where we left off. It was so easy to just start talking with her. . . . You know, I think I still love her."

The character could say, "I saw Sonia today and I think I'm still in love with her," but that means the thought process happened off-camera—when he saw Sonia. In the preceding dialogue, the audience and the actor have an opportunity to be a part of the thought process that draws the conclusion.

Threes are common in drama and surprisingly natural to our own experience. We perceive many patterns in threes. Notice the use of threes in clauses, prepositional phrases, and especially epithets—"You low-down, good-for-nothing creep!" Sometimes we'll find a dialogue bite or narration block that will use both patterns—three sentences increasing in intensity *and* three elements in the last sentence—to really drive a point home:

"I'm sorry, Greg. I'm leaving you for good. I didn't realize until last night you were such a two-faced, lying bastard."

or

"I'm sorry to see you stuck here in jail. It's really hard on your mother. Godfrey is still hopeful that maybe they'll change their policy, reconsider your sentence, and release you in her custody."

or

"Throughout their lives, the ancient Egyptians had one goal. They wanted to live forever. To this end, they created a mythology, developed herbal potions, and mummified their dead."

Notice also the use of threes in scenes where pressure is being added to a situation:

"Captain, we have twenty minutes to get off the ship before impact. . . . Captain, four minutes to collision. . . . Captain, abandon ship!"

In *The Unforgiven*, Will Munney (Clint Eastwood), who swore off booze through the civilizing influence of his wife, confronts liquor three times. The first time, in the saloon, though cold and wet and ill, he declines. He gets severely beaten and only manages to crawl out of the bar at the end of the scene. The second time, he takes a nip from the bottle before the murder of the young cowhand. The third time, he drinks the bottle dry after he learns of his friend Ned's (Morgan Freeman's) death. The scene opens with an empty bottle being thrown on the road as he marches into town for vengeance. We know he has now reverted fully to being the "man of notoriously vicious and intemperate disposition." Murder and mayhem will soon follow.

And certainly, drawing from our previous example, there are three little pigs who build three houses. The wolf threatens with threes, to huff and puff and blow their houses down, and they defy him by the hairs of their chinny-chin-chins!

Pacing

Given the unvarying forward pace of film and video projection, it is essential that scenes and sequences vary in their internal pacing. One way to vary pacing is to intercut between the A-story and the B-story. This gives flexibility to the pacing, especially if one of the story lines is fast-paced action or humor and the other is slower paced drama or romance. Intercutting isn't always appropriate, but when outlining story beats, remember that, in most comedies—even the slapstick classics of Chaplin, W. C. Fields, Laurel and Hardy, Abbott and Costello, and Lucille Ball and Vivien Vance—the fast-paced, uproariously funny, zany antics are intercut with slower paced dramatic or romantic moments. Most action films such as the James Bond films, *Robocop, Terminator 2, Raiders of the Lost Ark,* or the swashbuckling genre like Richard Lester's *The Three Musketeers* or Michael Curtiz's *Captain Blood* also have their quiet or romantic moments. Even the more serious films such as *Driving Miss Daisy, Terms of Endearment, Knife in the Water,* or most of Ingmar Bergman's works have moments of comic relief to offset the heavier moments of the drama.

Juxtaposition is another powerful pacing tool. We can play a quiet, romantic or tense but slowly paced scene for as long as we think an audience can stand it, then "smash" cut to something of high energy and action. This can often work right after the third three. The audience has just been given confirmation of an important point and then they immediately witness the action it precipitates. Expectation can also be drawn out, as when the point-of-view camera shot holds on a closed door behind which we think the alien may lurk, then wham! The door opens and in blasts the monster. Using pacing to surprise, to give comic relief, or to allow a moment of quiet—playing the tension of the production—are effective ways to keep the audience involved with our show.

Reminders

Most audiences never notice while watching Disney's *Dumbo* that the little mouse who helps Dumbo realize his flying abilities doesn't have a name. This is rare. Most individuals and characters on the screen do have names and just as we attempt—frequently without much success—to remember the names of individuals we meet, audiences like to know the names of characters they watch in films and on television. We frequently solve this problem in news, documentary, or interview formats by superimposing a person's name in the lower third of the frame. We can hold this label or even repeat it if appropriate.

In drama, names pose problems. In spite of all the care we take in selecting just the right name to suggest our character's personality, social status or role in the story, audiences don't easily remember names. To further complicate matters, we rarely refer to individuals by name in conversation, which makes them difficult to include in dialogue without sounding forced. Therefore, we carefully craft scenes in which we introduce a character so that we reveal the character's name effortlessly and unobtrusively. We may have one person introduce the character to another, call out the name to get the character's attention, or use the name as people sometimes do, in anger, admonition, or a sarcastic put down. Then, to help the audience remember the name, we can repeat it in later scenes, perhaps as one character speaks to another person about the third character.

Technical terms or product names are often something we want the audience to learn and remember. Much advertising is nothing more than a creative mnemonic device to help the audience remember the name of the product. Advertisers use both visual and verbal repetition to get product names stuck in our mind. It can help an audience to define technical terms when first used and also repeat them in the narration or dialogue shortly after. That reinforces what we have heard and helps us remember the term or phrase.

Sometimes it is possible to reduce the term or phrase to a shorter, more easily remembered form. However, there is a danger in reducing a technical term or phrase to its initials and using the acronym throughout the production. Some acronyms, such as FBI, CIA, IRS, DDT, TNT, or SCUBA, have general acceptance. Others may complicate or add confusion to the production rather than simplify it. One New England college orientation film referred to the student meal ticket allowance as the MTA throughout. This got laughs from most audiences who associated the acronym with Boston's famous Metropolitan Transit Authority. Repeating the phrase, "meal ticket allowance" begins to sound officious and cold in narration. But the college could have just used a shorter form referring to their MTA as the "meal allowance" or the "meal ticket." Once we have shortened or simplified the term, using threes helps remind and reinforce important names or terms in a production and make the audience feel familiar with the terms and comfortable with the characters.

Sequences: The String of Pearls

Film and television productions move forward by a series of sequences much like pearls on a string. A *sequence* is generally a fully developed vignette, consisting of a scene, part of a scene, or several scenes, which can be defined as having its own beginning, middle, and end. Each sequence mirrors the structure of the story as a whole, with rising, increasingly important, or intense action to a story reversal.

Occasionally, between sequences there are transitions, perhaps showing that the time has changed or the character has moved to another place. These transitions do not really contribute to the advancement of plot or story nor do they contribute materially to the development of character or relationships. The purpose of these transitions in well-crafted productions is to provide a big pause to let the audience think about what may have just happened. Or, perhaps it is to change the pace, giving the audience respite from the intensity of the drama at the end of a particularly powerful or action-packed sequence. These also work when we want to change the mood, pace, or rhythm of the piece. Quite often they work as a curtain for an act break as in the early morning foggy exterior shot in *Driving Miss Daisy* between the first and second acts.

Most sequences take place in a single location or on a single set. They will have real time unity and involve the same characters. Often there is only one major plot point to a sequence; however, it's not uncommon for there to be two or more.

The sequence, like "French scenes" in theater, may start with an entrance and end with an exit. Between the entrance and the exit is rising action in a sequence created by a character's confrontation with something, someone, or some elemental force. Confrontations that initiate the rising action can be caused by nature: tornados, hurricanes, blizzards, drought, fog, or time. The character or individual can be forced to deal with the powers that be, the mob, chaos, the bureaucracy, the deity, or any other formidable foe. Rising action can be new information or additional information to put pressure on an existing problem. Decisions or choices made by the protagonist or by someone whose decision affects the protagonist can also create rising action. In non-narrative productions, rising action occurs as the audience learns, grows more aware, becomes more involved, or begins to realize the implications of the production.

Additionally, good sequences provide subtext. The audience learns additional information from the characters' actions or how the characters deal with the story elements. We interpret their behavior as a reflection of their thoughts. Characters are like people who confront conflict. They learn and grow. When characters share experiences with other characters, especially during trying times, they tend to develop strong feelings for and about each other, whether love, friendship, or out-and-out hatred. Thus, as the story evolves, we also see the evolution of character and relationships. This gives texture to the sequence. More than one thing is happening. In nonnarrative, the audience members are the ones who are growing and developing as they confront new information and new situations and share new experiences.

In documentary productions, structuring and sequencing are planned during what often turns into months of detailed research. But, however well prepared, much of this planning is still done on the fly as the reality of the production alters the blueprint of research.

Exercise 1

Writing a good log line is a terrific exercise and not as easy as it appears. Flip to the index in the back of the book for a moment and look at the films cited in this text. Write log lines for two or three of the films. You'll find it an interesting way to focus on the core of a film.

Now, take an idea of your own and write several different log lines for it, emphasizing different interpretations and treatments for the story. This is an important step in focusing on the core of your project. Often you begin to find weaknesses and flaws right at this point. Select a log line that you like and then come up with a title—at least a working title. Finding the right name for your production helps you coalesce your ideas and define the uniqueness of your production even further. This is not just a cosmetic afterthought, but an important step in the creation of the work.

Exercise 2

Pick a video tape of a feature-length movie you are familiar with and fast forward to about 28 or so minutes into it. Can you find the break between act one and two? Roll forward to a point just ahead of the 60-minute mark and see if you can find the hero's action that changes the direction of the rest of the act. Now go to a place in the tape just before the 90-minute mark and see if you can find where act three begins.

Analyzing the film's structure sequence by sequence is a good exercise for potential writers, directors, and producers. Time the length of each sequence in the film. (This is useful if you remember that a page of script equals about one minute of screen time.) Look at each sequence for rising action as well as for what it does for the movie: develop character, develop relationships, provide exposition, move the story through action, create anticipation or other emotions, and so on.

Exercise 3

To help move from linear to sequence oriented thinking or writing, go through your treatment or script and mark off and number your sequences. (If you don't have a production in mind at this point, find a short one-act play or even a short story that appeals to you.) Make a 3 × 5 or 4 × 6 card for each sequence. In analyzing sequences on the card, record the following information:

Protagonist: _____

Confrontation with: _____

Reversal: _____

Action or reaction required: _____

On the back of the card, note the following information:

The sequence starts at: _____

The sequence ends at: _____

In this sequence, the audience sees: _____

Character growth is shown in the action or line: _____

Relationships are developed in the action or line: _____

Notes

1. Locale is sometimes referred to in film as the *diegesis*, or the world of the film. In television production, it may be called the *arena*.

2. After buying the title, Goldwyn discovered Paramount had already registered it and he had to pay another hundred thousand to buy the rights. *Then* he went through a long list of writers to come up with an actual story.

5

MOOD

The magic of cinema lies in its evocative power. Think for a moment about your favorite films and you are likely to remember scenes marked by a strong sense of mood:

- In *Apocalypse Now*, the scene of the helicopters surging across the screen to Wagner's "Die Walkyrie" or the dark, mysterious first meeting with Kurtz.
- In the final scene of *Butch Cassidy and the Sundance Kid*, as the two crouch, wounded in the little room in Bolivia and then explode from the door with thunderous weapon fire and we slowly pull back from the freeze frame.
- In *Chinatown*, Polanski, in his cameo role, slices Jake Gittes's nose. (See Figure 5.1.)
- In *Who's Afraid of Virginia Woolf?*, George (Richard Burton) returns from the closet with the gun and "shoots" Martha (Elizabeth Taylor).

It is the treatment of mood in a scene that contributes more than story or dialogue to creating these "memorable moments."

As an audience, we want to be moved. We watch films with the expectation of having our emotions aroused. We are drawn into scenes through the persuasion of mood. It sets the emotional tone and guides our reactions toward the story, action, and characters. Creating and controlling the mood of the film or video is a weaving together of all the elements of the scene or production—not only the action of the performer or subject of the film or video, but also the location, the design elements of the frame, the lighting, cinematography, editing, and sound. It's the building of a well-textured, emotional foundation for the audience on a nonrational level that supports the linear communication of story and information on a rational level.

FIGURE 5.1
The scene in *Chinatown* where Polanski, in his cameo role, slices Jake Gittes's nose is marked by a strong sense of mood.

"CHINATOWN" Copyright © 1995 by Paramount Pictures. All Rights Reserved. Courtesy of Paramount Pictures.

Although mood is such an obvious pleasure in the film experience, conceiving and describing mood—and planning its creation—are a surprisingly subtle undertaking. Mood is a subjective impression. People react to it with their own history and sensitivities. The fundamental difficulty in thinking and talking about mood is that we feel the qualities of mood at a nonlogical, impressionistic level that is difficult to translate into words. The words available to us to describe feelings—joy, sadness, exhilaration, melancholy, nervousness, desperation, awe, and so on—are simply too broad to express the rich tonal variations in most of what we feel. Try using words to describe the differences in mood between a John Coltrane saxophone solo and a Thelonious Monk piano improvisation, or between Grieg's "Peer Gynt" and Beethoven's "Eroica," or between a Kandinsky painting and a Rothko painting, or between Coppola's *The Godfather* and Scorsese's *Goodfellas*. Language must operate at the level of poetry and literature where it is connotative before it can truly capture the subtleties of mood.

One might think that creating mood and arousing emotions with the visual media would be easily understood, an almost natural undertaking. Surprisingly, as film and video producers, we may find it difficult to learn how to express mood and feeling. We may struggle to grasp the slippery notion of mood and find ourselves instead expressing abstract concepts, beating our audience over the head with the stereotypes and rhetoric, or confusing them altogether.

When trying to conceive and create mood with images and sound, we need to beware the trap of falling back on familiar word-based concepts. Instead of conveying mood, we end up trying to express ideas and abstractions by juxtaposing hackneyed representational images: crosses, circles, phallic symbols, weapons, voodoo dolls, the broken face of a child's doll, hypodermic needles, and the like.

When we see shots of expensive suburban homes, fancy cars, and well-dressed people juxtaposed with shots of homeless persons and inner city poverty, or long sequences of gravestones, or a montage of flags and honor guards, we may guess at the meaning such compositions are intended to rhetorically communicate. However, it is unlikely they will actually move us and establish mood.

An audience does not necessarily feel sad, in knee-jerk fashion, if they see a gravestone. Some people see a cemetery as a resting place of peace and tranquility; as a place of love and passion where an early romance bloomed, away from prying eyes; or even as a place where one's family and tradition are honored.[1] Similarly, shots of fancy cars, flying birds, waving flags, and so on don't necessarily make all of us react the same way. They just refer to some vague intention of an idea.

To actually create mood—to make an audience feel mood—requires technique, not a laundry list of symbols. Creating a scene of vaulting idealism and youthful romantic exhilaration in a dark, confining cave as in *Dead Poets Society*, for example, is only possible if we go beyond the cliché associations of the location to ask the questions: "What about the subject? How do we want the audience to feel about the subject? How will I create these feelings? What techniques can I use? *What's the treatment of mood?*"

Treatment of Mood

The source of treatment is in your analysis of what feelings you want to engender and grow in the audience as they watch a particular scene. As we pointed out in Chapter 1, technique serves treatment. There are subtle shifts in how we might direct the talent, paint the set, choose the props and wardrobe, and light the scene, where we would place the camera; what and how much we would shoot; what we would add for music and effects; and how we would edit the shots together. Changing the treatment influences how the mood will affect the audience, how it will arouse different emotions and evoke feelings.

Location and Setting

We usually associate mood with location, setting, and sense of place. Consider, for example, the differences in mood suggested by the following film locations:

- the confining, cluttered living room of a college professor and his wife in *Who's Afraid of Virginia Woolf?*,
- a forest in Appalachia made malevolent in *Deliverance*,

- the surreal, flaming landscape of a steel mill in *Black Rain,* where criminal chieftains meet in the night,
- a spaceship's terrifying cargo hold echoing and dripping in the outer reaches of the galaxy in *Alien,*
- a remote country road in *North by Northwest* lost in the openness of the Kansas corn fields.

Whether scouting locations or building sets, our first considerations are how a setting will contribute to the mood we want to convey and how it will provide photographic opportunities for our treatment of the subject.

Bonnie and Clyde opens with Bonnie Parker (Faye Dunaway), in her room playing with her makeup, flopping on her bed, casting about for something to do—stark naked. In essence, not dressed up and no place to go. There is no music. The set is a monochromatic yellow-brown, and we never see all of it in a wide shot. It seems small and Bonnie caged by it. This caged feeling is re-inforced by the bars and braces of her metal bedstead through which we see her, as if in jail. We believe she is bored to death. If we didn't, we wouldn't ac-cept her going off with Clyde Barrow (Warren Beatty) for a Coke and armed robbery so easily. Here, the mood of the film establishes the character motiva-tion and sets the narrative in motion before any dialogue begins. A similar use of setting occurs in *Moonstruck* when Loretta Castorini (Cher) first encounters Ronny Cammareri (Nicolas Cage). The volcanic roaring of the flaming brick ovens of the bakery are emblematic of the frightening animal passions of his personality.

The mood of a place depends on how the filmmaker makes us experience it. Sometimes we can make a familiar place unfamiliar just by experiencing it at unusual times or under unusual circumstances—a department store at night after closing time. Sometimes the mood is evoked by associations with the past—an abandoned amusement park or the living room in an old house be-longing to an elderly woman no longer there. Mood can be created from em-phasizing existing physical characteristics—the overpowering scale of a palatial living room, the claustrophobic crowding in a submarine, the vast emptiness of a desert, or the clammy chill of a rain-drenched forest.

When scouting and choosing locations for a scene and when selecting props for a scene, we should consider various effects. Do we want exteriors and daylight to accentuate the mundane and ordinary, the bright and cheerful, the harsh and realistic, the adventure? Do we want exterior night for unseen dan-ger and mystery or for romance or for psychological abandon? Do we want tight spaces for dramatic compression and entrapment or for a cozy nest? Do we want open spaces for a sense of freedom or for alienation and loneliness or for overwhelming vastness? Do we want hard surfaces or soft surfaces? Do we want old? How old? Antique? Do we want new? How new? Ultramodern? Do we want well kept or run down? Do we want plush, slick, funky, junky, formal, austere, stone or siding, hardwood or wall-to-wall? However, the main ques-tion is: What is it about the set that lends itself to the mood we want to create for the scene? If the answer is nothing, can we move the action to another set or can we alter the location with props or paint or can we crop our shots to give it the *feel* we want it to have?

Color, Texture, and Design

Closely associated with the choice of location are the choices of colors, textures, and design elements that dominate the frame. Locations and sets provide the photographic opportunities that are the material for visual treatment. Whether rooms are peach, white, red, or blue can have a major impact on the quality of a scene. Coloring the light with gels has similar effects.

Some basic tenets borrowed from elementary design are worth remembering—frames dominated by reds can feel enclosed, connote richness, suggest anger, support eroticism, portray high emotional arousal, belie degeneracy, or simply be warm. A blue frame can be cold, austere, and emotionless, suggesting cruelty or intellectualism or supporting feelings of freedom, liberation, the ethereal, spirituality, calm, and peace. We often use shifts or contrasts of color from one scene to another to establish changes or contrasts in mood. The important point is that color greatly affects the mood of a scene. It must be considered when choosing a location, dressing a set, and selecting gels for lighting. In *Quest for Fire,* the filmmakers selected the coldest, wettest, most barren tundra on which to place their band of cave men and women to reinforce the importance of their dependance on fire. Then, when the fire is lost, the scene is almost a monochromatic blue and appears to be shot with a fog filter to further enhance the feeling of cold and the mood of despair. A fog filter was used in the final meeting of Bonnie and her mother in *Bonnie and Clyde* to give the misty, surreal look of a world that Bonnie was no longer a part of, foreshadowing her imminent death.

Beyond the color of things, much of what is rendered in the frame is texture: hard polished marble, rough hewn wood, sand, mud, tree bark, flaking paint, rusting steel, rushing water. Surfaces bring the detail of reality to a scene and contribute to mood. The use of hard surfaces, without the softening textures of fabric, contributes greatly to the tough, brutal world of *On the Waterfront.* The use of silky textures in the early scenes of *The Last Emperor* emphasizes the sensuous decadence of the world within the walls of the palace. A major part of location scouting is finding settings with surfaces and textures to complement the mood we want to impart to a scene.

A powerful technique for the creation of mood is the use of basic design elements of line, mass, and pattern. Again, borrowing from the fundamentals of design—jagged, broken lines can express tension, chaos, nervousness, and anger, whereas long curved and flowing lines can project calm, harmony, equilibrium, flight, and liberation. A frame dominated by organic shapes feels very different from one filled with a construction of geometric shapes. Tight, filigree patterns convey a different sense than broad, simple patterns. A frame composed of strong vertical elements is very different in tone from one composed of strong horizontal elements. It's hard to build a state of high dramatic tension in a frame dominated by long, flowing horizontal lines. It's hard to build a sense of peace and calm in a frame composed of short, hard, jagged, vertical lines.

Lighting

The emotional palette of cinema is painted with light. Dark frames can evoke mystery or tense danger or romance or sadness and loss. Bright frames can be cheerful or stark or glorious. Sharp-edged shadows and hard lighting can connote glamour or meager existence or danger. We can use soft lighting with delicate shadowing to create moods of innocent playfulness or tranquility or institutional barrenness.

In Chapter 10, we describe basic lighting techniques and distinguish between lighting setups and lighting design. *Low-key lighting designs,* in which the frame is dominated by deep shadow, are so often associated with mystery and dark psychological forces that a major genre, *film noir*—black film or dark film—takes its name from the lighting style and the dark forces of human nature it expresses. The effects of low-key lighting are numerous and can complement such moods as mystery and suspense, loneliness, romance, or psychological release.

Multitudes of lighting designs fall within the general category of low-key lighting. There are frames in which the background is almost entirely dark and the subject is illuminated either brightly and frontally as when Polanski steps out of the dark at the waterworks to slit Jack Nicholson's nose in *Chinatown.* (See Figure 5.2.) Or, frames may be very dimly lit as when Jimmy Stewart waits in his darkened apartment for the murderer to attack him in *Rear Window.* Another familiar low-key design is a frame in which the black background is punctuated by a strong backlight and the foreground subjects are seen against the light in silhouette, as in the projection room scene in *Citizen Kane.* It is not unusual in some low-key designs to create a lighting pattern on a section of the background—either hard-edged or diffused depending on the mood—and to frame portions of foreground objects (a section of a wooden rocker or a person's arm or hand, for instance) against it in silhouette or near silhouette, allowing the audience to infer the identity of what they are seeing.

Our purpose here is not to attempt a comprehensive survey of low-key lighting designs, but simply to point out that many variations can be effective in evoking mood. A close study of favorite low-key lit scenes both for technique and for the effect of mood is well worth the effort.

High-key lighting designs, in which the frame is predominantly brighter than medium gray, also come in many versions and can support a variety of moods. High-key scenes range from idyllic pastorals such as the barn-raising scene in *Witness* and the bicycle interlude in *Butch Cassidy and the Sundance Kid* to cold, stark realism as in the train station bathroom murder scene in *Witness* and the final ambush scene in *Bonnie and Clyde.* High-key lighting character-

FIGURE 5.2
There are low-key lighting designs in which the background is almost entirely dark and the subject is illuminated either brightly and frontally as when Polanski steps out of the dark at the waterworks to slit Jack Nicholson's nose in *Chinatown.*

izes comedy, human-interest drama, and lighthearted adventure, which includes everything from *Kramer vs. Kramer* and *Driving Miss Daisy* to most of the James Bond films. High-key lighting is often associated with daylight and "the ordinary." Films such as *Driving Miss Daisy* or *Steel Magnolias* tell their human-interest stories usually under the "full light of day." When considering these types of films, as well as most Westerns, it is easy to dismiss the significance of high-key lighting by simply observing that, of course, scenes will be high key if the action takes place outside during the day. However, this misses the point. A scriptwriter or director can deliberately choose to set most scenes indoors or out, during the day or at night, to provide the lighting opportunities for the desired mood. In fact, the two items of information that appear at the beginning of a scene—whether INTERIOR or EXTERIOR, and whether DAY or NIGHT—are two primary decisions a filmmaker makes in laying the foundations for mood in a scene.

Suppose we want to set a scene in which anger and gloom dominate, although the scene itself must take place outdoors during the day. We can still subdue the brightness of the scene by choosing locations that provide shade and darker backgrounds. The funeral scene near the end of *Steel Magnolias,* when the mother breaks down, is an example.

On the other hand, high-key lighting with hot backlighting and glaring backgrounds can help create a kind of compressed, overheated, psychologically oppressive reality. Films as varied as *Chinatown, Treasure of the Sierra Madre, Bonnie and Clyde,* and *Who's Afraid of Virginia Woolf?* provide scenes in this high-key style used for powerfully disturbing mood. If we replace the background glare with more subdued tones, hot backlighting produces warm and glamorous effects.

Very flat, high-key lighting—little or no backlight on the characters to separate them from the background and minimal falloff from foreground to background—is sometimes used to create a sterile, institutional setting. Hospitals and asylums, government and corporate offices, barren public facilities, even the newsroom of *The Washington Post* (as in *All the President's Men*) can be treated in this way to create moods of cold, businesslike, even inhumane efficiency. Take care when using this lighting design because so much amateurish lighting (bouncing light off the ceiling as the sole light source, for example) produces exactly this kind of look.

Effective high-key lighting usually requires establishing a falloff of light from foreground to background and from center to the top of the frame. These shadings create depth—a sense of three-dimensional space—which is so important in motion picture design. Naturally, for a scene to be high key, shadings and shadows must be moderate. Backgrounds allowed to go too dark produce low-key effects. But the variations in depth, the pattern of shading, and the percentage of the frame that is shadowed provide a range of lighting designs, which can be used to complement subtle shadings of mood. A simple rule might be: the deeper the mood, that is, the farther we get from comedy, the more shaded the frame becomes and the deeper the shadows become. Obviously this is only a generalization and there are many exceptions. *Ghostbusters*, a wonderful comedy, for example, has shaded frames and deep shadows.

A third general type of lighting design is created when the frame is predominantly lit in gray tones. We often see these kinds of frames used to evoke dismal misery. The purgatorial, long-suffering emotions that this lighting expresses have been well used in such films as *Five Easy Pieces* and *Deliverance*.

Before we leave the subject of lighting for mood, we should mention one special technique that is separate from variations in low-key and high-key lighting design. This is the *eyelight*. Sometimes called the Obie, after the man who devised one version of it mounted directly on the camera, eyelights are critical to many mood lighting setups. Most medium and close-up shots—especially in romantic, demonic, or glamorous lighting setups—benefit greatly with a light in the eye and look flat without it.

A marvelous example of this effect is used in *Chinatown* in the night car scene just after Jake (Jack Nicholson) discovers Mrs. Mulwray (Faye Dunaway) visiting her daughter. When he confronts her, she lies to Jake regarding her past, but for the first time we see the depth of her despair. The two characters talk, the eyelights enhancing their attractiveness, until the powerful moment when the woman reveals her desperation. As she turns away from the detective, the eyelight vanishes, her eyes go dead, and for a moment we see Dunaway's beautiful face become lifeless and somewhat reminiscent of a dead fish.

The techniques for creating eyelights vary and we discuss them in detail in Chapter 10. However, do not underestimate the importance of an eyelight in the evocation of mood and character. If the situation calls for it, schedule the time necessary to set it up.

Camera Framing, Angles, and Movement

Camera framing and angles are the fundamental grammar of film language. The basic framings of the shots—wide shot (WS), medium shot (MS), and close-up (CU)—and the principle camera angles—low angle, high angle, eye level, frontal, three-quarter front, profile, three-quarter rear, and tail away—are the building blocks of visual storytelling. These are among the first topics taught in visual literacy, basic production, and critical studies courses. We discuss these in further detail in Chapter 8, but for our purposes here, we can summarize the usual commentary regarding shot framings and angles. A WS is used for an "establishing shot," emphasizing location environment; a MWS and a MS show action and body gesture, while allowing us to see both facial expression and environmental context; and the CU emphasizes small details of action, objects, or facial expression. Low angles tend to make subjects loom over us, large and dominant, whereas high angles tend to diminish subjects, making them look small and vulnerable. Canted camera angles that create a horizon not parallel to the bottom of the frame create an unbalanced view of the world, good for the portrayal of psychological imbalance and an unstable or chaotic world.

These general observations are all useful, but the effects of framing and camera angle are much richer—more complex and subtle. Although framing and camera angles do not convey mood by themselves, but need to be used in orchestration with other elements—color and design, lighting, lens focal length, and so on—they guide the audience's view and interpretation of a scene.

The camera frame is a window on the world. What the audience sees through the window, as defined by lens focal length, determines how small a detail or large a part of the scene they can watch and how close or far they feel they are to the action on the screen.

Scenes dominated by wide shots give an audience a sense of distance, a certain detachment and withdrawal from the action. Of course, panoramic shots of landscapes—mountains, forests, wheat fields, river bends, and waterfalls—can elicit a mood of peace and contemplation suggesting the beauty and grandeur of nature. Such shots with human presence seen small in the frame—a ranch house in front of the mountains, a lone human figure dwarfed by the forest, a covered-wagon rolling past the wheat fields, an angler at the river bend, a canoe approaching the waterfall—can set off the minuteness of human affairs against the immensity of nature.

The human figure in a wide shot, surrounded by environment—trees, office buildings, an empty room—might convey a sense of vulnerability, isolation, and aloneness. This can be effective, if we have established portraiture and the audience is involved so that they care about the human figure, the character. However, if we frame the action continuously in wide shots, the imposed distance quickly discourages audience involvement.

High-angle wide shots can emphasize scale and magnitude—looking down on Bogart's boat lost in a sea of reeds near the end of *The African Queen,* Butch and Sundance running from the law in the barren wastes of the desert in *Butch Cassidy and the Sundance Kid,* and the mountain hunting scene in *The Deer Hunter* are just a few from hundreds of examples. Also, we now recognize the convention of the camera being craned up to a high-angle wide shot as giving the audience the feeling of departure from the story, a technique used quite frequently as the final shot of the film.

Although not directly evocative of mood, using wide shots to provide space for large physical movement can be a strategy in action scenes. Theatrical directors also use wide shots to provide long takes and physical freedom for actors and actresses in emotionally demanding scenes.

Medium shots bracket human action and interaction. They provide enough of the background to maintain a sense of context, yet concentrate attention on the human subject. Medium shots show only part of the human figure so that large body movements sweep across the screen as more powerful gestures than in wide shots. Grabbing someone's lapels in a wide shot is not visually very arresting (though it may be dramatically arresting). The same action in a medium shot can be a powerful physical event.

Medium shots show facial expression clearly, together with body movement and location surroundings. In a single frame, the director and actors can show a full range of dramatic action and reaction, from facial expression to large body movement. Another name for a wide medium shot is the *two-shot.* As the term implies, the two-shot holds two people in interaction. Often, in a dialogue sequence, the widest framing in a series of over-the-shoulder reverses is the medium shot. A series of progressively closer angles accompanies growing dramatic tension in the dialogue. We can complement a relaxing of tension by reverting to the looser medium shot.

Some scenes, dominated by shots no wider than a medium shot, create a feeling of confinement and complement tense dramatic action. The interior treatment of *Who's Afraid of Virginia Woolf?,* as the night becomes more drunken and hostile, is an example of this claustrophobic use of the medium shot.

One important use of the medium shot, both for narrative and for the evocation of mood, is the close juxtaposition of significant subjects—characters and objects—in the same frame. We've already mentioned the two-shot, which composes two characters together in the same frame, sometimes in profile, but more often in the foreground/background relationship of an over-the-shoulder shot. This foreground/background framing in the medium shot is an important device for creating three-dimensional compositions in cinematography. Framing characters with objects or animals—a cat in the corner chair, a talisman or family totem, a weapon, a suggestive sculpture, a telltale professional tool—is a common technique borrowed from a painting convention that goes back to the Middle Ages to build mood and character by associating people with objects. One example is the silhouetted demonic statue on the desk in the suicide scene in *Dead Poets Society.*

The close-up of the human face is a powerful shot for the evocation of mood and the expression of emotion. All the subtleties of character, intentions, and feelings visible to us in the human face show in a close-up. A study of almost any well-wrought film reveals many "look" shots—CU shots of characters reacting by facial expression to the situation and other characters in a scene.[2] These reaction shots are especially effective in conveying mood and interpreting a scene for an audience.

Close-ups can exaggerate the force of sudden movements and magnify the significance of telltale gestures and details. They can confine the audience's view of a scene to pique curiosity, build mystery, or add suspense. They can enlarge and fill the screen with the world of the very small (the opening shot of the ants and scorpion in *The Dirty Dozen,* for example.) They can bring us into close confrontation with the beautiful or the grotesque.

Considering the mood of the scene or sequence is important in planning the juxtaposition of shots. We can often provide the required information in a scene by moving from a WS to a MS to a CU. This generally follows the increasing intensity of the drama as the scene builds to a climax, but this pattern can become repetitious and dull in its predictability. Two good scenes to look at for the juxtaposition of shots as they contribute to the mood of a scene appear in *Witness.* The first is the scene where the boy, Samuel (Lukas Haas), observes the murder and, in the tense moments after, McFee (Danny Glover) and the murderer search the stalls. This scene intercuts between the boy's face and the shots depicting their search for the witness to their crime. The second is the scene in the police station when the boy is confronted with the criminal in handcuffs and then sees the photograph of McFee, revealing his discovery to John Book (Harrison Ford) through his facial expression.

Camera angles, like camera framing, can be a powerful element in the creation of mood. Camera angles produce different effects according to degree. For example, a low-angle shot slightly below eye level causes the subject to appear somewhat dominant but not necessarily threatening, whereas a more extreme low-angle shot can make the subject appear to loom and seem very threatening or triumphant. Extreme low-angle shots, from the floor, can create an exaggerated and bizarre effect—the fantasy perspective of a tiny creature in a land of giants (as in *Citizen Kane* in the dialogue between Kane and the drunken Jedidiah in the newsroom office after the election is lost.)

Conversely high-angle shots slightly above eye level can make the subject seem somewhat yielding but not necessarily endangered, subjugated, or forlorn. More extreme high-angle shots can reduce the subject to a state of utter defeat. (In *Dead Poets Society,* after young Neil has returned home and is unable to confront his father, he sits in total misery and despair in the chair, presumably contemplating his suicide.) Because the large screen magnifies and exaggerates effects as well as actions and facial expressions, subtle and restrained shifts of angles are normally more effective and less conspicuous than extreme maneuvers.

Near-frontal shots, especially close-ups, involve the audience in character and focus the audience's attention on the subject's face and expression. It is a common technique to cut from a three-quarter front over-the-shoulder MS to a more frontal CU up to emphasize a character's emotions and reactions.

The most common of all angles is the three-quarter front MS. This angle opens up the face to show expression. It provides for a dynamic composition with perspective receding frame right or frame left. It allows us to see what a character is doing (action) or with whom a character is involved (interaction).

Profile shots are often used in formal compositions, especially in close-up. We've all seen the grand moment of love consummated by a kiss, the great chief lifting his head to the heavens for guidance and courage before the battle, and the squinting cowboy staring down his opponent in a shootout.

The violation of the rules of composition can create a jolting or uncomfortable effect on the audience. Generally we strive for balance in our compositions. We leave room in the frame for the weight carried by the eyes in the direction a person is looking. We avoid cutting limbs at the joint with the frame line. We allow adequate head room. We avoid placing people or objects that are the point of interest in the dead center of the frame or against flat walls. However, at the risk of making a production draw attention to itself, it is occasionally appropriate to violate these rules. For instance, we can stack the weight off balance in the frame, creating an instability that longs to be corrected. To balance the composition, we hold the shot for a moment and then fill the void. This technique can contribute to the tension in the scene in subtle ways if done carefully.

Moving camera shots, pans, tilts, and dollies can do more than follow action or open the frame. They can create an uneasiness in the audience, a sense of movement with someone else driving. For example, Stuart Rosenberg used moving POV camera shots (as mentioned in the beginning of Chapter 3) in the opening of *The Amityville Horror* after the couple has moved into the house and are unpacking. Although there is no established predator, the scene is made full of premonitions by using the moving camera with foreground objects between the lens and the subject, almost as if we were the wolf in Disney's *Three Little Pigs,* creeping from tree to tree keeping an eye on the tasty piglets. In another example, the slow zoom into the television screen in *Poltergeist* draws us into an object, which we ordinarily find innocuous. But, given the expression on the little girl's face, the other lighting in the room, and the growing sound of the white noise of the TV, we find the scene increasingly intense.

Thinking of movies as controlled dreams and of horror or thriller movies as controlled nightmares is a good guide for the scripting, direction, and production value we want. It can also guide us in our choices of camera movement. Things we find scary in our nightmares—primarily things that make us feel small and helpless—work well in scary movies. Perhaps it's what scared us as infants, and that's why it makes sense that the pursued always runs and the pursuer never does because most adults can catch infants without breaking stride.

Lens Focal Length

The lens focal length affects the angle of view, depth of field, and perspective. Changing the focal length can radically manipulate the image, influencing the way the audience sees the subject. Any good introduction to basic photographic techniques discusses the effect of lens focal length on depth of field. The rule is that when we focus on a subject, as we shorten the focal length of the lens, we cause more of the background and foreground also to be in critical focus. Conversely we cause the background and foreground to be more out of focus as we lengthen the focal length of the lens.[3]

Although throwing the background in or out of focus creates some obvious differences in the image, the actual effect of these variations is a bit more subtle. Short focal lengths, *because* they show foreground and background more in focus, cause the subject to be seen surrounded by the details of the environment. On the other hand, long focal lengths cause the space surrounding a subject to be out of focus and set in a diffuse pattern of light, shade, and colored tones. Middle focal lengths allow the general structure of the background to be visible, but suppress detail.

We can illustrate how mood is expressed through the effect that focal length has on depth of field with the following example:

> *An anxious, distressed young man waits for his date in an automobile junk yard. As seen through the short focal length lens, the young man's surroundings—twisted metal, old rusty automobile hulks, stacks of tires, tangled piles of wire—are clearly in focus. The hard-edged, inhospitable chaos around him intensifies the anxious mood.*

> *When his friend arrives, the young man is greatly relieved and the two become enveloped in a loving world of their own. By changing to long focal lengths, the scene of the couple is now rendered with soft, out-of-focus backgrounds, where soft shades, pastel tones, and starlike highlights reflected from unseen chrome surfaces transform their world into a feathery, spangled fantasy.*

Using focal length to alter the depth of field for the creation of different moods is easy to comprehend and visualize. Less obvious but no less powerful is the effect of focal length on perspective. The manipulation of perspective through focal length is a technique commonly taught in basic photography courses, but using this effect to express mood deserves some special attention.

Briefly, focal length affects perspective by exaggerating depth. When focal lengths are short, they make perspective lines converge more quickly than normal. When focal lengths are long, they flatten perspective, causing perspective lines to converge more slowly than normal. A "normal" lens (50mm in 35mm film or 25mm in 16mm film, for example) is so called because its focal length renders perspective similar to the way our eyes see perspective.

Using the effect of focal length on perspective, we can manipulate the way space is rendered in a scene, change apparent heights and distances, modify the perceived speeds of objects and camera moves, and even alter the facial features of our subjects.

The ways in which we can integrate these manipulations into the creation of mood are innumerable. The effect of a short focal length on the rendering of space can be used to exaggerate the length of a long hallway or alley down which a person must walk to reach safety (the long hallway shot in *The Shining,* for example). Or, it could be used to make a room seem larger, more spacious, or even cavernous (the huge living room of Xanadu in *Citizen Kane,* for example). Looking up at a building with a short focal length makes the building look taller. Looking down the extended and raised ladder of a fire truck with a short focal length makes the truck and scene below appear to be much farther down.

Looking up at a person with a short focal length makes a person seem taller, more imposing.[4] Looking along the length of an automobile with a short focal length exaggerates the apparent size of the car. A shot angled down the length of a high wall or fence appears to extend way into the distance when rendered by a short focal length. Someone running toward the camera appears to be running faster with a short focal length. A fist thrown toward the camera increases in size more rapidly than normal, emphasizing the impact or violence of the strike (the kitchen scene in *Raging Bull* when Jake coaxes his brother to hit him, for example). A camera mounted on a moving car appears to travel faster down the road when viewing the on-rushing scene with a short focal length. Many of these effects can contribute to the mood of a shot or scene.

A long focal length makes rooms look smaller, more compressed (the pressure cooker living room in *Who's Afraid of Virginia Woolf?,* for example). In over-the-shoulder shots, people talking or arguing with one another appear closer, more intimate, or more confrontational. When we study the methods of feature film technique, it is a revelation how often shots of human interaction are composed with longer focal lengths to compress the space between characters. This is even more significant when we realize that these longer focal length shots are more difficult and more time consuming to arrange, and require more room to set up than shots taken with shorter focal lengths.

Editing

Good editing is like a form of music. Joining and juxtaposing shots creates rhythms and pacing that contribute to mood. There is a musical, almost percussive quality to editing. The rhythms are visceral and felt. They can be fast—often associated with excitement, chaos and confusion, wild action—or they can be slow—often associated with melancholy, stealth and danger, or romance. As with any sophisticated use of rhythm, there can be counterpoint—cutting against the beats of an action to suggest the subject is in a psychological world separate from the surrounding action. Also, there can be cutting both on beats and on upbeats.[5] There are even "measures" in which we can cut shots by threes, twos, or fours.

Pacing is closely related to rhythm. Pacing refers to the speed of action in the frame as established by subjects or camera moves and by the durations of shots on the screen. Languid or flowing camera moves of gentle actions in long takes convey a much different feeling than short takes of abrupt actions. Interesting contrasts and manipulations of mood can be set up by filming violent, abrupt actions with long takes of slow, fluid camera moves (the fight scene in *Raging Bull,* for example).

Montage

Montage is the most purely evocative of editing styles. Some of the most memorable scenes in films are montage sequences. The opening of *Apocalypse Now,* the steam bath scene in *McCabe and Mrs. Miller,* the football game in *Dead Poets Society,* and the buffalo hunt and the wolf dancing scenes in *Dances with Wolves* are just a few of many beautiful examples.

Opening montage sequences in films establish mood quickly, as in the opening of *Raiders of the Lost Ark.* While we see shots of the explorers traveling through hostile jungle, the subtle ability to evoke mood and convey the kernel of narrative is so strong that we are unaware that the sequence is a montage. More frequently, however, editors use montage to eclipse time or set apart small jewels of the story when mood and meaning become more important than story continuity.

We can take inspiration from these examples and, as scriptwriters and producers, be prepared to digress from the inexorable march of story line into the associative world of montage when our purposes call for it. However, to decide to treat a certain subject, theme, or situation in montage is only the first step. The nature of the treatment itself must be defined and, as we have discussed, the essentially nonverbal subtle shadings of mood are infinitely variable.

For example, we may decide that we want to create a montage treatment of the fall season. Seasonal montages are common and subject to cliché approaches. For most of us, the images that probably first come to mind are falling leaves, multicolored stands of trees, and chevrons of flying birds, perhaps accompanied by the soft sounds of water gurgling over stones in a woodland stream, soft wind, rustling leaves, and geese honking in the distance. A contemplative, poignant and subdued sequence of images and sounds based on summer's gentle waning.

Suppose, however, that we want to push this natural treatment a bit toward a brighter, more vivacious interpretation. Perhaps we want to capture the energy that comes with cooler, crisper weather. We might shoot leaves in an extreme close-up, capturing bright abstract patterns of harlequin color and intercut this with brilliant, sunlit mosaics of multicolored trees in similar design. We might punctuate the sequence with shots of the sun sparkling off rivulets and droplets shaken from waterfowl taking flight.

We might wish to introduce a theme of industry and activity and abandon our exclusive use of natural images to include children climbing onto a waiting school bus, a couple hanging storm windows, or a man chopping wood. Or, we might wish to create a bleak, even grim mood in our fall montage by establishing a chill, gray scene with the wind banging the boards of an old, deserted barn; the dry, bare husks of long dead flowers in a garden; a lonely clearing near the riverbank with a rope dangling from a bare tree branch over the swimming hole; or a child's rusting wagon half-buried in the mud.

The point, to repeat a main theme of this book, is that subject is different from treatment and we can apply practically any treatment we choose to any subject. Once we determine the subject, the film or video producer then must ask: "What is unique about it? How do I want to treat it?" There are as many possible variations in the montage treatment of a subject as there are moods associated with it.

Cross-cutting, or parallel action, is generally cutting back and forth between the action in one scene to the action in another to give the impression of two simultaneous events. Editors use this technique to create dynamic associations similar to montage editing. An excellent example is the powerful sequence in *The Godfather* of violent murders intercut with Don Corleone in church. The sanctified mood of the church service is totally subverted and turned into a travesty by the slaughter, which Corleone has ordered, while the church service itself adds a patina of diabolical ritual to the killing. The effect is that the two scenes each modify the other, creating a mood mixing church and community with animal brutality and viciousness. Editing is usually the process of creating an unobtrusive, seamless experience. However, the ability to juxtapose images is a power to manipulate mood as well as interpretation.

Sound

Sound can impart emotional impact to a scene with enormous force. The dense and powerful soundtracks of such action films as *Star Wars, Terminator,* and *Apocalypse Now* heighten the excitement of scenes immeasurably and may resound in our minds for hours afterwards, dominating our memories of the films. Leonard Cohen's sad ballads throughout *McCabe and Mrs. Miller* gave a melancholy feel to scenes, including the opening scene, which could otherwise be interpreted as upbeat. In *Out of Africa,* classical European music was used with moving effect against African wilderness scenes. The musical transitions in National Public Radio's "Morning Edition" interpret news stories in terms of mood. In *On the Waterfront,* the sound effects of heavy machinery and ships' horns underscored scenes of intense dramatic impact. The audio composition for the "Dawn of Man" opening in *2001: A Space Odyssey* illustrates how film reality can be created by sound design. All the location sounds of birds, wind, flies, lions, grunts, screams, slurps, and so on are wildtrack sound effects added to footage that is shot silent. Ken Burns's PBS television series *The Civil War* depends heavily on multiple layers of sound for establishing mood and ambience.

Building mood in a scene with sound is done principally through the music and sound effect tracks rather than in the sync sound track. Music is the most purely evocative of all art forms and can express infinite variations of mood and feeling. Film, being the eclectic art form that it is, uses the expressive power of music well. Often the mood of a scene or even an entire film can be identified with a musical theme or motif (think of "Thus Spake Zarathustra" and "Beautiful Blue Danube" musical themes in *2001: A Space Odyssey* or the very popular original music from the scores for *Chariots of Fire, Cabaret,* and *Deliverance*).

Instrumentation, pace and rhythm, tonality, dynamic range, and style are the fabric of musical composition. Each instrument has its own character and can be used to establish a special mood in a scene. Music performed by solo instruments has a much different effect than fully orchestrated music. Different styles—rock, classical, jazz, and so on—obviously vary greatly in their influence on a scene, and there are tremendous variations within each genre.

The filmmaker must consider carefully when to accompany a scene with music and what type of music to use. Furthermore, the character of the mix—when to bring the music in, when to make it louder, when to make it softer, what kinds of audio transitions or segues to make (hard cuts, fast or slow crossfades, and so on)—determine whether the music contributes to or detracts from the mood of a scene. Not only must the selection of music, either prerecorded or composed especially for the film, be appropriate, but the audio design and execution must also be artfully done.

Naturally lyrics can have a strong interpretive effect on a scene (the Jim Morrison and the Doors song in the opening montage of *Apocalypse Now,* for example). Selecting a piece of music to accompany a scene because of the words can sometimes be effective. However, lyrics in music can also be very deceptive. We often find songs with words of sweet love and understanding, for example, written against a hard-driving, heavy metal score producing an ironic effect in the music. If a producer wants to convey a mood of gentle affection and selects such a song for the words alone, insensitive to the mood of the music itself, the effect will be far different from what is intended.

Again, the trap here is being too literal—mistaking verbal abstractions for mood. This can happen when illustrating a song using shots that show literal representations of the words when the words have no narrative continuity. The associative continuity that works for word imagery does *not* always provide the same continuity when we translate the word images into pictures. The result can be a chaotic jumble of unrelated images. The flow and rationale of visual imagery simply do not work according to the grammar of language.

Sound Effects

At the least, sound contributes to the realism of a scene by providing the ambient background that our audience would expect to hear in a location. To be convincing, a scene in a New York apartment shot on a quiet set might have added to it a wildtrack of outside traffic noise, distant sirens, and loud voices. Obviously we can compose this type of background wildtrack to complement the mood of the action. Listen closely to a film set in the city and you will find the harsh urban sounds augmented during moments of distress and confusion and faded out altogether during moments of intimacy and relative serenity.

Sound effects, however, can powerfully influence our perception. Hits, thumps, crashes, rips, and swishes when "sweetened" with properly timed, especially recorded audio effects dramatically heighten even strong action. Machines whir and clank better, doors slam louder, snow scrunches are squeakier, slurps are wetter, breaths are breathier. These augmented sound effects are within the range of the low-budget film or video producer who is willing to devote the time, care, and aesthetic sense to use them.

Combined, music and sound effects are marvelous tools in the creation of mood and ambience in motion pictures. Their use in contemporary feature films has achieved a level of finesse and power that makes the sound track a major aesthetic experience unto itself. Audio production is one of the most developed of the cinematic arts.

Voice

Finally, in considering important sound elements for creating mood, we need to mention the treatment of the human voice. Voice-over and sync sound are the two principle types of voice track. Each can be manipulated for effect.

In voice-over, simply selecting a male or a female voice can greatly affect the interpretation of the scenes covered. Tone of voice obviously carries emotional connotations that color a scene. The simple fact that voice-over is off-screen lends it a special character—it can be used to capture the intimacy of interior monologue (*A River Runs Through It* and *The Wonder Years*) or the authoritative voice of an unseen omniscient narrator (*The World at War*). Heartfelt confessions sometimes accompany the visuals revealing the events of a crime at the end of mystery shows. As a storytelling device, voice-over can keep us removed from the action and move us around quickly from one period to another (*Little Big Man*).

Sync sound is less susceptible to manipulation and usually serves the simple purpose of enabling us to hear dialogue. However, as is the case with music, sound effects, and voice-over, the tonal quality and dynamic range of sync sound can be manipulated through equalization so that men can sound huskier, or more menacing (the "fuck me" line growled by the killer after he's put on makeup in *Silence of the Lambs*), women sexier or more assertive (*Terminator 2*), and children more innocent (*Home Alone*).

These audio manipulations, along with the enormous evocative power of music and sound effects, combine with a scene's visual treatment to enable the film or video artist to impart the desired mood and interpretation to a subject and a scene.

Performance: Talent and Direction

Actors and even non-actors convey mood in their facial expressions, actions and delivery of lines. Part of the director and actor's job is to decide not only what information is being conveyed through the lines delivered and the action of the character, but also what is being conveyed through the delivery of those lines and the conduct of the character. It's like the famous line from Owen Wister's *The Virginian*, "Smile when you call me that." It's not what we say, but what we convey while saying it that's important.

Dialogue and action can play with the production's mood or against it. Although mood can contribute to the development of story or relationships or to the growth of individual characters, underplaying mood often works best. Then it subtly supports the narrative or information being conveyed. An example is Maxwell House's "1898" coffee ad. To stress their slow roasting and old-time flavor, all the shots are sepia-toned. This not only gives the feeling of age, but also reinforces the idea of "coffee" with color. To complement the design of the *mise en scène,* the shots are slightly slow motion. Supporting the mood of the visualization, the actors' actions, such as removing a hat, are all done with careful deliberateness, almost as if in a dream or the bygone era. Commercials are often excellent notebooks in production techniques for directors.

Occasionally the mood of a performance can even run in counterpoint to the mood of the visualization. A marvelous example of this is in *Network* when Diana (Faye Dunaway) and Max Schumacher (William Holden) are walking hand in hand along a beach at sunset. We hear gulls crying and waves lapping. We cut to Diana and Schumacher running playfully into a beach house, and there in the warm light of a lamp by the bed, they strip, as would eager lovers, and jump into bed, where they make passionate love. The use of familiar sounds, shooting style, lighting, set, and stereotypes tell us this is a "traditional" love scene, but the dialogue is of Diana going over rating points and programming strategies for the network. The mood works in contrast to the dialogue to reveal more about her character than in any other way.

Putting It All Together

The mood established in the opening of most productions is directed at taking the audience from their seats and placing them in the limbo world of viewer.

Often the mood is either startling or calming, with the goal of getting the audience's attention or soothing them. Mood engages the audience and entices them to understand, enjoy, and participate in the reality on the screen.

Mood can establish genre. Although each sequence of a production may reflect a different mood, there is usually a general mood that helps underscore the theme and genre of the work. In *Chinatown,* the opening of the scene in Gittes's office, lit in a "colorized" version of *film noir,* establishes the detective story genre for the audience. Robert Towne and Roman Polanski have so much fun with it they even have Curly biting the venetian blinds. Here, the blinds are not used just as a shading device (cukaloris), but as a prop that is a hallmark of the *film noir* genre.

The mood can also support the theme of the film. In the feature-length documentary, *The Thin Blue Line,* the general mood of the film is one of the inexorable grinding wheels of justice. At one point, late in the film, Adams's trial attorney says that the entire case against Adams took place because some cop in either Vidor or Dallas set the ball rolling in that direction and, once it got started, it was impossible to stop. This is one of those comments producers jump on because the phrase allows them to organize their research and provide focus for their approach. The mood reinforces the relentlessness of the legal justice machinery with Philip Glass's hypnotic music repeating the same figure over and over, with the recurring dreamlike reenactment sequences of the murder.

Audiences generally respond to moods that build, shift, and change. An example of one of the most memorable moments in the film *Network* is when Howard Beale (Peter Finch) begins exhorting the television audience to turn off their TVs and shout, "I'm mad as hell and I'm not going to take this anymore." The scene starts small, with Beale on a monitor in the control room. It then cuts to a full shot of Beale on the set as he begins his tirade. He starts quietly and rationally as the camera does a slow zoom into a MCU of him, with only occasional cuts to others, giving their reactions and guiding our perception of the event. However, he doesn't look rational. His hair is wet and messy. He's wearing a raincoat. He looks mad. The cutaways tell us that something out of the ordinary is happening, but they don't prepare us for what it will be. Our expectation is for an important scene, but the filmmakers take it beyond normal expectation and create a gripping and memorable event.

At the end of the zoom, Beale is on his feet and walking into the studio camera, seemingly right into the living rooms of his viewing audience, telling them to get mad. The pacing picks up with Diana's joyful reaction to the calls that the member stations are receiving. The final scenes become bedlam with people standing at their windows shouting out into the night as the rain and storm join their rage with thunder and lightning. The combination of Beale's appearance and Finch's brilliant delivery with the fast-cutting and urgent camera movement creates a building mood that seems about to explode. Then, when the sound has been layered with the yelling and the raging storm, the sequence does explode.

We create powerful sequences like this by adding extreme production elements to the camera, editing, and sound in an already hard-driving scene. This is especially effective when the audience isn't expecting the intensity of a scene to go as far as the film or video producer takes it. Pushing the mood by intensifying production elements is successfully handled at the end of Peter Brook's *Marat/Sade*, where the inmates appear to attack the screen itself while continuously banging their cups on the bars of their prison theater cell. Or, the convention sequence in Capra's *Meet John Doe*, where again the use of sound deepens our empathy with the hero's frustrating inability to explain his actions: paper boys shout, hired thugs disrupt the proceedings, rain pours, and it's all juxtaposed with Gary Cooper as John Doe standing, embarrassed and stifled from being able to explain the truth to his audience because the PA system is cut. Or, the first battle sequence in Lewis Milestone's 1930 production of *All Quiet on the Western Front*, where the French are machine gunning wave after wave of German youth in an uncomfortably interminable visual and aural pageant of killing similar to the final *danse macabre* in *Bonnie and Clyde*. Each is a textured weaving of performance with strong visuals and overwhelming and relentless sound.

These sequences are all well set up for the audience. They start quietly or come out of a scene with a contrasting quiet, poignant, or humorous mood. As each of these scenes builds layers of production elements and accelerates in pace, we know it's going to be a big, important moment in the film. However, we are not prepared for the visual and aural onslaught that moves us from a state of controlled dream to a state of controlling nightmare, from which we can neither escape nor wake up. We are no longer participating in the willing suspension of disbelief. We are glued to our seats, eyes riveted to the screen, incapable of withdrawing from the moment of the drama. Directors strive for these moments when the production really works.

Contrasting or changing moods within a sequence of action can create audience interest and weave texture into the drama. An example is in *Little Big Man*, when the Indians attack the stage coach carrying Jack Crabbe (Dustin Hoffman) and his wife. It begins as a humorous action scene as the guard refuses to relinquish the rifle he's too scared to use. Even the preacher smiles, when an arrow pierces his Bible as well as his heart. When Jack jumps on one of the horses and an Indian jumps on the steed in harness next to his, the film becomes a funny and exciting competition of Jack and the Indian jumping from horse to horse to driving upbeat western music. Then, the driver shoots the strap that the Indian and Jack are both holding. Jack falls into the water. Another Indian crushes the skull of one of the stage coach passengers. Jack's wife is abducted, and he is left sadly staring at the retreating band thinking he'll never see his wife alive again. The mood shifts play the audience like a violin, moving them through excitement, humor, and tragedy within a few moments.

Later in the film, another scene is made incredibly powerful by the contrast of visual mood and narrative action. The soldiers have herded the Indians into a reservation and told them, if they stay there, Custer's cavalry will leave them in peace. There has been a fairly slapstick scene where Little Big Man, at his wife's insistence, has to sleep simultaneously with his three sisters-in-law, while she gives birth to their first child. The mood shifts in the poignant scene that follows, where he decides that he is so happy that he vows never to leave the Indians again. Then the ponies whinny in fright and quietly, at first, he hears the lilt of "Gary Owen," the Scottish ballad the horse soldiers have adopted as their battle song. As the sounds begin to layer, out of the haze the soldiers attack the Indians and there is a massacre in the snow and fog. In the midst of this scene of already contrasting moods, Old Lodge Skins (Chief Dan George) in a very humorous bit, decides he is invisible and walks through the melee of the killing field and to safety. An unforgettable scene.

In *Bonnie and Clyde,* the film progresses along a path of light humor to a point where Bonnie (Faye Dunaway) and Clyde (Warren Beatty) go into a bank to rob it, while C.J. (Michael J. Pollard) waits in the getaway car. They enter the bank and the robbery becomes a comedy of errors. Clyde has to repeat his "this is a hold up" twice before anyone notices them, and when one of the patrons drops her money, Bonnie has to help her with it. It is a confused and funny robbery. Meanwhile C.J. sees a parking place open up, backs the getaway car down the street, and parks it. Bonnie and Clyde race from the bank to find there is no getaway car. They at last find C.J. and, while the pursuit starts, they try to get out of the parking place, smashing bumpers in close-ups in a scene worthy of Mack Sennett. The scene is colorful, bright, and filled with activity. The compositions are designed for humor: showing Clyde standing upstage and nondominant when he utters his ignored line in the bank, showing the two of them walk into an empty frame as they exit the bank to find the car missing, and showing the close-ups of the mashing bumpers. It's fun and hilarity. Then, as the car swings at last out of town, the bank teller jumps on the running board and Clyde, without thinking, shoots him in the face. There are two bloody close-ups of this shocking sight, and, for the balance of the film, the mood has been inexorably changed.

Stanley Kubrick, a master of the use of mood, re-creates the romantic period of eighteenth-century Europe in his film, *Barry Lyndon.* He carefully crafts his visuals to recall for his audience the English landscape paintings of the period. The film, thematically about deception, conveys in its mood the elegance and beauty of nature in contrast with the unpleasant human condition. The eye is constantly drawn to the beautifully shot landscapes, where fields, castles, and dramatic skies dominate the human subjects in the frame. We are "deceived" by the beauty until we become more aware of the contrasting story line.

A marvelous scene is the one in which young Barry (Ryan O'Neal), believing he has shot his rival for his cousin's affections, flees his home. In a beautiful wooded area, he is set upon by gentlemanly brigands. They, while being ever so polite and respectful of the lad's social status, rob him of all but his boots. All the while, the tone of the dialogue belies the reality of the pistols pointed at him.

Harmony of Mood

There is no aspect of a production that depends on coordinating so many elements as that of creating mood. The setting of a scene—the lighting, the colors and design motifs—paints a moving and evocative framework for the people and characters in our productions. They in turn arouse emotions in the audience through their expressions, their actions, gestures and words, which are colored by the choice of lens, camera placement, editing structure, use of sound effects, and music. Out of these interwoven relationships we can make our presentations, either theatrical or documentary, more rich and alive.

Exercise 1

Rent a movie you haven't seen, perhaps one of the films mentioned in this chapter, and watch the first five to eight minutes of it with the sound turned off. Take notes about the set or location, lighting, cinematography, and editing. Look at types and varieties of shots and how they are juxtaposed. Make some general assumptions about what is going on in that part of the film you have watched in terms of story, genre, mood, characters, and relationships. Watch the same portion of the film again, with sound, and make notes on the use of sound and effects. How close were you in your assumptions?

Finish watching the movie. Was there a particular scene that really grabbed you? Got you involved? Roll the tape back to that scene and watch it again and make notes on its production elements. Look at it with the sound off and see if some of the craft of the filmmaker is more apparent to you now.

Exercise 2

If you have shot one of the previous exercises, score the piece with two completely different musical selections. Select two that are both appropriate, one complementing the action and another in counterpoint with it. What effect does the sound have on your treatment of the visualization? Does it alter your original concept in any way?

Notes

1. We know one Eastern Shore (Maryland) family that meets annually at the ancestral cemetery to picnic, reminisce, and reacquaint themselves. It's hard to equate these grave markers with somberness or sadness because the family estate has long been transformed into a suburban housing development and the cemetery is in someone's back yard.

2. Watch Angela Lansbury in an episode of *Murder, She Wrote*. With her mobile face, she is wonderfully skilled at providing a wide range of "looks," and there are usually as many reaction

shots of her as there are shots of her with line delivery. For comparison, consider the range of reaction shots Clint Eastwood might deliver.

3. The effect of focal length on depth of field is, of course, modified by the f stop of the lens. Because increasing f stop increases depth of field, a shot taken with a relatively small aperture (f8, f11, f16, f22) causes a less extreme diminishing of depth of field as we lengthen the focal length of the lens.

4. Boris Karloff, a tall man (especially in elevator shoes), can be made to appear an even taller, more formidable monster when shot from a low angle with a short focal length. Jack Palance or Jack Nicholson, both men who are not very tall, can be made to appear bigger than they are by shooting up at them with a short focal length lens.

5. Hitchcock was a master of up-beat cutting for shock effect. One elegant example is in *Psycho* when we watch the man slowly climb the stairs in a series of cuts on the beat, to be shocked by a sudden cut on the up-beat taken from the ceiling above the stairs as a maniacal figure comes flying through a flung open door with an upraised knife and stabs the man in the heart.

6

CHARACTERIZATION AND PORTRAITURE

A Question of Balance

Most film videos and television programs are about people. Theatrical films, documentaries, and educational and training productions are virtually all—with notable exceptions such as the popular nature documentaries—about human action and interaction. Humans are homocentric animals. Information is interesting and a well-crafted story can hold our attention, but what truly fascinates us is people.

Suppose we are making a film or video about a craftsperson—a master potter and ceramicist. The situation is classic. As with most film and video subjects, we must decide how much emphasis to give to the potter and how much to give to the pot making. In both theatrical and nonfiction genres, whenever we show a person doing something, we must decide how much we will show what the person is doing and how much we show the personality of the person. We must balance our emphasis between portraiture and process, between characterization and action.

Only in the simplest, most mechanical "how to" production does portraiture become incidental or irrelevant. There is little room for developing the personality of the surgeon in a medical film demonstrating a surgical procedure, for example. Many instructional and educational films and videos primarily intended to show process and procedure, however, do need to devote some small attention to the person doing the activity. Disembodied, depersonalized demonstrations can put off our audience completely.

Film and video vignettes that show interaction between teachers and students, health professionals and patients, salespersons and customers, and so on are usually intended not only to show some procedure or method, but also to exhibit and motivate appropriate attitude and interpersonal skills. In these cases, we devote some attention to characterization. These kinds of activities and services exist because of individual personal need. If we don't develop portraiture in the scenes, we are ignoring the primary reason for the existence of these productions. We are neglecting the strength of film and video to show human interaction.

In productions in which process and procedure are the primary focus, the outcome of a character's dilemma is seldom an issue. Similarly, news, game, and talk shows as well as most science and nature shows do not put characters in jeopardy, but they often do rely heavily on a host or on-camera personality. In these cases, we should put our time, attention, and budget into casting someone who can comfortably convey an interesting and appealing personality in front of the camera.

At the other extreme, the structure of the production may revolve completely around portraiture. A production about a great painter, sculptor, or musician, for example, may show the maestro in action, but often this simply establishes the degree of their accomplishment, while portraiture is the main focus. Showing the great artist at work can be another facet of the portrait to show how this remarkable person approaches this particular craft.

In film and video, we often search for role models. We have a job description—a type—then we go find someone or several persons who will best represent the type. Productions that are ostensibly instructional can become great portraiture pieces when we select and present the right person for the role. A fine example is *All My Babies,* by George Stoney, which was made for the State of Georgia as an instructional film for midwives but is a classic work of documentary portraiture.

Narrative film and television balance character with story development. Action dramas, in which the character's actions are primarily driven by people and events that are external to the character, often sacrifice characterization for the sake of story complications and speed. Often they develop character only enough to motivate characters' actions in the story (*Batman, The Terminator,* or *Predator,* for example). These are basically morality plays of good versus evil, and associating the hero with good is the only character development necessary.

On the other hand, stories driven by characters going through change and inner conflict like *Thelma & Louise, Citizen Kane, Terms of Endearment,* and *On the Waterfront* depend much more on well-rounded, believable portraiture. They have to be complex enough for us to accept them as fully human characters, and we have to know about them at a level that enables us to understand the transformations they experience.

Generally the development of characters for the audience is as important as the story or content of the piece. It is dereliction of storytelling to show action performed by characters who have no dimension and serve only as generic human body units. We may sit in awe of their physical prowess, but if characters aren't believable, they cannot establish believable and involving action. We have to believe in characters at some level if we are to be involved in their actions and care what happens to them. We need to care.

The Quest for Personality

A friend has taken us to a party. We hope to have a good time, but we're not sure that we will. We don't know anyone at the party except our friend, who's disappeared, and for the moment we're hanging out in a corner of the room. Suddenly, across the room, we make eye contact with the host of the party and know deep in our socks that he is going to come over to where we're standing. What do we do? Wait for the inevitable or pretend our eye contact was merely a vacant gaze and urgently head for the hors d'oeuvres? We make our decision in a flash. We decide to stand our ground and wait for the inevitable. Why?

The situation is not far removed from one in which the TV audience sits on the sofa, remote control poised and ready to zap *our* production off the air. Or, the student watching our educational piece in class, prepared to fantasize a dream date in the blink of an eye. Or, the company employee faced with our corporate video who's got no time for nonsense and would rather be doing business, lunch, or both.

Let's go back and look at what we did during that snap decision when the as-yet-unknown party host headed in our direction. We made a snap judgment. In half a heartbeat, we defined the person, in terms of his look and demeanor, to the extent that he fits some familiar patterns based on our presumptions and prior experiences. In other words, our knee-jerk reaction was to label the person, to stereotype him.

That sort of stereotyping is not necessarily bad. In drama (as well as in life), we know that an individual isn't the sum total of their attributes and that our perception of a character will grow beyond original stereotype. But we also know that people do express inner qualities through outer manifestations such as body posture, facial expression, and clothing. We use this knowledge all the time. We seek clues that help us discover that precious yet elusive quality, a person or character's personality. Let's start with how we construct and label a stereotype and see how we build it into a well-rounded character, or delve into a person to create an honest portrait.

Physical Features

When we first see characters on the screen, what do we notice first about them? What do we look at and look for?

If we are close enough, we usually look at a person's face, especially the eyes. We are extremely sensitive in reading the human face. We look to a person's face to judge personality, age, attitude and mood, reactions, and even subtleties such as honesty and character. The face is the most personal and revealing part of an individual.

Film and video are personal media because they can bring us up close to characters. The face is a principal center of interest in most films involving the

human subject. Even antique, black-and-white still portraits in Ken Burns's
The Civil War documentary have tremendous expressive power and ability to
captivate an audience.

When we introduce a character in our production, we usually want to
bring the audience close enough to see the face without much delay. As we will
discuss later in this chapter, showing the face adequately is a principal task of
cinematography and should be considered when creating a shooting script.

In our metaphorical scenario of the party, whether or not we allow this
mythical party host to approach us is usually based on whether or not we
think the person looks appealing, attractive, interesting, and perhaps most of
all, friendly. It's not by accident that most actors, even those who play character roles, look appealing, attractive, interesting, or friendly. As already mentioned, we must care about the individual; otherwise, the story will be
meaningless. We have to care, not necessarily in the sense of being sympathetic,
but at least in the sense of being interested. If we are doing a documentary, we
have to want to share a character's interests and involvement in the subject.
Generally speaking, we enter drama and documentaries through sympathetic
characters.

This is not to say someone in the room pointing a shotgun at us won't get
our attention. Clearly, in such circumstances, the action will be more important to us than our getting to know the gunman. But even in action dramas,
we usually find the lead character sympathetic.

To be appealing, attractive, or interesting depends in part on the character's physical appearance and what we can guess from initial clues: age, sex,
coloring, height, body type, and general demeanor. Appearance is the collection of features that appeal or don't appeal to us, or at least, make us feel con-
fident in making a snap judgment about the person. Does this person appear
to fit one of our stereotypes? Arnold Schwarzenegger, Don Knotts, Julia Roberts, and Whoopie Goldberg strike us immediately as certain types of individuals based on how they look. Appearance is a helpful label in terms of
identifying a person in a crowd or cast and guessing what character this person
can play.

Appearance is certainly the first criterion we consider in casting a production. In an audition, even before we meet prospective talent, we often look
through a stack of 8 × 10 black and white photos (head shots) of actors to select
the type of person who looks appropriate. We may seek talent who are unusual
variations on cliché stereotypes so we can cast "against type" in interesting
ways. In either case, we are casting by looks.

Obviously clothing is important. Despite admonitions regarding books
and covers, the clothing industry is right: clothes do make the man—and the
woman and the child as well. We associate certain jobs with the clothes people
wear. Different age groups and social groups have their particular style of dress.
There are regional, national, and cultural differences. The California "look" is
different from the New England "look." Sweatshirts and tank-tops abound

with words, icons, and imagery that individuals wear as signs to define themselves. Like bumper stickers, clothes can announce who we are.

After casting, wardrobe is an essential consideration. In nontheatrical productions, talent may ask you what we would like them to wear. Give it some thought because it will greatly influence that important first impression our characters make. Should they look businesslike, folksy, outdoorsey, arty, youthful, or yuppie? What they wear will telegraph a message to the audience that we can play with or against.

Sociological Situations

Let's go back to our party scenario again and continue the quest for clues to personality and identity. As the would-be new acquaintance wends his way through the crowd to where we are standing, what else do we look for? We may notice other people's reactions to the host which provide clues to his personality. Do others find him funny, impressive, sexy, intimidating? How does the host relate to those he meets? We can learn about characters from the reactions of friends, associates, family members, and acquaintances. What are our characters' attitudes toward other characters?

In a good ensemble cast, as in most television comedies and dramas, each character has a unique relationship with the other characters. In *Murphy Brown,* Murphy's relationship with Miles is different from her relationships with Corky, Frank, Jim, and Eldin. The reaction of the townspeople in *High Noon* tells us just how bad the bad guy is who's coming in on the train.

We also get clues from their physical environment. What sort of home do they keep? How is it decorated? What books, magazines, and CDs do they own? What pictures hang on the walls? What is the *mise en scène* associated with the character? Individuals make choices that distinguish themselves. People manifest their own uniqueness. They live and exhibit their preoccupations as jocks, environmentalists, techies, artists, punks, and so on. Furniture, decorations, and wall hangings from fine art and posters to cute kitten calendars define taste and personality.

An automobile is often an expressive extension of a person's persona. Does a character drive a muscle car or a sensible sedan? What does it tell us when we meet a CPA driving a Corvette? Does it reveal a hidden persona or a poser? An important characteristic is posturing. People often do things, wear clothes, listen to music, and espouse ideas merely to impress others. A sycophant like Mel Cooley (Richard Deacon) on the old *Dick Van Dyke Show* is a wonderful character. By being observers, we can decide whether characters fit into their environments or not.

We can set characters up and build audience anticipation by introducing characters in scenes in which they react to situations and other characters, displaying their unique styles of behavior. In the opening scenes from *Raiders of the Lost Ark,* for example, we don't see Indy's (Harrison Ford's) face for the first several minutes of the film, yet we learn about his character from the way he moves, the type of environment he is in, how he is dressed, the types of weapons he carries, and especially from the reactions of his bearers to him. In Scorsese's *Cape Fear,* we first see Max Cady (Robert De Niro) in shots of his tattooed back and muscles rippling as he works out. Only at the end of the sequence, do we see his face.

External factors are merely clues to internal personality. Tangible facts anchor the intangible qualities of people—who they *really* are. It is the mystery of the psyche ultimately that keeps us fascinated with other human beings.

Let's go back to the party scenario. At last the person arrives and we hear him speak. We already know quite a bit from our observations. We've drawn some conclusions based on his face, physical appearance, clothing, and the way in which he has dealt with others. But now we begin to elaborate our impressions at a more complex level. Our first interaction with a person and a character is the most important. We hear the person's voice—the quality of speech and the use of language. It tells us about where people grew up, gives us clues about their social background, and tells us something about their energy and the way they relate.

Does our character speak softly, open with an intellectually challenging comment, gush inanities, act tough, show genuine good nature, seem patronizing, or fish for approval? Like the face, language and diction are expressions of character. The first words out of the host's mouth anchor our impressions and begin the basis for our feelings about this person and our relationship with him.

A person's name is probably the most important label for anyone we meet. It is often the first bit of factual information we want to know about a person. The same is true with important characters. We need to give thought to how we name our characters. We will perceive a young man differently, at least initially, if he is named Billy, Bubba, or Bernard.

Generally, when we are first introduced to a character or person, we look for patterns that parallel our own experiences and reality. We may find an area of mutual interest or past history. These may be very specific such as going to the same school, coming from the same town, or knowing the same people. They may be more generic such as having similar interests, jobs, or political beliefs or enjoying the same sports or pastimes.

As with real people, we associate a character in a production with several labels, which usually derive from the circumstances of these first encounters. The physical presentation is usually the first label. The next label is often a social role, such as a teacher, student, parent, banker, restauranteur, doctor, gambler, pimp, or henchperson. In a narrative, our character will have a primary role in the action of the drama—journalist, investigator, brother, sister, partner, love interest, crook, murderer, suspect, and so on—that will complement the primary label established in the portraiture. Often, we can set up intriguing contrasts by assigning a story role that is unusual for the primary label. We can put a monk into the role of solving a murder (*The Name of the Rose*), for example. Primary labels usually should be set up in the first moments of a story, through dialogue or narration, if we have not established them from appearance and surroundings.

A one-label, one-dimensional character is a very thin stereotype and will probably fail to get us interested unless there is arresting action. Saturday morning TV cartoon characters are one-dimensional: the greedy, maniacally fiendish scientist; the brave, heroic, courageous kid; the faithful, funny, lovable sidekick. The better ones may reveal a little wit, but, generally speaking, the audience will not get very involved with a one-dimensional cartoon personality. This includes the good-looking, golden-throated narrator as well as the optimistic corporate executive, the artistic artist, the reserved farmer, and the glib politician. Portraits or interviews that reveal only one dimension of a person are basically one-dimensional cartoons and turn dull very quickly.

Knowing more about a person's background gives depth to characterization and creates a more rounded portrait. Even if the person is a reputed expert in some field, we usually want to push our knowledge beyond mere reputation and find out something else, something more personal, and not simply associated with the primary stereotype.

Sometimes there is no room for contrasts in the characters or documentary subjects we are profiling. In these cases, start again with the stereotypical point of view and push it beyond the audience's expectation. In the short documentary *Salamanders,* a young blonde coed at a frat party is swallowing live salamanders with a beer chaser. To many in the audience, this probably represents the height of stereotypical activity at a frat party. The film continues through some fairly standard sequences giving exposition about the practice of swallowing salamanders and then returns to the young woman who continues to swallow the creatures. The shots grow in intensity. It becomes erotic. The competition rages and, by the end of the short film, she has swallowed over 25 of the live amphibians. It's extreme. It's outrageous. It's *beyond* what most audiences will (forgive us) swallow.

A two-dimensional character is much better than the Saturday morning cartoon. It provides two areas for us to draw on to understand a person's or character's actions and emotions. Most people have at least two arenas for their lives: the work or school and the home environments. We know that characters behave differently in each. Murphy Brown is different in her attitudes at the office with her co-workers than in her townhouse with Eldin. Charles Foster Kane exhibited a different persona in his public life than in his private life.

If we choose a character type, a football player, for example, and simply show the person playing football, there is no sense of depth in the characterization. We have a stereotype. When we establish a character on the screen, the first question to ask is: "What is unique?" Answering this question lifts our character out of the realm of stereotype. The idea of a football player has several stereotypical associations. However, when we ask, "Why is this football player unique?" we might answer that this football player also performs professional ballet. Immediately we have added to the portrait an intriguing second facet that potentially breaks away from many of the anticipated stereotypes.

Two-dimensional portraiture gives us the opportunity for unexpected combinations that contradict stereotype—a poetry-writing insurance executive, an investment-wise pizza parlor owner, a sensitive taxi driver, or the spiritualist who owns ten Rolls Royces. The most interesting portraits often feature aspects of a personality that seem unexpected or contradictory. Think of others you have met, heard about, or seen portrayed in films and TV shows.

Three-dimensional characters, characters with complexity and multiple facets, have depth and even greater potential interest. Thus an interview or portrait of a woman raising a family *and* going to night school *while* also being a volunteer firefighter gives us several areas to explore. As a theatrical example, *Raging Bull* is a story about a second-rate boxer who can withstand incredible punishment *and* is a loser in his personal life *while* having a poignant self-awareness.

In the documentary *Eduardo the Healer,* we are introduced to Eduardo, a Peruvian healer who uses a peyote-like drug and the entrails of guinea pigs to diagnose diseases and demonic possession. When we meet Eduardo, he looks the part. He does a diagnosis. Then, while we are watching him prepare for a major exorcism, we also learn he is university educated in art and religion, well read, and has led the architectural reconstruction of some Incan ruins. His library is filled with books on psychology, including Jung in several languages. What we first think is a backward man becomes an educated and enlightened Indian who practices witchcraft, fishes, and is a gifted artist. The contrasts and multiple facets of the character are fascinating.

Look for the inherent contradictions in individuals. Eric Hoffer captured public interest in the early 1970s as a stevedore on the San Francisco docks who was also a philosopher.[1] Stevedore/philosophers are unique. Similarly, we are not ready for Yoda to be a Jedi Master in *Star Wars.*

Portraiture does, however, require selectivity. Although we need enough elements to make our character interesting, we should not overload our portraiture with too many elements. We must pare down our rendering to a selection of relevant elements. Suppose we are doing a documentary portrait about a Salvation Army woman who is a caretaker, nurturer, and supporter of street people in a neighborhood where she serves. We must realize that we cannot portray the whole real woman on the screen. The woman may be an avid bowler, be all thumbs and unable to put a nail in a wall, or have a matchbook collection from all the towns she has visited, but these aspects of her personality are likely to be irrelevant to the portrait.

Probably we will select one major theme and a complementary minor theme to draw this person's portrait: she works on the street serving food from a storefront which she tirelessly runs from early morning to late at night in an efficient and businesslike way. And, she is a warm and caring person who takes time with each individual and mothers those who never had a mother. Showing her attempting some minor carpentry might give us a lighter moment, as in the scene in *Witness* where we see John Book in the barn surreptitiously listening to rock and roll on his car radio. Such moments give us insight into characters' personalities, but we don't want to pursue them as themes, just notes. For our Salvation Army woman, hardworking efficiency and warm motherliness are the two themes that will constitute this portrait.

Psychological Profile

In our party parable, after our first introduction to the person and a brief conversation, in something like a minute and a half to three minutes or so, somewhere in the back of our mind, we make another decision. We will either excuse ourselves politely, perhaps by first introducing him to another unwitting guest and then beating the proverbial hasty retreat, or stay with him and enjoy an emerging relationship. Our decision is again akin to a member of the audience about to tune out physically, mentally, or electronically after satisfying an initial curiosity about a program. Perhaps it was only passing interest or an attractive face that caught our attention, but what is going to hold it?

Primarily it is a character's involvement in something that absorbs us. In narrative, the story is the hook that keeps us attentive. In nonnarrative, it's whether we feel we will continue to be informed about something that interests us.

Beyond the character's association with story or topic, the character's point of view and attitude are also very important. Is the person's outlook surprising or funny? Does it make us laugh? Are we curious as to why the person acts or what the person says? As long as there appear to be more pieces to the personality puzzle, we will stay actively interested.

Is there a resonance between the character and our own experience? Can we reach the character's feelings and reactions to events through analogous echoes in our own life? What we are talking about is the character's humanness and how it is shown through acts, deeds, and words, even if the topic is something totally unrelated to our background and experience. We expect characters to behave in believable, even if bizarre, ways. If we see action that is arbitrary, without recognition or development of human motivation, we dismiss the scene as shallow, a poor rendering of dramatic reality.

A person or character's attitude is to some extent a product of physical characteristics as well as social environment. Our physical characteristics and the places, environments, and situations in our experience combine to shape our likes and dislikes, loves and hates, fears and desires, dreams and nightmares, weaknesses and strengths. It's what gives us our attitude on life—how we approach and react to people, places, and situations.

It is important to develop the psychological baggage that characters carry with them. It prevents them from being inert pawns in the plot. Characters should not be simply driven by the story. They should express their attitudes through their actions and decisions as they confront the problems and other characters in the story. Avoid the tendency to script action without regard to characterization. It results in zombielike humanoids acting out broad emotional gestures—sadness, anger, stealth, fear, happiness, passion, bravery—without any resemblance to real people. Even action requires believable motivation.

The characters we develop in theatrical or documentary portraiture will generally have, along with their primary and perhaps secondary labels, a general attitude or outlook on life. We often make knee-jerk assumptions about an individual's general attitude just as we do about their physical type. We define an attitudinal or personality stereotype and use it to label a person's basic nature. Again, that's not necessarily bad. In drama (as well as in life), our perception of characters grows beyond the original stereotypes of their attitudes or personalities. We see characters respond to life in their own unique, if predictable, fashions. Look at the list of attitude labels in Table 6.1 and think about the lead characters in the films and television shows referenced for this chapter. What attitude label would we pick for Han Solo, Luke Skywalker, Daisy Werthan, Roseanne, Thelma, Louise, or for some secondary characters such as Yoda, Darth Vader, Miles, Corky, or Jim? We probably can find an adjective in the list to associate with each of these characters and, significantly, we probably can select other adjectives to describe secondary and tertiary character attitudes, and these will often be conflicting.

Moods shape our attitudes. Thus a character in a vile mood may approach something or someone with a different attitude than when the same character is in better spirits. Generally we don't think of mood as part of a character's or person's label unless the label we associate with a character is "temperamental." But it is important in developing characters or researching subjects to get a feel for how their moods affect or alter their attitudes and outlook because that can affect behavior and speech, and potentially add new twists and depth to our stories.

Vitality and Power

The combination of physical, sociological, and psychological characteristics is what makes people and characters interesting. In addition, a powerful attraction of some people is their energy, passion, and fire. Such people charm us with their intensity and attract us like moths to a flame. They have drive and ambition.

Most important for both drama and portraiture is personal power. In drama, characters do more than merely interact. They lead, entice, persuade, move, and manipulate each other. How they do it depends on their personality. They use guilt, innocence, dominance, authority, prestige, position, cunning, a commanding presence, strong voice, good looks, and, often, plain and simple blackmail. They have presence on the screen.

Lasting Relationships

Characters that linger in our mind long after the movie is over or portraits that continue to haunt us are unique or complex, and exhibit strong personal power.

TABLE 6.1   Character Attitude Labels

absent-minded	fresh	offensive
abusive	frugal	old-fashioned
accident-prone	genteel	omnipotent
aloof	grasping	opinionated
ambitious	greedy	organized
anile	grouchy	patronizing
apathetic	gushing	philanthropic
athletic	harebrained	procrastinating
bashful	helpless	proud
bigoted	hen-pecked	prudish
birdlike	high-minded	pushy
bookish	hot-headed	quaint
breezy	humorless	regal
carefree	hungry	rowdy
careless	hypocritical	self-centered
caustic	idealistic	self-destructive
charming	impractical	self-effacing
chaste	impulsive	self-pitying
cheap	inane	sensitive
chicken-hearted	indolent	servile
childish	infallible	shameless
chivalrous	ingratiating	shrewd
churlish	inquiring	shy
clownish	irresponsible	slow
cocky	jealous	sneaky
complaining	jumpy	snide
conceited	kindly	snobbish
confident	lazy	sophisticated
conniving	lecherous	stiff-necked
cowardly	logical	strait-laced
cranky	loquacious	stubborn
deceitful	loud-mouthed	stupid
devilish	loutish	subservient
disconnected	lusty	testy
disdainful	magnanimous	timid
dishonest	malicious	treacherous
disloyal	maneuvering	trustworthy
dynamic	maternal	unappreciative
eager	mean	uncertain
edgy	mousy	uncivilized
egotistic	naive	unforgiving
extravagant	narrow-minded	unmanageable
fastidious	nasty	unsociable
fatuous	Neanderthal	untrustworthy
fickle	negative	warm
flamboyant	nervous	worldly
flighty	nervy	wormy
foolish	neurotic	xenophobic
formal	nonconforming	
foxy	oafish	

Individuals and characters are like puzzles. We remain interested in putting the pieces together as long as something continues to take shape. Just as we don't pour out all the story clues at once, we reveal the character over the course of the drama or portrait. Clearly we need to give the audience a strong first impression, and a character's opening lines or the opening lines about the character are crucial. Then, in each sequence of the show, we reveal more and more through action, dialogue, and narration, and by expanding the world in which the character moves to include new locations, characters, props, and situations. The process is familiar to the audience because that's how we learn about people as well. We learn the more personal and subtle facets of a person as we see them in expanding circumstances.

Secondary Characters

Because the reaction of others is so important in revealing the nature of a character, we need to select or create other characters who will provide this function for us. Often, the most interesting reactions come from a character who is of a different type. This might include the nice contrast of Rose to Charlie in *The African Queen,* Max Schumacher (William Holden) to Howard Beal (Peter Finch) in *Network,* Thelma to Louise in *Thelma & Louise,* or Daisy Werthan to Hoke in *Driving Miss Daisy.* Contrasting characters—Oscar and Felix in *The Odd Couple,* or George and Martha in *Who's Afraid of Virginia Woolf?*—have their own unique individuality and eccentricities. Contrasts can be pushed for comic effect as in the case of Vincent and Julius in *Twins.* (See Figure 6.1.) Each provides the mirror for the other, and the contrasts make for excellent and in-

FIGURE 6.1
Good characterization and casting provide contrasts, as with the characters of Vincent and Julius in *Twins.*

Copyright © by Universal City Studios, Inc. Courtesy of MCA Publishing Rights, a Division of MCA Inc.

TABLE 6.2   Characterization Template

Name	Age
School	Sex
Work	Dress and appearance
Hobbies	Walk
Other interests	General demeanor
Pastimes	Passion
Family	Drive
Home	Ambitions
Hometown	Unique, basic nature
Neighborhood	Outlook
Friends	Philosophy toward life
Enemies	Sense of humor
Problems	Power

---

triguing drama. Good characterization and casting provide contrasts and elicit traits through the relationships, which we would not otherwise see.

Making Vital Characters

The characters in our film or video need careful development in a way similar to the way we meet and develop relationships with individuals. In a dramatic situation, the job of creating the character is ours. With documentary, we need to research and interview the individuals keeping in mind that our purpose is to develop these people as characters for the audience. In either case, we need to know much of the information listed in Table 6.2.

Based on this information, we decide what is the dominant characteristic by which our audience will know the character and what are the secondary and tertiary characteristics that give texture and depth to the character. In a documentary portrait or interview, our research should easily identify the dominant way we see this person. But, our job is also to find the secondary and tertiary facets of that person's life that make the character come alive for us. This will likely take careful reflection, and the choices will no doubt be less obvious and more elusive.

The Treatment of Character in Production

Preproduction: Casting

Reconciling reality to the vision in our mind begins with casting. It is at this moment we have to begin to let go of our script or idea and recognize that film, video, and television are collaborative much like an orchestra, football squad, or army platoon. As writer-producers of television or directors of film and video, we set the tone and interpretation—the treatment—of the piece. However, contributions from each member of the production help shape as well as make the project successful.

All productions take on a life of their own. If we are producing a project that is our original idea, we are simply the first to contribute to it. Along the way, on-camera talent, behind-the-camera crew, and a variety of people behind the scenes will all conspire to bring the project to the screen. To the general audience, the most important of all these contributors will be those who appear on the screen. Our job as writer, director, or any of the behind-the-camera participants is to collaborate to make those who will appear on the screen believable and captivating.

Casting characters requires knowing the qualities at the centers of the characters that are the most important, the ones that motivate them through the story, and then finding people who can understand and convey those qualities. How they convey these qualities is their craft. They may surprise you. Generally the writer, producer, or director has a certain type of person in mind based on physical appearance and, generally, those are the people we look for to cast in our production. But, there are scads of semi-apocryphal stories about parts written for and offered to a particular actor who turned it down for some reason and the role was later performed successfully by someone quite different.

Jo Beth Williams was associated with the part of Murphy Brown before Candice Bergen became involved. It's now hard to imagine anyone but Bergen in the role. It's been said that Tom Selleck was considered for the role of Indiana Jones. The role of Sergeant Emil Foley in *An Officer and a Gentleman* was supposedly conceived originally for a white actor with a totally different body type and manner, but Lou Gossett, Jr., proved he understood and could convey what was at the core of the part and got the job. The role of Ripley in *Alien* was originally written for a man until Sigourney Weaver was given the script.

Before casting, we need to do our homework on the script to discover or rediscover the essential kernel of the character. Then, during casting, we must be open to the interpretation an actor brings to the part. Just as different musicians bring different interpretations to a song, different actors approach a character differently.

In documentary production, we need to be clear in our mind what it is that attracts us to the idea of the piece. Then we find the individual who not only embodies that idea, but can display it in front of the camera. Sometimes, someone we have met sparks the idea for portraiture as an approach to our production. We are struck by this person's presence and find in it the perfect expression of the idea we want to convey.

Production

In planning to shoot our portrait or introduce our character to the audience for the first time, we need to make two important decisions: where will we meet our character and what will our character be doing.

Setting/Arena

Portraiture depends on context. People do not exist in a vacuum. It is impossible to talk about characters exclusive of the environments in which we find them. In the previous section, we assumed our character was at a party. Those are probably not the best circumstances under which an audience is introduced to a character, but it gave us both people and things in the room from which to gain clues about the person. Where we meet the character or what environment we find the character in tells us a great deal and, therefore, we should give it considerable thought. We often see the character's environment before we see the character, and it begins our quest into the character's basic nature. Consider the following settings:

- The cold, colorless, misty mountain mining town where we are first introduced to McCabe (Warren Beatty) in *McCabe and Mrs. Miller*
- The austere, anachronistic, religious farming community where we are first introduced to Rachel (Kelly McGillis) in *Witness*
- The stark, dark, concrete and steel world of *Batman*
- The steamy, cramped hotel room at the beginning of *Apocalypse Now,* where we first meet Captain Willard (Martin Sheen)
- The hot, confining bedroom at the beginning of *Bonnie and Clyde,* where we first meet Bonnie (Faye Dunaway)
- The precise, orderly bedroom of Daisy Werthan in *Driving Miss Daisy*
- The bustling diner where we first find Louise (Susan Sarandon) in *Thelma & Louise*
- The tough running-course through the woods in *Silence of the Lambs* where we meet Clarice Starling (Jodi Foster)
- The hot and possibly dangerous environment of the bakery in *Moonstruck* where Loretta (Cher) is first captivated by Ronny Cammareri (Nicolas Cage)

Think about what kind of character we expect to find in a particular location: a police station, a dank and dreary castle, a cabin in the woods, the mayor's office, a sculptor's studio, or the deck of a ship. Sometimes we want to use a location that is immediately recognizable to reinforce or tell us something about the character, or we might want to contrast the character with the location (as with Crocodile Dundee in New York City). If the personality of the subject of our portrait has several facets that can be revealed by location, for example, the sheer ice wall of Mt. Everest and also the grill of a diner, we may want to establish our character first in one location and then expand the world in which our character lives to include the other location. The Butch Cassidy we first meet at the bank is different from the Butch we see with the Hole in the Wall gang. These are different from the Butch we see when he visits Sundance's friend, Etta. We may want to start in a person's normal habitat, then develop the other locations as we unfold the character on the screen. *Raiders of the Lost Ark* starts in a highly adventurous setting in the title sequence, but then retreats to the normal setting of a college classroom where Indy teaches, before building the story back toward the exotic.

In television, we want to establish the arena of the story immediately. The arena in television is the regular, repeatable *mise en scène,* the milieu in which the drama takes place. In *Cheers,* it's the bar; in *Murphy Brown,* it's FYI. When we first meet the characters of an episodic television show, the set, the situation, or what we call the *arena* immediately helps to define the characters. The FYI set in *Murphy Brown* immediately establishes Murphy, Frank, Jim, and Miles as a broadcast news team and provides a context for us to meet the types of characters we find in the show.

The arena establishes what kind of story and characters we will meet and the kinds of conflicts that will occur. Characters become involved in action that somehow can be made logical given the arena of the show. A feature, movie of the week, or a single episode is different. It's all right for a reporter to chase a murderer in one show, but it's hard for a reporter to always be chasing murderers week after week. It's outside the arena for reporters. Once we set the arena, we simultaneously set primary physical and sociological character labels. Then we add the attitude labels, and we get a Murphy Brown who is an ex-alcoholic, tough, experienced, respected, investigative, broadcast journalist or an Indiana Jones who is a tough, gutsy, resourceful adventurer and archeologist.

In addition to the sets, think of the set dressings that can contribute to the development of character. What speaks either specifically of a character's taste or occupation, or speaks symbolically about the character's inner nature that could contribute to the *mise en scène*? In the opening of *Network,* the television monitors each show one of the network news anchors and one shows Howard Beal. This association, plus the hectic, serious business of producing an evening news show sets up the credibility of Beal as a network anchor.

As with set or location, give thought to colors, shapes, and forms as well as to specific objects to hang on a wall or stick on a table. If shooting in a person's home or place of work, don't be afraid to move objects that belong to a person into the shot. Don't let subjects clean the house or rearrange the office so they will appear to be someone they really aren't if our goal is to show them as they really are. Think carefully about where you want to introduce the audience to them and what the place will look like.

Props

Props are also important. A single prop can become so associated with a character that it becomes a part of the physical features of the character, as in Charlie Chaplin's Little Tramp character's hat and cane. Props can help convey sociological information, as with the black lunch pail carried by Ralph Kramden on *The Honeymooners,* which tied him into his blue-collar background, or Fonzie's black leather jacket in *Happy Days,* which was specific to a certain social status, setting him up on the cool fringe of high school society.

Guns have served this purpose for everyone from Wyatt Earp with his Buntline Special and Davy Crockett with "Old Betsy" to James Bond with his Walther PPK. The Lone Ranger's silver bullet became his calling card, and Paladin actually had a calling card reading "Have Gun Will Travel." And, of course, Indiana Jones has his trademark whip.

Archie Bunker's chair in *All in the Family* not only reflects middle-class social status but is a constant reminder, center stage, of his authoritarian role in the plot, as well as in the household, through his refusal to allow the other characters to use his chair. The chair also represented the psychological nature of his character as one comfortably set in his ways. In the *The Wizard of Oz*, Dorothy's ruby slippers regularly remind us of her mission in Oz as well as her strong desire to return home.[2]

In creating the character of Murphy Brown, who hits the audience with the initial label or stereotype as a hard-nosed career woman who dominates the show, producer Diane English had the problem of how to make her accessible to the audience without undermining Murphy's rugged professionalism. Yes, we'd probably like to meet a Murphy Brown, but would we like her to visit us in our living room on a weekly basis? The Murphy Brown character needed an area of vulnerability, something we could empathize with. Not many of us are at the top of our careers as news anchors. What are the patterns or traits that parallel our own experiences and reality? What is the resonance between Murphy Brown and our own experience? Can we reach her feelings and reactions to events through analogous echoes in our own life? What is the humanness of the character?

English's solution to the problem was to create another character, Eldin, who views Murphy from a different perspective than the rest of the cast. To Eldin, Murphy is not a tough professional, but a regular person. Since Eldin is not on the FYI set, English also introduced in the pilot episode that Murphy was returning to FYI after a stay at the Betty Ford Clinic overcoming alcohol and tobacco dependencies. Rather than build reminders of Murphy's vulnerability into the dialogue of each show, English used the prop of a number two soft pencil which Murphy would chew when her level of need got high. The pencil prop then became an important recurring emblem of Murphy's vulnerability.

Other Characters, Narration, and Commentary

If our character is going to relate to others in some specific way, we may want to introduce a recognizable group of people whose attitudes can be referenced quickly: homeless, fraternity or sorority types, BMW drivers, commuters, and so on. Or, we may want to introduce secondary characters for this person to play against. For instance, in a piece about a nurse who works in a hospice, we may want to show some of the patients and perhaps even hear their comments regarding the nurse before she is introduced. By their commentary, these secondary characters then set up the entrance or create concern for the primary character.

The actions of lesser characters often intrigue us and set up the entrance of the star. As mentioned, the porters in *Raiders of the Lost Ark* set up the character of Indiana Jones. Peter Weir sets up Rachel (Kelly McGillis) in *Witness* in this way. She is made prominent in a shot at the church during the funeral scene so that when she is identified later, we already have that sense of acquaintance with her. Then, in the scene where he finally identifies who she is, Weir first establishes the lesser character, Daniel (Alexander Godunov), visually and lets him lead us through the farmhouse in his purposeful search through the minor characters. Daniel then comes to a door. He clearly hesitates, in contrast to his fairly determined actions up to that moment. The hesitation sets up our curiosity. What has given him pause? Rachel is then introduced. That little hesitation in this obviously strong character is enough to set her importance above his as the major player on the scene.

First Action

Once we have in mind the qualities of character we want and have cast the person that can embody those qualities in interesting ways, we are ready to plan the visual introduction of our character. The character needs to be established as important to the audience.

In narrative or productions that rely on portraiture, when we bring on the protagonist for the first time, we need to have him or her do something that sets up the first stereotype of the character, that creates a strong impression, and that arouses the audience's curiosity to know more about this individual. Showing a character waking up, turning off the alarm clock, showering, getting dressed, drinking coffee, and leaving the house could expose us to personal items and articles of decor that might provide clues about the character. However, because the character's first action needs to intrigue the audience and make them want to know more about the person, having the character do something so tiresomely mundane will likely kill audience interest unless it's done in a remarkably interesting way. We introduce our character in a way that will make the audience want to know more, and we establish action that gives clues about the person. Daisy Werthan's first action was to get in her car and have an accident, thus setting up her dependency on her son and ultimately on Hoke.

Arousing our curiosity about a character before we are actually introduced, much as we did in our party scenario, is a standard convention. In *McCabe and Mrs. Miller*, the title sequence is a series of wide shots of a lone rider winding his way up a cold, misty, mountain trail. Warren Beatty's face is deliberately kept out of the shot. As a gambler, Warren Beatty's McCabe wants to arouse curiosity and attract the moths to his poker game. Altman accomplishes this with props. When McCabe first enters the dingy mining town, the men in the bar instantly focus on McCabe's gun and wonder what kind it is. One thinks it is a Swedish gun—clearly a rare item. Then McCabe clears a table, and there in the drab, colorless room he spreads out a red and white checked tablecloth, bringing color for the first time to the set. Not only is this a wonderful device for McCabe to use, but it becomes symbolic of McCabe's role in the town, bringing color and a hint of the exotic that raises, for a while, the vitality of the town.

The first actions of a character are very revealing. If the scene is scripted to be meaningful, we will see how a character reacts to a given situation. In narrative, we want to show the character's potential for achieving the goals of the narrative. Think of the opening sequence of *Raiders of the Lost Ark*. We are exposed to dank, mysterious, uncharted jungle. Again, Indy is not seen except in shadow or from the rear, a man moving purposefully, but obscured from us. We are introduced first to his team of native bearers, and through them we get the impression of a dangerous mission as they react to poison arrows in the trees. Finally, one pulls a gun to shoot their intrepid leader when, with his first definitive action, he snaps the gun from the underling's hand with a crack of the bullwhip and we are given the close-up of Indiana Jones. (See Figure 6.2.)

In Scorsese's *Cape Fear* and in *Terminator 2,* the principal characters are introduced working out in a prison environment. The scenes convey toughness, independence, tenacity, tautly contained anger, and threatening physical power. They portend events that soon follow.

First action doesn't always set up characters capable and ready for action. Often it is through the course of the story that we discover them to be extraordinary people confronted with extraordinary circumstances. This development of character over the course of the story is called the *character arc*. The

FIGURE 6.2
The first actions of a character are very revealing. Only after he snaps the gun from an underling's hand with his bullwhip are we given a close-up of Indiana Jones in *Raiders of the Lost Ark*.

Courtesy of Lucasfilm Ltd. ™ & © Lucasfilm Ltd. (LFL) 1981. All Rights Reserved.

characters introduced have strong, clear labels, but these are stretched, changed, and added to during the drama. Our introduction to both Rose and Charlie in *The African Queen* gives us strong impressions about them, but no clues to their capacity to resolve the problems that eventually confront them. Thelma and Louise seem very ordinary. Rachel in *Witness* does not initially strike us as particularly heroic. Rocky Balboa seems incapable of staying in the ring with Apollo Creed. Kevin in *Home Alone* is just a kid. But, as they confront major challenges, they draw us into the drama by our concern—Can they make it? Suspense is created as we watch characters struggle to rise to the circumstances.

Subtle changes in makeup, wardrobe, and hair can sometimes suggest changes in the character's arc. In films such as *Crocodile Dundee, Romancing the Stone,* and *Black Widow,* as the female characters become freer spirits, their wardrobe becomes more casual and their hair comes down and softens. Subtle changes in hair and wardrobe affect male characters as well in such films as *Rain Man, City Slickers, The Fisher King,* and *Wall Street.*

Lighting

The lighting in a scene not only directs our attention and allows us to focus on the protagonist as more important than the others in the same shot, but it also influences our attitude toward the character in terms of mood and genre. Do we see the character's environment as aggressive, relaxed, bright and cheery, drab and dreary?

Remember the lighting in *Ghostbusters* in the scene where we first meet Bill Murray's character, Peter Venkman. It's very low key and sinister, which makes a nice contrast to the humor of the scene. Venkman is playing zap-the-nerd as he hustles his way toward a date with a beautiful blonde student. The light on Murray is always slightly brighter. The light falls off a little on the two volunteers and the rest of the set is dark, creating a cameo effect on the principals.

Lighting has a major effect on the rendering of a character's face. Character lines in a person's face are revealed by shadows and subtle movements or reaction. They are seen best when shadow patterns model and define the face. How our lighting creates these shadow patterns greatly affects how the audience sees the character. (For a more in-depth discussion of these techniques, see Chapter 10.)

Placement of the *key light,* or principal light source, greatly affects portraiture. Key lights set frontally and near eye level minimize shadows, illuminate the eyes under the brow, and generally produce a smooth-skinned appearance. Such lighting diminishes structures of the face—the nose, brow, chin, and cheekbones—as well as wrinkles and skin texture. This placement of the key light is often used to smooth a person's appearance and reduce apparent nose size. It also makes a character look young, innocent, and vulnerable.

Frontal placement of the key light slightly below eye level provides this effect and causes a reflected sparkle in the eyes, which can be very attractive in romantic scenes. Look at any scene in which candlelight motivates the lighting (the restaurant scene in *Moonstruck,* the candle scene in *Cabaret*) to see this effect.

As we move the key light farther to the side and higher up, brow shadows and nose shadows increase, bone structure in the face becomes more pronounced, and skin texture is accentuated. This kind of key light placement makes the person look rugged and, generally, makes characters look craggier, older, rougher, and tougher.

If we move the key light all the way over to the other side of the subject's face from the camera in a narrow lighting setup, we can emphasize the eyes, model facial structure, and articulate expression.[3] If we strongly back light the subject or put an actor or actress in front of a brightly lit set or window, as in the opening of *Thelma & Louise,* we can isolate the individual against the background, giving good three-dimensional separation and produce a halo effect on the hair. We can add soft frontal fill to these setups to avoid melodramatic shadows and to create natural-looking scenes. We can add an eyelight that puts sparkle in a subject's eyes for a scene that can be very appealing and greatly enhance a romantic treatment.

Another lighting choice that affects portraiture is the quality of light used to illuminate the character. Hard lighting creates strong contrasts and sharply outlines facial features and skin texture. Soft lighting produces delicate shadow effects, which make the face appear gentler with velvety skin.

The amount of light used to fill in the shadows on a person's face also affects portraiture. A deeply shadowed face is generally more appropriate for dark moods and somber characters. Greatly reducing shadows with fill light gives us an open, candid face appropriate for less stylized characterizations.

Image Size and Camera Movement

Portraiture depends on face. As we've mentioned, expectation and curiosity can be created by not showing the face for the first few moments of the production, but we won't really begin to care about the individual until we can see the face. Intentionally obscuring the face to shroud the character in mystery or make the character more of a generic "Everyman" ultimately distances the audience if their initial curiosity is not going to be satisfied. We need to make the character's acquaintance. If, after seeing the work, we were to see the person in the same room with us, would we recognize him or her? Characters can go through all sorts of interesting action, but they do not truly involve us if we never see a clear view of their face.

It is important not to get so absorbed by the complexities of production that we forget that the audience needs the close-up. This can happen when we are concentrating on action without giving sufficient attention to who the characters are. We can either shoot scenes so wide as to make room for broad action, or so close as to emphasize moving feet, legs, and other body parts. In either case, we obscure and conceal the face.

Another reason we may fail to adequately show a person's face is that much action involves characters looking down or turning their backs to the center of a room (preparing a meal at a stove or counter in a kitchen, for example) or moving away from one place toward someplace else. In these situations, without thoughtful camera placement and blocking of action, all we will see is the character's back turned toward the camera. It's no accident that kitchens in many television and film productions have islands or separate tables where action can be staged.

Usually the showing of face involves nothing more than making the effort to move the camera in for medium shots (MS) and medium close-ups (MCU) during the action and getting in front of the action so that the character faces the camera, allowing for at least a three-quarter front shot. If locked into a restrictive location, we can sometimes cheat the furniture out from the wall enough to get the camera in front of the actor. In a tight shot, nobody will notice. We might even try using mirrors, but remember to light the face, not the mirror.

Another problem can occur in a simple dialogue between two people. If the characters are facing each other and the camera is placed to see each one equally, the result is a not very satisfactory shot of both profiles. Profiles can be effective in formal, romantic-style close-up portraiture or in comic "nose-to-nose" confrontations, but usually they simply show a lot of ear and hair, neither of which are very expressive. These shots deprive the audience of their desire to see the face. In theatrical productions, the solution is easy—the interaction is simply staged shot by shot in a series of over-the-shoulder three-quarter front and near-frontal reverse angles, allowing us to see both eyes and the face of each character more fully. In documentary, the problem is a bit more difficult, but the solution is the same. We usually decide which person to emphasize, and then place the camera in an over-the-shoulder position to show the dominant character in a three-quarter front shot. We can cover the other person by some reverse angle, three-quarter front reaction shots. Sometimes in documentary, we can emphasize one person in a dialogue and then the other. The purpose always, however, is to show clear near-frontal face shots of our subjects.

Of course, the medium close-up (MCU) and the close-up (CU) are the most powerful shots showing the human face. These shots can be overused and should be used in combination with medium shots, which also clearly show facial features and expressions, to give variety to the sequence of shots. Video is considered a "close-up medium" and, because of the smaller screen size and lower resolution, our shot scripts must include many more MSs, MCUs, and CUs to show characters' facial expressions.

Close-ups denote power. For example, Robert Redford is introduced in *Butch Cassidy and the Sundance Kid* through a long, protracted close-up. According to William Goldman in his book *Adventures in the Screen Trade,* it helped Redford, who was then unknown but had been given equal billing with the well-known Paul Newman, to become a power on the screen as well as establishing the character, a little-known gunslinger, as an important threat.[4]

Focal lengths of lenses used in portraiture have a profound influence on the rendering of the human face. Because of their effect on perspective (see

Chapter 11), very short focal length lenses exaggerate the features in close shots, causing the brow to jut forward, the ears to set back, the nose to extend outward, and the jaw line to recede. The result is a gargoyle caricature, which can be horrific (Jack Nicholson's maniacal face grinning through the broken bathroom door in *The Shining*) or used for comic effect in shots of Paul Reubens's Pee Wee Herman or Jim Varney's Ernest.

Used less extremely, short focal lengths can cause a person to appear more round faced and youthful. Conversely, long focal lengths flatten the face, shortening the nose, squaring the jaw, and pulling the ears forward. The effect can be a kind of a pug look. It can be used to make some people look rougher, whereas on others, it can be flattering, shortening the nose and accentuating cheekbones.

As characters move, they motivate the camera to move with them. We realize that the character is clearly the focus of our attention. In *Thelma & Louise,* the camera is stationary for a moment as we open in the diner. Then, as Louise moves with the coffee pot, the camera takes off with her, tracking her action against the brightly lit window of the diner, making her prominent, and revealing the set as she moves. Similarly, bold movement, especially in the direction of the camera; bright colors; or other contrasting, noticeable features—hair, size, and so on—will draw our attention to a character in the frame and make that character the center of our attention.

Cutting on incomplete action and camera movement, cutting together shots that would normally be awkward juxtapositions, shooting extreme angles, and engineering bizarre manipulation of the camera can intentionally unsettle the audience. Hitchcock went to these extremes in *Psycho* and *Vertigo*. Scorsese's *Cape Fear* uses an upside-down shot to reintroduce Cady (Robert De Niro) after he gets out of prison, and later in the film, during the storm, Scorsese spins the camera to disorient and involuntarily disturb the audience.

Portraying Characters

In our discussion of characterization and portraiture, two major points should now be evident. One is that portraiture is what involves us in action and makes us care about what is happening on the screen. Without the establishment of subjects that we care about, we cannot sustain narrative for any length of time.

The second point is a bit more subtle. If we have an interesting subject and simply point a camera at the person, we do not automatically get an interesting film or video. What the audience sees on the screen is not the person, but an image of the person, a portrait created through the application of an aggregate of various production techniques. Audiences do not see real people in a film or video, they see portraits, and our ability to effectively portray character is crucial to inducing the audience to be interested in our work.

Exercise 1

Watch the first three to five minutes of a movie or television show with the sound turned off and make notes about how much we learn about the lead characters. Make notes on their physical appearance and what it tells you. What can you discern about their sociological background from what you observe? Can you tell what their dominant attitudes are? What their attitude or commitment to the plot is? How is their vitality shown? How do they exercise power? If you can watch a tape of the movie or TV show, now go back and look at the same three to five minutes *with* the sound on and fill in the gaps. See how much you could pick up nonverbally from the actions, reactions, and physical surroundings, and from the way the director portrayed them in the scene. Now, go watch people interact at work, school, in a restaurant, and so on and see how much you can discover about them. How would you film the interaction you are watching?

Exercise 2

Create three characters who know each other. Write a monologue for each of them describing the other two characters. Create a scene in which we meet these three characters for the first time, but make one character clearly the hero or the character from whose point of view we are seeing the story. In this scene, reveal something about one of the characters that goes beyond our expectation or presents another facet that expands our knowledge about the person.

Exercise 3

Research an individual in your community whom you think might make an interesting portrait. Develop questions that explore his or her area of expertise as well as extend into secondary and tertiary areas of interest. Can you explore the subject's problems in an interesting way? Can you discover a sense of humor? By the end of the interview, do you feel that the audience can define the subject's unique qualities, outlook, or philosophy toward life?

Notes

1. We recommend his book, *The True Believer.*

2. Fonzie's jacket, Archie's chair, and Dorothy's ruby slippers are such prominent symbols of character, story, and historical periods that they are today preserved in the Smithsonian Institution in Washington, D.C.

3. We refer to a narrow lighting setup or a broad lighting setup to denote the area of light from the key on the subject's face. In a narrow lighting setup, the key is on the opposite side of the subject from the camera. In a broad lighting setup, the key is on the same side as the camera and the subject's face is broadly lit.

4. William Goldman's *Adventures in the Screen Trade: A Personal View of Hollywood and Screenwriting* provides a good look at the problems facing most screenwriters. It was published in New York by Warner Books in 1983.

7

MISE EN SCÈNE AND DESIGN

The Philosophy of *Mise en Scène*

The Material Content of Shots

The French term *mise en scène* has proven useful to English-speaking producers and critics because it encompasses so many elements that contribute to the look and meaning of a scene. Literally translated as "putting in the scene," the phrase refers to all the visual elements of set, set dressing, props, costumes, makeup, lighting, and even physical body posture that are arranged and placed before the camera lens. Designing and exploiting *mise en scène* are basic to the art of production and provide expressive and artistic means for the manipulation of scenes and the interpretation of subjects.

Locations, props, costumes, and lighting make up the visible substance of the world in which we set our characters and our story. They constitute the reality that we conjure for our audience. These are the elements with which we visually design our compositions. *Mise en scène* is the stuff from which shots are made.

The power of *mise en scène* is so central to production that it has led to an important aesthetic and philosophic approach in film theory articulated by André Bazin and writers in *Cahiers du Cinéma,* the journal of the French New Wave. Through the ideas advanced by this French school of film theory, the term *mise en scène* has become associated with a style of filmmaking that emphasizes the reality before the camera as opposed to artificial juxtapositions created by film editing (montage).

Productions dominated by this *mise en scène* style are characterized by long takes, deep-focus photography, and extended, flowing camera moves. These long takes with moving camera and deep focus are used to change the camera point of view rather than imposing point of view by cutting from one shot to another in editing. Actions are carefully choreographed with the movement of the camera and in the depth of the frame. It is considered by some producers and theorists to be a more "democratic," truthful, and less contrived approach to creating a scene. It certainly creates a distinctive style that can be quite striking.[1]

The Production Elements of *Mise en Scène*

Although the term *mise en scène* has special meaning to film theorists and can be used to describe a specific style, in most film, video, or television productions, *mise en scène* is not a theory-laden concept. It is a way of referring to the selection of locations, sets, set dressings, props, costumes, and lighting for their visual interest, their visual storytelling abilities, their graphic possibilities, and design features.

Evocative Locations and Photographic Opportunities

We craft the *mise en scène* to make our scenes articulate, cohesive, and engaging visual experiences. We select locations or create sets that are unique, exotic, or evocative for their purely visual potential. In fact, the photographic opportunity or visual possibility of a specific location may be the springboard for a production.

Producer A. B. Cooper, Jr., had been captivated by the visual possibilities presented by a motel swimming pool, closed for the winter and covered with a huge blue bubblelike cover supported by an air blower. (See Figure 7.1.) Because of the captured humidity, all the house plants from the motel were kept inside and with the pool lights on, especially at night, it was transformed into an eery, iridescent blue, tropical oasis. Cooper, scripting a horror film at the

FIGURE 7.1
Director A. B. Cooper recognized the visual possibilities presented by this motel swimming pool, closed for the winter and enclosed with a huge blue bubble-like cover, for his horror film *The Mutilator.*

"THE MUTILATOR," O.K. Productions. Courtesy of A. B. Cooper Jr., Producer.

time, used the photographic opportunities of that location, which became the visual gemstone of the film *The Mutilator.*

Baltimore's old Lexington Market, with its predawn activities of farmers, fish mongers, butchers, and flower-sellers hauling in their meats, fish, and flowers; uncrating them; packing them in ice; cutting them into steaks and roasts; arranging great loops of sausages; arranging their flowers, all the while making the sounds of their work, camaraderie, and the sizzle of breakfast, was another location that offered enormous visual possibilities. The sequence was about weights and measures inspection. It could have been shot anywhere that the inspectors operate, but the earthy Lexington Market, seething with the character of commerce, presented itself as an area filled with visual interest while content could be played out on the screen.

Whether it's the unique location or the need for it that comes first, we can often create an exotic-looking place by using an unusual angle or unique approach to our everyday surroundings. For all the people and tall buildings in New York City, few have seen the fascinating architectural features atop the skyscrapers, yet Dan Aykroyd and Harold Ramis drew them from their visual arsenal to provide a unique urban environment for the final confrontation scene in *Ghostbusters.*

Remember the peculiar long, steep stairway down which the priest throws himself in *The Exorcist?* There is no house overlooking them as scripted for the scene, but it is such a terrific location that William Friedkin, the director, had a false wing built onto a nearby house exterior so that a window would overlook the steps, allowing him to shoot the priest's spectacular suicide. (See Figure 7.2.)

FIGURE 7.2
This peculiar long, steep, stairway in Georgetown provided a terrific location for William Friedkin in *The Exorcist.*

Sometimes we can isolate an interesting feature to good use in our production. By keeping the frame tight in a medium shot or close-up, we can often take advantage of the features and lines of a building without having to reveal the exact location, which might destroy the effect we are trying to create. In that climactic suicide scene in *The Exorcist,* we never see the gas station or parking lot that was, at the time, right at the bottom of the steps! (See Figure 7.3.)

It is worth the effort to comb your area for the exotic, unique location or architectural detail that will provide an evocative backdrop for your production. Many buildings with distinctive ornamentation and facades are treasures tucked away for the imaginative producer. Architectural styles provide worlds of different looks and settings. Art deco entrances, Federalist-style townhouses, Modernist glass corporate towers, sterile concrete commercial offices, Spanish mission stucco simulations, Georgian pomposities, concrete block industrial parks, old wooden warehouses, log cabins—these styles and many more can be found in various parts of the country to provide backdrops that can contribute visual interest to a scene. Public buildings—court houses, city halls, libraries, museums, train stations, and churches—often are designed in some revivalist period architecture or stylistic extravagance that can provide expressive settings for exterior action. Even old, rundown structures with broken boards and peeling paint can provide excellent settings for interesting scenes.

Naturally many sites require permission to be used, but many fine locations are accessible without permission and often it is easy to obtain permission for those locations that do require it. Use good sense and always make

FIGURE 7.3
In the climactic suicide scene in *The Exorcist,* we never see the gas station or parking lot that was, at the time, right at the bottom of the steps!

proper inquiries regarding any needed authorizations for access. Don't take unnecessary risks with yourself, your talent, or your equipment just for a "spectacular" shot. No shot is worth injury. Police and trespass charges can ruin a good shoot.

Creating a Catalog of Visuals

The serious producer is always on the lookout for locations that have striking visual and evocative potential. Don't choose locations for action indifferently—somewhere, anywhere, just someplace convenient. When conceiving a scene, if your attention is primarily focused on story line, character, and perhaps on an intriguing situation or an exciting action, you might overlook this graphic aspect of visual storytelling. As the camera shifts from angle to angle, shot to shot, much of what we see in the frame is not the subject of the shot, but the background. The visual interest it provides may make the difference in the audience's mind between a production that is a richly textured visual tapestry or a flat, uninteresting presentation.

As you become increasingly visually oriented, you should begin to catalog, at least in your mind, locations for scenes that lend themselves to visual treatment: snow-covered trees seen through steam swirling around people in Colorado hot springs; the repetitive, robotic motions of machinery in an auto plant; or the optical effect of driving by fields with rows cultivated perpendicular to the highway. For the film and video producer, having a repertoire of interesting visual locations is as important as building your vocabulary. Visualizing significance through the concrete and interpreting the concrete in significant and beautiful images constitute the essence of the photographic arts.

Wooded areas are generally easy to find and provide a lace of branches in winter or a lush of foliage in a sweeping array of subtle shades of green in spring and summer. Weedy lots, gardens, barren flats, or open fields used as backgrounds can be anything from desolate, monochromatic areas filled with jagged, broken stalks and canes to rich colorful areas of form, line, and pattern. Locations unique to your area such as rock quarries, gravel pits, swamps, bogs, waterfronts, cliffs, orchards, old forts, urban and suburban streets, military bases, and even college campuses can add dramatically to the visual interest of the scene. Become a connoisseur of photographic opportunities waiting for the right project.

Exterior locations are, of course, greatly affected by season and time of day. As you familiarize yourself with the location possibilities in your area, pay attention to how they look at different times of day under different lighting conditions with different lengths and depths of shadows, and with different levels of diffusion depending on weather and different seasonal conditions. Winter can provide snow and stunning beauty as in the snow palace scene in *Dr. Zhivago* or the Indian mountain camp in *Dances With Wolves*. It can also provide lighthearted playfulness as in *It's a Wonderful Life,* or even gray, gloomy cold as in *On the Waterfront* or *Silence of the Lambs,* or even truly life-threatening, elemental danger as in *Misery* or at the end of *McCabe and Mrs. Miller.*[2] Summer can establish warmth, freedom, energy, and joyfulness as in the barn raising scene in *Witness*, or oppressive heat as mentioned in *Bonnie and Clyde*. Spring and fall seasons each contribute their repertoire of possibilities. Rain (during the climactic battle on the boat in Scorsese's *Cape Fear*), mist and fog (the hunting scene in *The Deer Hunter*), and all variations of weather provide wonderful visual opportunities to complement the sense of a scene.

Sometimes a location we envision is quite different in reality. One shoot for the United States Navy was scheduled for Yorktown, Virginia. When we arrived, a cold mist and driving rain greeted us. The crew was disappointed and expressed a concern for their bodily comfort. They also knew it would take a lot of extra work to protect the equipment in such bad weather. But the mists and diffuse light on the rolling green of the old battlefield were quite spectacular. With ponchos, umbrellas, and plastic bags we got some of the most beautiful footage in the film. Flexibility and a willingness to put out a little extra effort make locations work and yield their visual potential.

Visual Storytelling

The locations chosen for our actions can powerfully influence a scene, whether we intend it or not. The effect of a location can depend on differences that, at first, may not be realized as being significant. For example, suppose we want to set a scene of two people falling in love even as they drive along a road and run out of gas. The inopportune quitting of the engine interrupts their romance and growing intimacy. What kind of roadside do we want to choose for this vignette? Various roadsides have different characteristics and provide different visual details. The scene on the side of a road after the car has run out of gas will play very differently if the setting is a remote two-lane country road surrounded by corn fields, or a busy freeway with passing cars and trucks, or a city street packed with people, or an industrial park of massive unlandscaped buildings.

Action plays differently in different settings and choice of setting significantly affects the overtones and the look of a scene. A love scene in the back seat of a car has a different look than a love scene in a swimming pool. Furthermore, a love scene in the back seat of a new Cadillac convertible on a scenic summertime hilltop carries a different visual connotation than a love scene in the back seat of a steamed-up old Dodge during a snowstorm. Similarly a luxurious pool in a mansion (*Black Widow*) provides a much different setting for a love scene than in a prosaic school gymnasium pool (*Children of a Lesser God*).

As early as the scripting stage, activities and occupations can be invented for characters to provide visual design elements both complementary to the story and contributing to the total look of the film. For example, nothing in the plot of *Moonstruck* requires that Ronny Cammareri (Nicolas Cage) work in a bakery. Logically he could just as well be a courier, a telemarketer, or a bartender. But, in scriptwriter John Patrick Shanley's catalog of locations, the subterranean confines of a bakery oven came to mind as a visually expressive way to set up his introduction to us. The heat, flames, and sweat; the antique stone walls; and the classic action of baking bread in an old-world tradition reverberate archetypal Italian background and values. It suggests the mythic blast furnaces of Vulcan and smoldering desires. All of this provides a wonderfully evocative setting for the tormented, ferocious, and possibly mad figure who confronts Loretta (Cher) and us.

Examples abound in well-designed films of settings chosen from the writer's, director's, or photographer's visual repertoire that not only support the story, but are unique, exotic or at least provide a variety of interesting photographic opportunities for the visual backdrop of the scene: the steel factory where the Japanese crime bosses meet in *Black Rain,*[3] the face of Mount Rushmore in *North by Northwest,* Wilson Observatory in *Rebel Without a Cause,* the old man's clothing factory in *Klute,* the planetarium in *Manhattan.* These visually rich locations are not accidents and commonly are not totally dictated by theme, character, or the logic of the story. They are chosen to provide interesting and expressive visual settings for action.

The "Look" of the Production

A film, video, or television production is a graphic work of art, painted with light, which has the dimension of time as one of its aspects. The role of the DP (director of photography) is to work with the director to create the general "look" of the production that supports the director's approach, point of view, or interpretation of the project. As an easy illustration, we can think of the look of the *film noir* genre with its dark shadows, perhaps a 1930s or 1940s costume and set design, or locations that illustrate contrasts between the luxurious and lavish and those from the darker, seamier side of society.

Visuals are not merely setting a backdrop. They are integral to our storytelling. Just as the narrative of the drama or logical thrust of a nonnarrative, documentary production is built by the succession of scenes, the total visual impact of our production—the look—is carefully crafted from each set or location selected. We should review the script or treatment of the project to determine the look we want. We then select locations or settings to support it.

All well thought out and planned productions have a certain look. We use words like slick, heavy, earthy, ominous, rich, cold, hard, cheerful, and steamy to characterize the overall graphic quality of the production. Often it helps the DP if you define the look by comparing the project to a film or television show you've seen that has a similar look, perhaps *Miami Vice, Twin Peaks, Batman,* or *Blade Runner.*

Ultimately, the look of your productions becomes your signature. It bespeaks your style. Just as a Monet painting is not a Van Gogh painting, neither is a Peter Weir film a Woody Allen film. A rose, in fact, is more than just a rose. Your selection of visuals that appeal to you and your approach to putting them on film or tape represent your personal technique, your taste, your individuality. Your style affects the projects you choose and the people who choose to work with you. It is the defining factor of you as a professional.

Designing the Frame

In designing the scene, we manipulate the *mise en scène* to direct where the audience will be looking in the frame through the sequence of shots. Forcing the audience to discover where they should be looking interrupts their involvement in the events of the production and destroys the fragile suspension of disbelief. If we rely on the audience to discover something of interest, especially in sweeping wide shots or ambiguous, meandering panning shots over scene detail, we run the risk that they look at the wrong spot and may not discover the right place to look before we cut to the next shot or scene. An essential for audience comprehension is to use line, light, color, and movement to direct the eye. It is also crucial for editing. Careful scene design ensures that the audience's eye is already in the right place when the scene cuts to the next shot, which makes the edit go by unnoticed and gives the production a seamless feel.

We strongly encourage students beginning a study of film, video, and television production to take courses in both design and photography to help them develop their eye for color, composition, and design, and to build a vocabulary of visual references.

Design elements provide pleasing compositions. Learning to recognize design elements in pastoral as well as urban locations and to make them work for us in our productions adds greatly to the visual interest of our works. When scouting locations for photographic opportunities, we look for areas we can isolate with design elements that complement the subject and action of the production. When looking at a location, it helps to take along a still or video camera and use it like a director's viewfinder to help visualize where the action will take place.

Sometimes a clean, simple white or monochromatic background is an appealing way to isolate the subject. Some television commercials use such a background quite successfully to give a straightforward approach to the message. The concrete-clad bed of the Los Angeles River was used successfully as such an uncluttered setting for Jake Gittes (Jack Nicholson) to literally face a blank wall in *Chinatown*. The same location provided a uniquely isolated chase scene in *Terminator 2*. Although settings such as this may be too simple to provide visual variety for an entire film, locations like this often provide a clean frame that can be photographically intriguing.

Sometimes we want to accentuate lines or geometric patterns that will add interest to the frame. Some locations that can provide such elements for composition are railroad switching yards, freeway overpasses, areas of cultivation, and areas near airport runways such as the one used in *Easy Rider.*

Shooting *Mise en Scène*

Day Exteriors

Normally we think of sunny days as bright and cheerful, or at least routine. Many actions just naturally occur in daylight exteriors and must be scripted and staged accordingly. Going to an office, leaving school, plowing a field, driving or riding through rural areas and open country, watching kids at playgrounds, partying on the beach, moving cattle, making a speech in a city park—these everyday, nine-to-five kinds of situations simply require daylight exterior settings. Films with dark moods may never show any of these kinds of activities or may keep such scenes to a minimum.

We may choose to set a scene as a daylight exterior for specific purposes. At the simplest, we may wish to do it for a comedy or lighthearted drama for the brightness of the setting. A device that can cause interesting dissonance is to lighten up a scene or an entire film that might otherwise be more somber by setting action predominantly in daylight. *Bonnie and Clyde* uses this technique powerfully for an almost perverse effect of exhilaration and gaiety overlaying murder and mayhem.

Although a sunlit scene is characteristically high key and is often associated with humor, routine, and lack of conflict, the direct sunlight of a day exterior can photographically look very stark and produce hard, harsh shadows. As discussed in Chapter 10, we usually must go to some length to soften hard sunlight and fill shadow just to make our shots look normal, let alone attractive. This is especially true in medium shots and close-ups, when the eyes of the audience seek the features of a character's face. Only if we want hard light to accentuate the cragginess of features or have a scene set in a desertlike environment and want to emphasize the glare of the sun or for some reason want to create a stark effect would we choose to do portraiture under direct, bright sunlight.

Time of day is another element of *mise en scène* that can have a tremendous impact on the interpretation of a scene. The warm glow of late afternoon sun is so important for its golden, angled light that we call it the "magic hour." Directors often plan to shoot scenes during this time of day to capture the special light that transforms their images into exceptional, golden moments. The time available to shoot in late afternoon when the light turns golden and the angle of light etches textures and shapes three-dimensionally is about one hour. This is very little time to execute a scene and shooting requires maximum planning and efficiency. The results are so photographically rewarding, however, that directors such as Coppola, Herzog, and Cimino have been known to risk revolution and reputation keeping cast and crew waiting all day for the few moments of magnificent cinematography available to them at the end of the day during the magic hour.

Night Exteriors

Night exteriors may be challenging to shoot, but they can reward us with scenes that are instantly unique or mysterious, shrouded in danger or madness, or sparkling with the excitement of fireworks or the beauty of a gem on black velvet. Here are some examples:

- The bridge scene in *Apocalypse Now*
- The waterworks scene in *Chinatown*
- The fire ceremony in *Dances with Wolves*
- Digging in the courtyard in *Rear Window*
- Marian's driving up to the motel in *Psycho*
- The priest's first visit in *The Exorcist*
- The night battle sequence in *Patton*

In the same way that we can choose settings for their cinematic qualities for many scenes that do not logically require specific locations, so too can we stage many exterior scenes either during the day or at night. Directors choose one or the other for dramatic, thematic, and photographic purposes. The firefight in *Platoon,* for example, could have been staged as a daytime scene, but clearly Oliver Stone wanted to capture the special terror that comes from a fast-moving, stealthy enemy attacking out of the darkness and the surprise, shock, and stark effect of flashes of gunshots and explosions violently breaking up the night.

Exterior night scenes provide us with much the same level of control over lighting design as we have with interiors. Any style is possible, although usually the dark and distant backgrounds of exteriors at night lend themselves to low-key lighting designs. Night exteriors provide a black background against which subjects can be set, cut by light as in a cameo. The parade of characters around the tower at the end of Fellini's *8½,* and the two couples outside the bar in *Who's Afraid of Virginia Woolf?* are two examples. An even more brilliant effect can be achieved when lights, flames, or brightly lit objects are filmed against the black of night as in the secretive horse timing scene in the rain in *The Black Stallion* or in the street battle in *The Year of Living Dangerously*. We can enhance the sparkle of night street scenes by wetting the streets down, creating a sheen that will reflect the light of cars and buildings. This is an inexpensive effect, and the rewards are exceptional.

Night exteriors, of course, can be more subdued. They can have the simple effect of peace and quiet (the walk home from the restaurant in *Moonstruck*), or the sinister effect of lurking danger (the alley before the truck attack in *On the Waterfront*). Some very memorable scenes in film are night exterior shots. They vary in scale from a simple close-up to broad, dramatically shadowed street scenes (waiting for Harry Lime in *The Third Man*) and grand panoramic night shots explored in *Black Rain* (the high angle, extreme wide shot of the limousine dropping Michael Douglas off in the grape fields outside the country villa of the Japanese yakusa don) and in *Thelma & Louise* (the haunting night shots driving through Monument Valley).

We often think of exteriors as establishing shots that are followed by the interior scenes, which supposedly take place inside the location shown in the exteriors.[4] A common pattern in many productions is for most scenes to be staged interior with a few action or transition scenes set as exteriors. In some films, however, the settings for most scenes are exterior and then the locations become a dominant element in the film. The woods and river of *Deliverance,* the southwest expanses of *Thelma & Louise,* the cool Puget Sound forest of *Five Easy Pieces,* the enclosing jungle of *Platoon,* the river in *The African Queen,* and the open plains of *Dances with Wolves* are all examples of films that depend heavily on natural locale for their story and their ambiance.

We have enormous creative control over the quality of exterior scenes by the thoughtful selection of location and time (the first items specified in the scene of a dramatic script) and the season in which the action is to take place.

After an initial exterior establishing shot, however, most scenes occur in interiors. Selecting interior locations gives producers a great deal of control over the quality of *mise en scène.*

Interiors

We have already made the point that many locations are not logically necessary to a story (the bakery in *Moonstruck*) but are selected for the dramatic, thematic, and photographic contribution they provide. Here is a short list of interior locations some directors have used to provide striking photographic opportunities to complement their stories:

- The grain elevator in *Witness*
- The marble-columned train station entrance and stairway in *The Untouchables*
- The public library in *Ghostbusters*
- The opium den in *McCabe and Mrs. Miller*
- The projection room in *Citizen Kane*
- The meat locker in *Rocky*

Interior locations can be closely tied to plot, but inventive directors also use them for visually powerful settings as well (the newsroom in *Citizen Kane* and the high-security cell block in *Silence of the Lambs*).

As producers, we consider both of these issues:

- How can a location required by the plot be used for photographic treatment?

- How can the action, which could be set in a variety of locations, be placed in an interesting surrounding to provide strong, complementary visuals?

Again, choices that seem subtle can have dramatically different effects.

Imagine, for example, the scene of a thirty-ish, urban professional couple slightly drunk and fighting over their perceived lack of savings. The scene of their argument is in their apartment. An important question to ask as a director is: What kind of apartment do we want as a setting? Chances are, even as low-budget producers we can find several different alternatives. A broad, open contemporary apartment with lots of glass might work against their argument and make it appear that the couple is, in fact, doing quite well. Or, we might select an apartment that suggests a cold barrenness and distance between the characters. A closed, old-fashioned apartment with small rooms and windows might compress their hostilities and fuel the conflict in the scene. First, then, is the selection of type of location, but equally important is the subsequent decision of how to shoot it.

Consider what the apartments in the following films tell about the characters and their situations:

- The Japanese detective's neat and orderly apartment in *Black Rain*
- Bud Fox's (Charlie Sheen's) new apartment in *Wall Street*
- Susan Alexander's apartment in *Citizen Kane*
- John Book's sister's urban working-class apartment in *Witness*
- Travis Bickle's (Robert De Niro's) barracklike apartment *Taxi Driver*
- John Keating's (Robin William's) cramped but cozy little room in *Dead Poets Society*

Characters' homes, whether apartments or houses, provide the setting for many interior scenes. In a well-conceived film, their size, shapes, styles, and furnishings truly are the worlds that reflect the themes and personalities in the story. To make the point as obvious as possible, try comparing the exteriors and interiors of the house in *Driving Miss Daisy* with the house in *Silence of the Lambs*. Simple set design decisions—for example, neatness versus clutter, clean versus dirty, well-maintained versus rundown, crowded versus spacious, cheap versus expensive, urban versus rural, dated versus modern—have powerful effects on the way we interpret scenes, character, and action.

Naturally not all interiors are houses and apartments. More interiors are probably shot in offices, hotels, restaurants, bars, and factories than in private, domestic settings. Researching these locations is much the same as the way we look for exterior locations. Again, make a list and keep adding to it. Whenever you visit public or commercial space, note interiors that are interesting and different.

Universities, by the way, can provide a wonderful variety of settings. Private offices vary from large, neat, and formal executive suites to tiny, cluttered, pigeon holes. The variety of university facilities—labs, classrooms, hallways, departmental offices, storage rooms, photocopy rooms, theaters, mechanical rooms, seminar rooms, and galleries—provides a wide range of *mise en scène* for the producer in search of a set.

The interiors of retail shops, malls, churches, terminals, factories, libraries, banks, grocery stores can be selected for scenes by a director to complement an action, or the script can be written to deliberately lead the action to these locations for the photographic opportunities they provide.

Set Dressings and Props

Our discussion now leads to a consideration closely related to the selection of interior locations—the choice of set dressing. The items we find in a setting tell enormous amounts of information about the kind of place we are in and the kind of people who are there. As with locations, this is an element that the aspiring producer can inadvertently take for granted, at the expense of diminished control over interpretation and visual impact in a scene.

How many productions have we seen that begin with a close moving camera shot over the objects of a room—photographs, personal artifacts, memorabilia, decorations, a clock, books, sporting gear, stuffed animal heads, wine glasses, discarded clothing, dirty dishes, weapons, whatever? These shots are the most obvious examples of using set dressing to set the scene, convey character and mood, and suggest story.

Set dressings are the items in the scene such as furniture, pictures on the wall, curtains, knickknacks on tables, lamps, rugs, and anything that dresses the bare walls and floor of a set. Props are objects that actors or people use in the drama—a picture of a loved one, a baseball glove, a gun, a bouquet of flowers, or a pizza that will be delivered to the door. Sometimes the line between them isn't clear. When the actor hits someone with a chair or uses the television, is the object a prop or a set dressing? Generally props are involved in the action of the scene and set dressings are not.

Props are integral to story and character. Consider the importance of the props in the following examples:

- The gin bottles trailing behind the boat after Rose empties them in *The African Queen* (associated with the relationship of the characters)
- The teddy bear in Scorsese's *Cape Fear* (a part of the alarm system)
- The pistol in *Bonnie and Clyde* (Clyde's surrogate manhood)
- The green convertible in *Thelma & Louise* (a metaphor for freedom)
- The camera, telephoto lens, and flash in *Rear Window* (a plot device)
- The bow and arrows versus stringed musical instruments in *Deliverance* (instruments of personal expression)
- The body armor in *Taxi Driver* (the physical manifestation of lethal paranoia)

If we don't provide talent with adequate props, they may either stand stiffly with nothing to do, gesticulate self-consciously, or fill the void by attempting nonsensical business with set dressings. John Sayles's early film *Return of the Secaucus Seven* has scenes with actors pointlessly playing with toilet plungers and pointing to tires to cover action while delivering their lines.

Often we can enhance the story line, action, and character, lifting them out of cliché, by introducing unique or suggestive set dressings or props. The selection of these items requires thinking out the possibilities suggested by character and situation.

Suppose we want to set a scene of a young man, Frank, who has accepted an invitation to dinner at the apartment of a young woman he has recently met. He doesn't know much about her, but she seems very nice and has promised to cook something he especially likes. Frank has never been to her apartment before. Let us assume that the general location for the film's story line is urban and that the two are both young professionals. For the sake of purpose and direction, let us suppose that the plot will reveal that the young woman, Susan, is a risk-taker who is flirting in a relationship with a powerful international drug baron, strictly for the thrill of it. The potential danger of her situation excites her, but she is naive to the real dangers that threaten her. She is under the illusion that she can handle the situation. Finally, let's also assume, for purposes of this example, that Susan's and Frank's actual jobs are irrelevant to the story line.

What kind of an apartment should we create for Susan? What should Frank and the audience see when he arrives for dinner? If we take our method from what we have learned so far, we know that narrative treatment is the art of the specific.[5] Casual generalities will not do. If we want this scene to play with rich overtones, we need to invent some elaborations that can provide us with texture and detail to complement the scene. Now, as producers, we reverse the process described in Chapter 6 where we discussed looking for clues to personality. Now we plant the clues that reveal character and serve the narrative.

For example, if we ask ourselves what kind of professional she is, that could lead us to the design of a suggestive *mise en scène* in her apartment. Suppose Susan is a lawyer or a legal aide; that might give us books, bookshelves, a desk, a computer, and perhaps some paintings and an expensive Persian rug—generally, a well-to-do environment that is paper-cluttered, suggesting educated taste, intellectual competence, and hard work. Perhaps some plants will suggest an attempt to add greenery to this otherwise urban environment. In such a setting, an unusual and extravagant gift from her dark and powerful friend—a large, intricately carved, Oriental jade figure of a demon riding a dragon, perhaps, or a bejewelled but garish and grotesque Indonesian mask—could be made to stand out as incongruous and foreboding.

Suppose Susan is a television producer. Now we can have paper clutter (scripts, contracts, crew calls, and so on) and books, but we might also include a more diverse collection of art and graphics, cameras, musical instruments, perhaps some crafts (quilts, maybe), VCRs, TV monitors, and even a few action toys (a dart board). Such a setting could suggest an energetic person, broadly curious, eclectic in tastes, comfortable with high-tech but also with folk art, looking for action. In such diversity, Frank notices in the corner a collection of war memorabilia from some recent hot spot. Included in the mix is some live ammunition and a grenade with the pin still in it. A startled Frank discovers the grenade while waiting for Susan to bring out the meal from the kitchen. After finding out she brought the weapons back from a recent journalistic sortie behind the battle lines, he and we realize Susan is a person who has more taste for danger than for good sense and self-preservation. Although this may not be the final selection of props for the scene, the point is that this is the kind of brainstorming that will eventually result in effective, not arbitrary, *mise en scène.*

We can use set dressings as elements in creating the composition of the frame. Our primary concern is usually composing the main subjects within the frame. However, it is also important to consider the whole composition. If we don't, the result is a bare background, a kind of visual vacuum to set the action against. It is as if the picture is incomplete and we have left areas of undefined open space that lack form.

It is interesting to watch the professional growth of a producer and see the discovery of full-frame composition. Even in feature film production, we occasionally see young directors develop the technique of using set dressing for full-frame composition. For example, note the difference in compositional richness in the work of Spike Lee as he progresses from *She's Gotta Have It* to *Do the Right Thing.* In the former, Lee's frames are bare with only the foreground subjects composed. In the latter, Lee has discovered the importance of full-frame composition and judiciously places set dressings that complete the frame composition.

Once we understand the technique of placing set dressings for full-frame composition, scenes in films begin to reveal interesting discontinuities. Pictures and clocks on the walls move inconspicuously from one shot to another to provide better frame composition. Potted plants, fish tanks, lamp shades, and sculptures become recognized for their actual purpose—to provide framing devices for shot composition.

The technique of using set dressing for full-frame composition is important in professional film and video production. It is not unusual to bring a collection of flat wall hangings and three-dimensional decorations to a set, placing them strategically in the scene to help composition. Often, various objects in a location such as a home or office are rearranged or brought to the scene from other rooms in the building to augment the design of the shots.

Even in documentary production, the use of props for full-frame composition is common. We know one documentary producer who keeps a wonderful collection of prints, calendars, potted plants, bird cages, toys, and odd stuff that he constantly uses for dressing sets. The joke is that the decorative bird cage that he uses both as a foreground framing device and in the background of many of his compositions has appeared in so many of his productions it has become his trademark.

Costumes

Unlike the stage, where costumes are often cut and marked in an exaggerated way so that their character can be distinguished from the theater's back row, costumes for film usually must be believable in close-up. We select or design them for authenticity. Here are some examples of effective and characterizing costumes:

- The tweedy writer meets the hot pants dog trainer in *The Accidental Tourist*
- Female commando chic in *Terminator 2*
- Motorcycle jacket machismo in *Black Rain*
- The Philadephia cop's wrinkled suit contrasted with unpressed homespun in *Witness* (which is given an interesting twist when the detective hides out in the Amish community and dons Amish clothing, looking wonderfully out of place)
- The grubby fringed jacket and hat in *Midnight Cowboy*
- The bowler hat in a world of mountain men in *McCabe and Mrs. Miller*
- The extravagant, binding costumes of *Dangerous Liaisons*
- The red suspenders in *Wall Street*

Though authenticity is important, leads in theatrical pieces will have clothes that set them apart from other characters. Some of this may be to assuage the ego of the actor by giving them a finer wardrobe, but it is also true that we want the leads to subtly stick out in the crowd. The most obvious way in old Westerns was to give the hero a white hat. During the 1968 Democratic convention in Chicago, Haskell Wexler had Verna Bloom, dressed in a highly visible yellow dress, running through actual riot scenes. He was later able to use the scenes in his ultrarealistic film *Medium Cool*, where she certainly stood out amid the police and rioters.

Many productions take place in contemporary time because of the expense associated with sets and costumes. Although students seldom undertake period drama because of the enormous difficulty and expense involved with settings and costumes, it is often easier and cheaper for students than for professionals to get these things. Sometimes the problems of period costuming can be overcome by seeking out the resources of historical societies. If there is a chapter of the Society for Creative Anachronisms in your area, their members outfit themselves in everything from medieval armor to pirate garb. In the Southern and Middle Atlantic states, local Civil War enthusiasts reenact various famous battles regularly. It is possible to find these organizations and gain permission to not only use their authentic attire but often they will agree to be extras in your films for the fun of the experience and the price of a good lunch. In addition, many places regularly have living history exhibits such as some maintained by the U.S. Park Service and state historical societies.

Of course, not everyone has access to colonial or Civil War costumes, but some research may reveal unexpected resources. Many towns have festivals for immigrant groups in their area ranging from Hispanic and native American to Basque, Russian, German, Italian, Polish, Chinese, and so on. Or, in the West, many towns have jamborees and pioneer celebrations. Participants keep costumes for these annual events stored away in their attics and closets.

Foreign settings cause similar problems of finding unusual but convincing costumes. Some foreign attire—especially clothing worn by peasants—is simple in design and can be made quite inexpensively. More elaborate costumes are another matter. In both historical and foreign settings, authenticity usually requires research. If we are going to set a scene in nineteenth-century France in the Bordeaux country on a farm, we should find out what nineteenth-century French Bordeaux farmers wore.

There are costume rental places in most urban centers, but many of these costumes are designed for the stage or costume parties and may not be suitable for a film production. Finally, don't forget to check out the costumes worn by waiters and waitresses in your area. One secret of good production is to work with what's available and not to leave any stone unturned.

Usually, effective costuming does not involve the special problems associated with historical or foreign scenes. Again, the approach is not to be arbitrary or unspecific, but to give distinctive and idiosyncratic costuming to your characters, based on their identity and activities.

Suppose our character is a middle-aged sales agent from Chicago visiting a small Midwestern town on a sales trip, meeting a local store owner who is an older man short on patience and with an active dislike of Chicago sales agents. The two men know each other well because they have been trading for years, but they come from different worlds and different backgrounds and their interactions are strained at best. We want to dress the Chicago man in a suit, but what kind of suit and in what condition? Well, we might want to specify what he sells. If he sells hardware, he could wear a suit that is likely to look different from one he would wear if he sells pharmaceuticals.

Depending on the plot, which we have not elaborated here, we must make those simple but important decisions regarding whether the sales agent is wearing polyester or 100% wool, dark blue or plaid. We must also decide whether he is trim and pressed with the shirt tucked in, or baggy, wrinkled, and hanging out. One thing is for sure, we know he will not be wearing a double-breasted European cut unless he is a radical misfit.

Lighting

At its essence, light creates *mise en scène:* the patterns of light and shadow formed by the intensity of light and that light as it reflects off objects in the scene into the lens. Lighting design is fundamental to the photographic arts. Together with camera placement and lens selection, it is the principal expertise of the photographer, gaffer, or DP. Lighting design, then, is a very powerful tool for rendering the image to affect the look of the frame.

Lighting designs, like works of any art, are infinite in their variety. Although it may be considered no more than a craft, it nevertheless can be a major artistic concern, challenging the sensibilities and intelligence of maturing producers throughout their professional careers. Although the variations of lighting design are endless, there are specific strategies that provide order and structure to our approach to lighting design. Much has been written about lighting. Whole books are devoted to lighting techniques, and most production texts devote one or more chapters to the subject. There is no point in repeating this readily available information in detail, but it is worthwhile to set down here a basic approach to lighting design, which can serve as a foundation and as a method for thinking about film and video lighting. This can act as a framework for production students as they develop a mastery of lighting techniques.

The beginning of a systematic approach to lighting design is first to distinguish between lighting design and lighting setups. *Lighting design* refers to the look of the image in the frame. It is the pattern of light and dark on the screen that results from the photographic rendering of the lit scene before the camera. *Lighting setup,* on the other hand, refers to the actual selection and arrangement of lighting instruments, devices, and materials (such as diffusion, reflectors, and cutters) used to produce the desired lighting effects. Lighting setups are the physical placement of the hardware necessary to achieve lighting designs.

Various lighting setups are especially useful at creating specific lighting designs. It is awkward and probably pointless to try to discuss lighting designs without reference to the setups used to produce them. However, for the audience, lighting setups are invisible. All we see are the results—the image on the screen. Our discussion here focuses on that "look," the visual design of the frame, but it will help to consult Chapter 10, on practical lighting procedures, as a complement to this section.

Lighting compositions are most commonly defined as either *high-key lighting* designs or *low-key lighting* designs. Although the definitions of these terms vary somewhat, high-key lighting designs usually refer to frames that are predominantly lighter than medium gray, whereas low-key lighting designs refer to frames that are predominantly darker than medium gray. We often associate comedy, musicals, and lighthearted drama with bright, broadly lit scenes, characteristic of high-key lighting. We also associate mystery, horror, and serious drama with the dark, shadowy scene characteristic of low-key lighting.

Most films, of course, include both types of lighting, although films will use one type of lighting more than the other to create an overall look or to support a specific genre. For example, *Thelma & Louise* includes a preponderance of high-key scenes, with some very critical scenes designed as low key. Staging most of the exterior scenes in bright daylight reflects the spirited, upbeat mood of the film that supports the theme of liberation and friendship. However, a few low-key scenes—the attempted rape scene and the contemplative night drive through Monument Valley, for example—strike darker, more serious tones. As mentioned earlier, the drive through Monument Valley did not have to be staged at night. For purposes of plot only, it could have been staged during the day when it could have been shot much more easily. Setting the scene at night instead allows a low-key lighting treatment that reinforces the mood of the scene (and is a *tour de force* of grand-scale, night exterior cinematography).

Naturally, high-key and low-key treatments not only depend on lighting, but on the colors in the scene as well. A large room with dark paneling, drapery, and furniture occupied by characters dressed in dark clothing reproduces as a dark scene despite the lighting, if it is properly exposed. Light-colored backgrounds (walls, for example) and costuming normally work well in high-key lighting designs. Dark backgrounds and costuming are more usually found in low-key lighting.

There are, of course, other types of lighting that do not fall into either of these two main categories. One lighting design that can be very moody if done well is a flat, even gray lighting throughout the frame. Bergman captures this bleak look in some of his overcast exteriors such as those in *Through a Glass Darkly.*

As already mentioned, there are countless variations on these two major types of lighting design. At the basic level, we see these variations primarily as the product of the following factors:

1. The degree of contrast between the key and fill lighting on the subject(s)—the contrast ratio
2. The degree of contrast between the lighting on the subject and lighting on the background (and the foreground)—the lighting ratio
3. The quality of light that serves as the principal illumination in the scene—hard lighting or soft lighting
4. The angle of light that creates the amount and pattern of light and shadow visible on the subject and in the background—broad lighting, narrow lighting, or cross lighting
5. The application and amount of light we use to illuminate the head and shoulders of our subject(s) to highlight them and separate them from the background—backlighting and kickers.

We discuss contrast between key and fill lighting and between subject and background lighting, as well as basic differences with quality of light, in this chapter. In Chapter 10, we will describe lighting setups, the effects of key lighting, placement, and types of backlighting.

Contrast Ratio

Contrast ratios refer to how dark or light the shadows are on the subject. Contrast is much more exaggerated by film and video imaging than in the way the human eye sees contrast. Lighting that looks "normal" to the eye has much more contrast when reproduced in film or video. The solution to this problem is to reduce shadows with enough soft fill light to make the contrasts on the screen pleasing to the eye. Experimenting with the amount of fill to add in a scene is time well spent. Keep in mind that copying camera original through the editing or printing process creates a build-up of even more contrast. Therefore, it is generally a good idea to add more fill than seems correct to prevent shadows from being rendered black. Compare the lighting on the subject in Figure 7.4(a) to that in Figure 7.4(b).

Once our eye has begun developing a sense of how much fill is enough and we know the methods of adding fill to shadow areas, we can hone these techniques to create any degree of shadow wanted. Obviously low-key lighting design tends toward dark shadows and the use of less fill. High-key lighting designs usually include very light shadows resulting from the use of more fill. The goal is usually to plan and to execute a depth of shadow and contrast between these extremes.

Lighting Ratio

Lighting contrast is the degree of darkness of the background[6] compared to the illuminated subject. It is a primary element in the creation of lighting designs. Just as *mise en scène* involves not simply a concern for the subject in a shot but for the entire frame, lighting design involves lighting not simply the subject but lighting the entire set.

When we go into a location and illuminate our subjects with hundreds or even thousands of watts of light, the background will be extremely dark in contrast if left unlit. (See Figure 7.5.) After lighting the foreground subject, we must light the background as well. This means if our subject is in a room and we can see a hall or an adjoining room through a doorway, that room—at least the visible part—has to be. If we are working in a hallway and it is possible to see the length of the hallway in the shot, we need to light the hallway. Usually this is quite difficult without a lot of lighting instruments and the time to conceal cable from the shot. When we can avoid shooting in halls, we probably should. There is a good chance that our "hall shot" is transitional anyway and we can easily omit it.

Again, once we learn the basic techniques of lighting sets, the degree of light falloff from subject to background becomes a major concern. Naturally, we light high-key scenes with much less falloff than we would low-key scenes.

An equally important concern is how the pattern of light on the background—as well as on the basic design elements of the set—directs the eyes of the audience to our subject or another interesting element in the scene. This requires manipulation of color and gradations of light and shadow to paint the background with light. One common and effective technique is to *cap* the

FIGURE 7.4(a)
Subject lit by key light, without fill light.

FIGURE 7.4(b)
Subject lit by key light, with shadows reduced by fill light. Subject is near wall so spill from the fill light also brightens background.

light, that is, to use barndoors or flags to cause lighting on the background to fall off toward the ceiling or, more accurately, toward the top of frame. Even in a close-up, diminishing the background light toward the top of the frame

FIGURE 7.5
If we light a subject but
not the background,
the background will
come out very dark.

makes the scene look more natural. Causing light to fall off toward the top of
the frame creates a more realistic, dimensional rendering of the scene, as
shown in Figure 7.6.

Similarly, we often find that our set lighting will look much better if we
use a flag or a side-mounted barndoor to shade the light toward the corners of
a set. It is common in a room for light to fall off toward the corners, and we
usually see a corner of a room as the convergence of deepening shades of two
adjoining walls. Shading our background lighting toward the corners with
barndoors or flags produces more realistic set lighting and helps create a three-
dimensional illusion of space, as shown in Figure 7.7.

A common technique to set off foreground subjects from the background
and give balance and depth to frame composition is to reverse the direction of
dark to light in the background from the foreground lighting pattern. In other
words, if the foreground subject is lit from screen left with the shadow side (fill
side) of the subject on the right, we light the background so that there is more
light on the right side of the frame with the darker part on the left. We achieve
this background lighting by gradually feathering the light. We can get a similar
but harder edged effect by illuminating doorways, windows, or other architectural structures to contrast against the foreground lighting design. The result
of these opposing lighting patterns is that the lighter part of the foreground
subject is set off against the darker part of the background, and the darker part
of the subject is set off against a lighter toned background. The subject is sep-

FIGURE 7.6
Shading the light toward the top of the frame (capping the light) creates more realistic lighting designs.

arated nicely from the background with variation, gradation, and spatial depth throughout the frame.

Hard and Soft Lighting

Hard lighting and soft lighting produce very different kinds of effects, and the choice of light quality greatly influences the look of the frame. Directional,

FIGURE 7.7
Shading the light into the corners with barndoors or flags also creates more realistic lighting designs.

sharply focused, hard light creates hard-edged shadows, glistening highlights, and little falloff over distance. This kind of light can accentuate facial structure and skin wrinkles if angled properly and generally can be used to emphasize texture. In high-key lighting designs with two people facing each other, we can set our hard key to backlight one subject while keying the other. (Compare Figures 7.8(a) and 7.8(b).) We usually use hard lighting for backlights, kickers, and any other kind of rimlighting effect.

FIGURE 7.8(a)
When two people are facing each other, some lighting setups use one person's key light as the other person's backlight.

FIGURE 7.8(b)
The reverse angle of the shot in Figure 7.8(a).

In high-key lighting designs created by broad lighting setups (see Chapter 10 for a discussion of broad, narrow, and cross lighting setups), a hard key causes the background to be brightly lit in the frame due to the minimal falloff of spill light falling behind the subject. In low-key lighting designs, a hard key in a narrow lighting setup can easily be kept off the background. We can focus it and direct it off-frame with very little spread. We can also barndoor or flag it if necessary. With this kind of lighting, we can use hard light on the subjects, sharply etching them against dark backgrounds. (See Figures 7.4(a) and 7.5 and Figures 10.3 through 10.7.)

A traditional lighting style known as *glamour lighting* uses a hard key with strong backlighting. (See Figure 7.9.) The subject is often set against darker backgrounds with just enough fill to bring out detail on the shadow side. In this design, the key tends to be frontal to avoid accentuating skin texture and we use a silk or diffusion filter over the lens to cause backlights to flare.

Hard lights are very effective when shooting extreme wide shots. Hard light can travel long distances with little falloff, and it can be tightly focused with little spread. Also, we can barndoor and flag hard light on the sides very effectively. These qualities make hard lights ideal for selectively illuminating subjects from far enough away to be off-frame in extreme wide shots.

Since hard lighting produces sharp shadows, it is the type of light we use when we want to cast distinguishable, hard-edged shadows on the back-

FIGURE 7.9
A hard frontal key with strong backlight, little or no fill, and diffusion over the lens produces a classic effect known as glamour lighting.

ground. A hard light source is ideal for creating the Venetian blind pattern of *film noir,* palm tree shadows, shadows of people on walls, and angular architectural shadows. (See Figure 7.10.)

Soft lighting, on the other hand, tends toward being shadowless. Depending on the degree of softness and the distance from the light to the illuminated subject, soft light can vary in degree from being shadowless to producing very soft shadows with edges trailing off into feathered gradations. The closer a soft light is to a subject, the more it becomes shadowless and "wraparound." Because it tends toward being shadowless, its use as a key softens features and minimize wrinkles and blemishes. As a key, soft light produces a warm glowing illumination with gentle shadowing that can be very attractive. Close to a subject, the softly graduated shadowing and wraparound quality usually makes any additional fill light unnecessary. (See Figure 7.11.)

A common lighting design in a dialogue between a man and a woman is to illuminate the man with a hard key at an angle to accentuate skin texture and produce a craggy appearance. In contrast, a diffused key illuminates the woman to smooth out her complexion and soften her features.

Soft or diffused lighting can produce delicate patterns of light and shade on backgrounds. We can achieve this by placing the light at an angle or by the using shadowing devices or silks in front of the light. The look of this kind of modulated shadowing on the background is very different from the look of the sharply defined shadows cast by a hard light.

FIGURE 7.10
We can cast a sharply defined, identifiable shadow on the background with a hard light source.

FIGURE 7.11
We can use a soft light as a key, producing soft, glowing, wrap-around lighting that may not need additional fill light.

Design

In this chapter we have discussed photographic opportunities that afford possibilities for interesting compositions and visual imagery. The selection of locations, props, and costumes must reflect the milieu of the story and the personalities of the characters. Once we have selected these tangibles, they become design elements aligned and framed in the shot. With the addition of lighting, these visible components translate into our photographic composition on the screen. The audience does not just see trees, buildings, rooms, people, and other objects in a film or videotape. They also see projected patterns on a screen.

If our scene includes a horse, the audience does not see an actual horse. What they see is a visual rendering of the horse. If we put the horse in the surf, as in *The Black Stallion,* we've created the possibility for some interesting shots, such as hooves splashing, underwater shots, and silhouettes against water and sunsets.

Our pictures are of people, places, and objects, but they are also compositions. They have line, shape, color (or shades of gray), texture, and pattern. Consequently film and video do not just provide the experience of story and character, they also provide a unique visual event of their own. One pleasing aspect of a production can be the visual composition of the piece, and these visual compositions are the product of an interplay between camera technique and *mise en scène*.

Shots are merely parts of scenes that express the fully developed visual styles that dominate an entire work. In producing these shots, directors and photographers take advantage of the visual possibilities provided by the action, setting, props, costumes, and lighting that they have orchestrated for the camera—all for the sole purpose of adding visual dimension to the drama.

We all have memories of notable shots and visually expressive scenes. Here are some of ours:

- Toward the end of *Black Rain,* when Nick Conklin (Michael Douglas) is dropped off in the rural vineyard before daybreak, to approach the villa of the Japanese mafia don on foot, we see a beautiful high-angle EWS of the limousine on a narrow road in the rolling fields, with each tier of hills receding into the background in wavy, faint bands of color—a study in peace and tranquility. This rural location provides a terrific setting later in the motorcycle chase, when the jagged, staked grapevines serve as barbed-wire-like fencing—a flesh-ripping and hellishly imprisoning environment.
- Every frame in *Witness* is beautiful. Even the bathroom scene in the train station where the boy witnesses the murder is rendered in powerful images. One of our favorite shots is the simple MCU of Rachel (Kelly McGillis) standing in the door of her home, watching John Book (Harrison Ford) leave to go back to Philadelphia at the end of the movie. It is a classic rendering of soft, portraiture lighting, carefully controlled shading and color in the background, and white painted architecture on the side to gracefully frame the face.
- Martin Scorsese offered us an unusual and unforgettable treatment of boxing when he shot the slow motion sequence of the fight in *Raging Bull,* which he cut against silence in a slow, brutal, rhythmic dance.
- The playful bicycle montage sequence in *Butch Cassidy and the Sundance Kid,* although it feels somewhat dated now, is one of the loveliest interludes in film. Remember the trucking shot through the board fence creating a kind of stroboscopic view of Butch Cassidy (Paul Newman) on the bike, or the beautiful desaturated close-up shot of the apple and his hand snatching it off the tree.
- Roman Polanski is a visual storyteller and, although all of his films from *Knife in the Water, Repulsion,* and *Chinatown* to *Tess* are marked by his strong visual style, one shot in particular comes to mind. He uses the setting of the sailboat and the sea for surreal visuals in *Knife in the Water* when he shows the lone figure of the young man and the becalmed boat afloat in a glaring, glossy sea.

The list goes on. We're sure you have your own favorites. The point is, when we plan action and *mise en scène,* it is important to remember that everything we choose will ultimately be material for use in our shot composi-tions. We should plan so that we will have strong shots available.

When we see a beautifully shot film such as *The Black Stallion,* we under-stand that many elements of the film have been especially conceived to pro-vide a pleasing visual experience. Strong design-oriented films do not simply use an occasional artful shot. Instead, they use design and rhythm to motivate editing and the relationships between shots. In the moving image, design can-not long remain static, as in a postcard or still photograph. We choreograph design both as movement within the shot and as rhythmic cutting of design relationships between shots.

The ultimate truth of *mise en scène* is that everything we see in a produc-tion is an artifact—a creation representing the choices made during the pro-duction process. In making films and videos or in producing for television, the locations we select or the sets we build and the placement of every person, ob-ject, line, or shadow are colors on our palette, the elements with which we paint our stories in light.

Exercise 1

Create a design project in film or video. Shoot for a finished length of approximately 5 minutes. Try relating interesting geometric forms to other similar forms, remembering that changing perspective by moving the subject or the camera often changes a form or pattern from a rectangle or cube to a square, from a circle or sphere to an oblong, and so on. Look for lines and angles. Use the macro lens to obscure or explore objects for their design elements. Look for unusual comparisons in scale and let the audience see patterns in your production that they might have missed in the natural or con-structed subject. Play with motion. Look for color and texture relationships and for flowing patterns of light and reflectance as the camera or the object moves. Work for total visual coherence and cohesiveness. The project should stand alone. It can be a lot of fun.

Exercise 2

There is a tradition in the theater of casting opera and plays, especially Shakespeare, in different times and locales from the original, giving new treatment to the script and a different angle on interpretation. Take a short scene from a favorite film of yours and set it in a different location than the original. Perhaps change minor details such as sex-es or occupations of characters, or the time of day. Use one or more of the unique loca-tions from your personal catalogue. Remember, sometimes you can combine locations through editing to create a fictional edifice or even portray gardens, streets, or yards next to buildings that in reality are nowhere near them. The challenge here is to see how a different setting reinterprets the theme or story.

Notes

1. Bazin held up Orson Welles's *Citizen Kane* and William Wyler's *The Time of Their Lives* as models of mise en scène style filmmaking.

2. The use of winter in *McCabe and Mrs. Miller* supports a central theme in the movie. At the beginning, the lone figure on horseback is immersed in the harsh, dismal, bluish cold of the mountain snow. McCabe brings color to the little squatters camp when he first spreads out the red checkered tablecloth. As the casino is built, the golden warmth of the comfort that the structure and the dream provide is set against the cold surroundings. In the end, when McCabe is shot, it is the unforgiving cold of the snow that remains unvanquished and lethal.

3. Well-designed films are not necessarily excellent films. Critical reviews and box office receipts for *Black Rain,* for example, were not exceptional. But films that may be flawed (which is most films) are more enjoyable than they otherwise would be and even provide their principal pleasure because they are well designed. On the other hand, there are few if any excellent films that are not well designed.

4. Think of the exteriors used to fix locale and neighborhood in TV series. What does the trucking shot along the row houses at the beginning of *All in the Family* tell us? How is that different from the exterior establishing shot of the large gabled house in *Designing Women?*

5. "Moment by moment authenticating detail is the mainstay not only of realistic fiction but of all fiction." John Gardner, *The Art of Fiction*, p. 23.

6. As discussed in Chapter 10, shot compositions often involve *three* levels of subject matter within the depth of the frame: a) a *foreground* framing device such as the back of the head and shoulder in an over-the-shoulder shot, b) the *midground* subject, and c) the *background* of the set behind the subject. Consequently lighting contrasts in many shots involve the comparison of contrasts (how dark or light) from foreground to midground to background.

TECHNIQUES FOR INTERPRETATION

A major theme of this book has been that treatment of subject is as important as the subject itself. We create a coherent and effective treatment by consciously and deliberately considering our purposes. Then, in executing our treatment of the subject, we select the appropriate production techniques to best achieve these purposes. This approach, simply put, is to think about and envision our artistic goals and then employ techniques to realize our vision. Successful productions execute the vision of those involved in them from the writer, producer, or director to every craftsperson involved. Often, new techniques, such as those provided by the integration of computers with video and film, are created specifically to stretch production capabilities to execute new visions.

At whatever point we enter the production—the initial idea, the pitch, the treatment, script, the first day of shooting, or at the beginning of the editing process—we need to envision the finished production. We envision the frame that the lens sees, its colors, shapes, and designs. We see the action within it and the play of shadows and light. In our mind's eye, we create the juxtaposition of these images into the single thread of the production. We need to see in our mind what we hope to see on the screen.

Then, the question becomes: How can we use the environment, people, and technology to execute our vision? We choose every element within the frame to paint the pictures of light the audience sees. We stage the action or move the camera to capture action based on our vision. Even if we were to walk in cold on a location for a documentary and have three minutes to set up and shoot, our first thought is not to simply ask, "How do I shoot this?" It is to begin immediately to see the finished project flash across the synapses of our brain and quickly move to execute it through techniques of production. Vision defines technique.

We would not be doing justice to the creative process, however, if we did not recognize that purpose, planning, and vision can only go so far. Although they can serve as illuminating guides, much of the creativity in film and video must occur in the act of production, in the actual lighting, shooting, and editing. Artists create through their art. A painter may have a subject, a color scheme, and a composition in mind, but the expressive act of painting occurs through the medium, while putting brush and paint to canvas. Similarly musicians conceive their art in the act of composing or performing the music. A writer may have a story line, a cast of characters, and some interesting scenes in mind, but the actual shaping of the work—the selection of words, the depiction of places and persons, the rhythms of language, the invocation of moods—does not take place until the writer sits and composes the words. Each art form provides the terms with which artists express their thoughts and, even more, with which artists think. Art forms are modes of thinking as well as means of expression.

In mastering the techniques of language, the writer becomes more proficient at conceiving and at expressing thought. Similarly, the painter must master color, form, and the use of the brush and pallet knife before conceiving and expressing fluently on canvas. As the musician practices and masters the instrument, the music becomes more eloquent. In film and video, as in every other art, developing technical expertise means far more than simply learning mechanical skills. As in the mastery of a musical instrument, technical proficiency is the basis of technique, and technique is the vehicle for artistic conception and expression. Technique informs vision.

Camera, lighting, and editing techniques are fundamental to the moving image. These craft areas, each of which produces work of impressive artistic merit in its own right, are so interdependent it is difficult to discuss one outside the context of the other two. Thus, in the following three chapters, the discussions are not so much divided into clear-cut divisions of camera, lighting, and editing as much as they are aimed at presenting how to employ each of these fundamental techniques for purposes of interpretation.

The final two chapters in the book deal with meaning. The best intended communications are often misunderstood. Eye contact during a conversation helps speakers to know when the other party understands what they are saying. Actors on the stage can sense the electricity of a receptive audience. However, in media productions, no one is there with the audience during the viewing experience and yet, we have all been in movie houses where the audience spontaneously erupted in applause at the end of the show. The communication has to work in the absence of the communicator. The audience is the ultimate receiver of the vision and interpreter of technique.

8

USING THE CAMERA FOR INTERPRETATION

Lensing the Image

The Eye of the Beholder

When we think about directing a film, most of us probably think of defining the action and directing the work of a production crew. However, our most important job as director is to direct the audience's attention in a scene.

We can shoot action in an infinite variety of ways, but how we break the action up into separate shots, the framing and angles we choose, the lenses we use, the compositions we design, the placement of the camera, and whether we move the camera during a shot—all the camera techniques—enormously influence the essence of our scene. Second only to the audience's involvement in the reality we create on the screen—the fantasy, if you will—is the pure aesthetic pleasure the audience takes in fine camera work. In the early days, simply seeing a moving image on a screen was sufficiently entertaining. Viewing a train pulling into a station from the comfort of a theater seat was a marvel for audiences of the Lumière brothers' films. Stories and plots actually came later.

In modern productions, we usually work with the camera as an invisible participant in the action. More than simply providing views of a scene, the camera places the audience in the scene. There, they shift their view from one place to another, approach and retreat from objects and people, and are often as involved in the actions of the production as the players themselves. The camera leads the audience around by the eyes.

Though the camera's visual rendering of scenes is such an integral part of the pleasurable experience for the audience, it is worth noting that what the audience lacks, in most cases, is free will. *We,* as producers, decide where the audience's interest should be, as well as where they will want to look as the scene unfolds. Usually we are accommodating. We anticipate where the audience would look if they were invisible voyeurs in the scene and we shift the camera to that view. However, there are times, such as in Alfred Hitchcock's *Rear Window,*[1] when we restrain the audience, preventing them from seeing what they want to see in order to increase the tension and build empathy with the main character with whom our point of view is associated.

Inside the Fourth Wall

In theater, we witness a scene as an audience normally confined outside the space in which the dramatic action is occurring—we are on the outside looking in. The theatrical convention of the "fourth wall" describes the stage as an enclosure with three walls formed by the sides of the stage and an invisible fourth wall separating the characters from the audience. Characters on the stage behave and interact as if in a real world, without recognizing the presence of an audience looking in from the other side of the proscenium. If a character momentarily steps out of the drama and directly addresses the audience, that person has broken the fourth wall and the illusion of reality created on the stage is suspended.

Theatrical productions sometimes use a thrust stage, or present plays in the round, or even move actors into the audience. However, moving the action closer to the audience is different from moving the audience into the middle of the action. With a camera, the point of view of the film, video, and television audience can move within the space in which the action takes place. Consequently the first principle of camera technique is that, instead of simply placing actions and subjects in front of the camera as on a stage, we move the camera into the space with the subjects. There the audience watches the action from the camera positions, framings, and angles that show what we as directors want them to see.

Even in film and video, there is a version of the fourth wall. Characters on the screen usually do not recognize the presence of the camera in the same way that characters on the stage ignore their audience.[2] The camera serves as an invisible eye for the audience, freely moving around in the space with the action without characters acknowledging its presence. Except in point of view (POV) shots, once a character looks into the camera, directly at the audience, the fourth wall is broken and the illusion of reality is dissolved. This is why eye contact with the camera can be such an intrusive distraction, or such a powerful device if used well (the final freeze frame in Truffaut's *The 400 Blows,* for example).

Visual Variety

The camera presents a scene—subjects, actions, settings—in a series of shots that render images on a screen. The second principle of camera technique, then, is that instead of just placing the camera where an audience can watch the action, we place the camera to provide the audience with engaging visual experiences.

Variety is important. If a scene is rendered simply by a continuous series of wide shots, the eye soon tires of the repetition. The sequence is likely to appear visually uninteresting. A good shot script and shot sequence will usually contain a variety of camera framings and angles, offering an orchestrated blend of compositions on the screen. This, of course, depends on the needs of our subject and theme because we can shoot most scenes in as many variations as there are visual styles.

Camera Placement

Once the director knows where the action will be taking place, the next decision is where to place the camera. Camera placement decides two primary elements of a shot—framing and angle. Framing refers to how much of the scene in front of the camera is included in the shot; or to think of it another way, how close to or how far away from the subject the camera seems to be; or to think of it a third way, how large or small the subject appears in the shot. Angle refers to how far to the side and how high or how low we place the camera in relation to the subject. Camera framing and angle are the principal means for creating composition with the camera.

Framing

When framing a subject, what we exclude from the frame is as important as what we include. The composition loses cohesion and power by arbitrarily framing a subject with a clutter of irrelevant items scattered around. The audience assumes the clutter is intended and searches the mess for meaning much like a hidden pictures game. Sometimes a cluttered frame is the effect we want, but when composing a shot, we usually tighten or reframe the shot to rid the picture of unwanted and unintended distractions so that the audience's eye quickly locates the objects in the frame that are important to see. (See Figures 8.1(a) and 8.1(b).)

Wide, Medium, and Close-Up Shots
Camera framings fall into three main types: wide shots or long shots (WS or LS), medium shots (MS), and close-ups (CU). Wide shots show the full human figure, usually with the height of a person occupying somewhere between one-half and three-fourths of the frame's height. Long shots usually show the same. The difference is that calling for a wide shot usually means shooting with a wide-angle lens, whereas a long shot requires a lens with a long focal length. (More about that in a moment.) Medium shots show only part of a person, from about the waist up. Close-ups frame a person's head, with perhaps a bit of the neck and shoulders included. (See Figures 8.2(a), 8.2(b), and 8.2(c).)

There are elaborations on these general shot framings. Extreme wide shots (EWS) or extreme long shots (ELS), for example, are essentially landscape shots

FIGURE 8.1(a)
Clutter in the frame
can distract the
viewer's eye.

FIGURE 8.1(b)
We should tighten or
reframe these shots to
remove unwanted
distractions.

with the human figure occupying only a small portion of the frame, as in
Figure 8.3. We use extreme wide shots to convey the sense of environment—
natural or manufactured—engulfing the human subject. They convey scale,
distance, and geographic location.

FIGURE 8.2(a)
A wide shot (WS).

FIGURE 8.2(b)
A medium shot (MS).

Medium wide shots (MWS) show human figures, usually cut off across the legs above or below the knees. We often use this framing for a "two-shot," a shot showing two people. In film, a medium wide shot is wide enough to show the physical setting in which the action is taking place, yet it is close enough to show facial expression.

FIGURE 8.2(c)
A close-up shot (CU).

Television and film present information in the frame differently. In video and television, the image the audience sees is smaller and has less resolution (shows less detail). We can see this effect when viewing a videotape of a grand-scale film (David Lean's *Lawrence of Arabia,* or George Lucas's *Star Wars,* for example), in which huge, panoramic shots simply lose their power when displayed on the tube. When we shoot for video, we place our cameras closer to the action so the audience can see facial expressions and other details.[3]

When shooting any type of wide shot, we need to decide how far back from the subject we want to set the camera. Don't get too far back! Usually wide shots are more effective if we are still close enough that the subject occupies a significant portion of the frame. If we move the camera back too far, subjects become distant and actions lose dramatic impact. Audiences feel removed and care less about the fate of our subjects. Often in a scene, not only is an extreme wide shot too far removed from the action, but even a wide shot does not bring the audience close enough to see facial expression and be

FIGURE 8.3
In extreme wide shots (EWS), we get a sense of distance, and the surroundings engulf the human figure.

moved by the emotions and cues of interpersonal communication. Consequently the medium wide shot is frequently the widest shot used in a scene.

Medium close-ups (MCU) are head and shoulder shots, as in Figure 8.4. They are close enough to clearly see subtle facial expression, but they are not so dramatic as a full close-up. Often we use them in over-the-shoulder shots, with the back of one character serving as a foreground framing device as we look at the face of a second character. Medium close-ups are common framings for shooting interview and dialogue, both for shots of the person speaking and for reverse or reaction shots of the person listening.

When describing the medium wide shot, we made the point that television and film present information in the frame differently. Because of this, we find that video shot scripts and production sequences contain many more medium close-ups than we normally would find in film-shot scripts.

Extreme close-ups (ECU) fill the screen with the details of a subject, as in Figure 8.5. Ingmar Bergman, when shooting *Scenes from a Marriage* as a six-part television series, filled his production with them for the reasons just mentioned, giving extraordinary intimacy to the production but an almost overpowering intensity for the audiences seeing it in its film release. Extreme close-ups have to be carefully defined. For example, it is not enough simply to call for an extreme close-up of someone's face. We need to know what part of the person's face we intend to show—an eye, a mouth, or maybe an ear or a twitching mustache. Both close-ups and extreme close-ups can have enormous power if used judiciously, but they can also become empty and tiring gestures if used too often in overdramatic treatments of a subject.

FIGURE 8.4
A medium close-up
shot (MCU).

Terms that refer to framing are approximate and a cameraperson's medium shot may not be the same as what the director has in mind. Because of these variations, the director in the studio or on location should consult with the photographer (cinematographer, videographer, shooter, or cameraperson) to agree on what is intended by various framing terms. It is common practice for a studio director working with a new crew to ask each cameraperson to frame a medium shot, a medium close-up, and so forth. Then, while viewing the compositions on the monitor, the director asks each to adjust their framings— looser, tighter, a bit more headroom, and so on—until the director is satisfied that they all agree on the basic definitions.

In single camera work, it is especially important that the cameraperson understand what the director intends by different framing terms. Shots that are meant to be cut together in a match cut are often taken out of sequence. Sometimes a director won't bother looking through the camera lens before a shot, especially when working with a trusted cameraperson. A successful match cut requires that there be a definite change in framing or angle. A director might call for a medium shot and then, later, call for a medium close-up of the same subject with the intention of making a match cut between the two. The cameraperson, because of shooting out of sequence, may not realize the two shots are meant to match cut and might frame the MS too tight and the MCU too

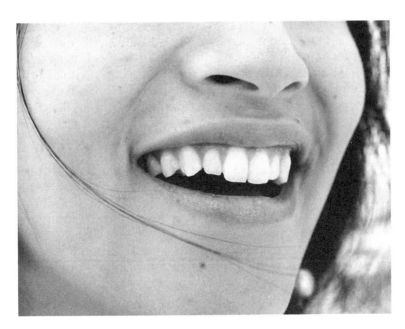

FIGURE 8.5
An extreme close-up shot (ECU). When scripting or directing an ECU, it's important to specify what part of the subject should be seen in the ECU (mouth, eye, hand, and so forth).

loose, resulting in two shots that are so similar in framing they cannot be cut together smoothly.

Angles

Depending on where we place the camera, we can enable an audience to view a subject from any angle:

- Frontal
- Three-quarter front
- Profile
- Three-quarter rear
- Rear (or tail-away)
- High angle (from above eye level to overhead)
- Eye level
- Low angle (from below eye level to underfoot)

Camera angles help us see action from revealing perspectives, they help us create the illusion of three-dimensional reality in a two-dimensional image, and they help us create pleasing compositions.

When presenting a film or video to an audience, we usually want the audience to suspend their disbelief and, for the time they are watching the action, imaginatively become involved in an illusion of reality on the screen as a world unto itself. Part of this illusion is the sense that action takes place and characters live in a three-dimensional space. To create this illusion requires the knowledgeable use of technique because the image itself is two-dimensional. We create film and video images with the monocular (one-eyed) vision of the camera, which cannot duplicate the depth perception of binocular (two-eyed) vision. Without binocular vision, angles become an important tool for creating spatial depth in the frame.

Frontal Angles

Besides rendering depth in the frame, angles also help us to render the three-dimensional physical presence of objects and people. We can illustrate this with a simple exercise in visualization. Suppose we are looking at a simple shape such as a box. If we look at the box straight on, we see only the front surface—a square or rectangle. If we move to the side, we now see both the front and one side, which recedes from us from foreground to background. Viewing the box at an angle, we see more of the three-dimensional features of the box. Finally, staying at this angle, but rising above or dropping below the box somewhat, we see the front, one side, and either the top or bottom. By viewing the box from an angle a little to the side, and from an additional angle above or below, we see the three-dimensional aspect of the box most dramatically.

Given the need to render space and three-dimensional objects in a scene, we find that camera angles are very important in their ability to render the illusion of reality. If we are doing a setup and find the camera pointed squarely into a wall, an alarm should go off in our heads. We may truly want the flat composition that results from shooting straight into a wall, as in Figure 8.6. More likely, however, a camera position angled into a wall, with the wall receding from foreground to background in converging perspective lines that create an illusion of depth, is the shot we want. (See Figure 8.7.)

Beyond rendering three-dimensional space, the use of angles enables us to create dynamic compositions in our shots. Consider the simple situation of two people facing each other having a dialogue. A shot from the side would show both characters in profile, each person on an opposite side of the frame in a symmetrical composition. Such a static, symmetrical composition is sometimes desirable—in the formal depiction of a wedding ceremony, for example—but, more often, the dialogue can be more interestingly handled by shooting over-the-shoulder, three-quarter front reverse angles. With this strategy we trade symmetry for dynamic composition. We see depth in the frame with the back of a head and shoulder serving as foreground, framing the person farther back in the depth of the frame. The head and shoulder also act as a weight in our composition, counterbalancing the mass of the person we are facing, as in Figure 8.8.

The preceding example also illustrates another very important advantage of angled camera positions. If we were to settle for the profiles of two people by shooting squarely at them, we would see ears, hair, some jaw line, the side of one eye, but very little face. (See Figure 8.6.) By angling our shots in three-

FIGURE 8.6
Shooting straight
against walls produces
flat compositions with
little sense of depth in
the frame.

FIGURE 8.7
Angling our shots into
walls produces reced-
ing perspectives and a
greater sense of depth.

FIGURE 8.8
In an over-the-shoulder shot, the back of the head and shoulder act as foreground framing, providing depth and balance to our composition.

quarter front positions as in Figure 8.9, we can see each person's face openly and, consequently, clearly. Angles enable us to see faces more fully, which is critical to effective portraiture and characterization.

In documentary as well, the technique of favoring one person with a three-quarter front shot while shooting over the shoulder of the other person is preferable to a profile shot of both. Usually the person being favored is the person dominating the conversation. We can show the other person in cut-away reaction shots. If the course of the dialogue takes an unexpected turn and the person over whose shoulder we are looking becomes the dominant character, we can simply move the camera around to the reverse position and shoot over the other person's shoulder.

High and Low Angles

High-angle shots are those with the camera above the subject's eye level. Conversely, low-angle shots are those with the camera below eye level, usually around the chin or chest or even slightly lower. A low-angle shot gives power and a subtle sense of dominance to the subject. It can also give the impression of height. Setting the lens a little below eye level produces a complementary portrait of our subjects.

It's interesting to look at the shots of Jack Nicholson in *Batman,* most of which are below eye level. In our first shots of him, the camera stays below his shoulder level. In his first confrontation with Eckhardt (William Hootkins), all of Nicholson's shots are low angle, giving him a particularly menacing look.[4]

FIGURE 8.9
The reverse angle of the shot in Figure 8.8. In theatrical productions, we can avoid profiles in dialogues by shooting three-quarter front reverse angles that show more of the face. This is more difficult to do when covering action in documentaries, but showing the face is just as important.

Chinatown paired Nicholson with Faye Dunaway, who is tall compared to him. To disguise their mismatch in size, Polanski shot Dunaway from higher angles and Nicholson from lower angles. He never shot them standing together in the frame from an angle that showed their true comparative height.

The slight shifts from high to low angle or vice versa often mirror the shifts in power or dominance in the scene. A typical situation involving the use of these angles is in a dialogue where the dominant person is shot from a low angle and the other person from a high angle. These differences in angle are usually subtle and not usually evident to the audience. A good idea is to review some particularly good dialogue scenes on video and pay close attention to if, when, and why the angles shift from high to low.

A typical situation involving the use of high and low angles is in a dialogue in which one person is standing while the other is sitting. Although these are not point-of-view shots, we often take reverse angles from a position near the height of the person over whose shoulder we are looking. Consequently, when we take a three-quarter front shot of the person who is standing, we often place the camera near the head level of the person who is sitting, looking up at the subject from an angle below eye level, as in Figure 8.10(a). Then, in the reverse angle, we place the camera near the head level of the person who is standing, looking down on the sitting subject from a high angle above eye level, as in Figure 8.10(b).

A similar situation occurs when we see two people of significantly different heights standing and talking together. However, to diminish the apparent difference in height, it is not unusual in these situations to bring the two nearer to each other's eye level, even if it is necessary to cheat and place the shorter person on a box.[5]

FIGURE 8.10(a)
In reverse angle three-quarter shots, we usually place the camera near the eye level of the person not being shown. Someone sitting is usually shot from a high angle, if the other person is standing.

FIGURE 8.10(b)
In a reverse angle, a person standing is shot from a low angle if the other person is sitting.

When we want to make a person look small, vulnerable, subdued, or defeated, we commonly use a higher high angle, over the subject's head, often in a medium wide shot, to look down on the subject. A medium high angle, if you will. Although this, like any technique, can seem simply mechanical and unconvincing, it can also be quite effective. In *Dead Poets Society,* for example, we see young Neil (Robert Sean Leonard) sink down in a chair in total defeat after his father has forbidden him to participate in theater at his school. The high-angle shot of him crumpled despondently in the chair, which amplifies his despair, directly precedes his suicide. Another good example is the opening of *Terminator 2.* After the camera tracks through the now devastated playground in the Los Angeles of the future and the robot's foot smashes the skull, the camera cranes up, but also maintains a low angle on the robot. Throughout the balance of this sequence, shots of the humans are a medium high angle, just over their heads, whereas shots of the robotic machines are from about chest height looking up. Then the camera moves in on John Connor (John McIntire), and we are just slightly below his eye level, giving him a strong and determined presence. We don't need a guide book to figure out who is winning this war. The angles tell it all.

Extreme high and low angles that are not dramatically motivated can seem contrived, distracting, artistically heavy handed, and self-conscious. However, there are occasions when extreme high angles, even full overhead shots, can be very effective. One powerful use of an overhead shot, for example, occurs in *Psycho* when Detective Arbogast (Martin Balsam) comes to the Bates Motel to investigate Marion's (Janet Leigh) disappearance and is himself killed after he climbs to the top of the long staircase. The shot of Norman's "mother" running out of a room with an upraised knife and slashing at Arbogast is taken from an extremely high overhead camera angle. The angle is disorienting, suddenly throwing us high up in the air above the stairwell and setting up the next shot, a high-angle close-up in which the stunned and mortally wounded Arbogast, his face slashed, falls backward down the stairs.

Conversely, extreme low angle shots make a subject look big, aggressive, dominant, or victorious. Kurosawa uses the extreme low camera position throughout *The Seven Samurai.* Welles's use of extreme low angle to create the towering figures of Kane and Jedidiah (Joseph Cotten) confronting one another in the newsroom at night after the election in *Citizen Kane* is an impressive use of camera position to turn mortals into mythical giants. Orson Welles was particularly fond of extreme low angle shots to make his characters tower above us in the scene. Extreme low angle, menacing shots of him as the murderous Hank Quinlan in *Touch of Evil* are particularly memorable.

Focal Length

The focal length of a lens greatly influences the way an image is translated to the screen. It can alter apparent distances and heights. It can change a person's face. It can exaggerate speed or cause motion to appear suspended. It can cause objects to look small or big, far away or close up, and it can make backgrounds appear sharply focused, slightly soft, or completely out of focus. The lens turns the hard reality before us into a plastic medium and molds it like clay.

The most distinguishing property that separates one lens from another is focal length. The impact of focal length is defined in terms of the angle of view and apparent size of the scene before the camera, depth of field, and perspective.

Angle of view and apparent subject size are the most obvious effects of focal length on image quality. Depth of field—how much of the scene in front of and behind a subject is in focus when the lens is focused on the subject—is a bit more subtle. However, it becomes clear when looking through the lens with a reflex viewfinder,[6] at a monitor, or at the final image on the screen. The effect of focal length on perspective is the least obvious, yet, in many ways, it is the most significant, consequence of lens selection on image quality.

We rarely need to measure the focal length of a lens. It's enough to know that focal length is an optical property of a lens that has little to do with its size. Lens focal lengths are conveniently divided into three types—short, normal, and long.

Short Focal Length

Lenses with a short focal length exaggerate distances in front of the camera. Objects seem farther away than they actually are. They are called *wide-angle lenses* because they take in a broad view of the scene before them. Because of their wide angle of view, they are often used for establishing shots. We have seen them used for those wide, panoramic shots in films like *Out of Africa, Glory,* and *Dances With Wolves.*

Short focal length lenses have great depth of field, that is, when focused on a subject, they also show the background and much of the foreground in focus. Because of their great depth of field, many wide-angle lenses do not even have focusing rings. They are "point and shoot" lenses, their deep depth of field causing everything from about four feet out to infinity to be in focus. Inexpensive still cameras without interchangeable lenses often have short focal length lenses that do not require focusing. This enormous range in depth of field is not the way the human eye perceives the scene in front of it. Our eyes select objects and planes of focus. Thus, in shots using short focal length lenses, unless the purpose is purely panoramic or establishing the scene or set, there needs to be some design element or movement in the frame to give the audience cues about where to focus their attention. Otherwise, they will scan the scene for meaning and perhaps focus on some unintentional or irrelevant scene detail. (See Figure 8.11.)

Short focal length lenses, because of their great depth of field, make camera movement easier. A camera can move through the space where action is taking place without the need to change focus. Furthermore, because short focal length lenses show a scene in a wide angle of view, they diminish any

FIGURE 8.11
Short focal length, wide shots with fore-grounds and back-grounds in focus and no center of attention cause the viewer's eye to search for significant detail.

bumpiness in a camera move. Short focal lengths, therefore, lend themselves to moving camera shots because they help make moves appear smoother. In a news or documentary situation, a cameraperson attempting a walking shot with a camera on a shoulder or bodypod mount usually prefers to get as close as possible so that the widest possible lens can be used. In the more elaborate world of feature production, short focal lengths enable the complex, moving camera shots of long-take style production described at the beginning of Chapter 7.

Short focal length lenses exaggerate perspective by causing parallel lines in the scene to converge more quickly than we normally see with our eyes. If we look up at a building with a short focal length lens, the parallel lines of the building—the walls, window frames, corners, and so on—converge toward each other sooner than we see with our eyes. The convergence of lines is an especially important cue for height in the monocular media of film and video, which lack the depth perception made possible by binocular vision. The effect is that the building looks higher than it actually is, as in the scene where the Ghostbusters look up at the skyscraper where Gozer awaits them. Conversely, if we look down the outside of a building with a short focal length lens, as in the shot above Batman looking down at the crime in the streets below in the opening of *Batman,* we see the parallel lines of the building converge in an ex-aggerated way. It makes our point of view seem higher than it really is. (See Figures 8.12(a) and 8.12(b).)

The exaggeration of perspective caused by a short focal length applies to all objects, not just buildings. It works with the apparent height of people as well. Look up at a person, as we do at Batman when he first drops into view (from a low angle with a short focal length lens), and the person, Michael

FIGURE 8.12(a)
Short focal length, low-angle shots exaggerate the height of buildings.

FIGURE 8.12(b)
Short focal length, high-angle shots also exaggerate perspective, making the point of view seem higher.

Keaton, in this case, appears taller. In *Terminator 2,* when the Terminator, played by Arnold Schwarzenegger, already a fairly big person, leaves The Corral in his new biker clothes, there is a wide angle tilt up from his shoes. He looks enormous.

A short focal length lens exaggerates interior heights as well. Shooting someone seated (at a desk, for example) from a standing position makes them appear as if we are observing them from near the ceiling. This can be deliberate, but it can also happen accidentally—the result of not moving the camera down closer to the eye level of the seated subject. The results can be disappointing, making us feel remote from the action and showing us lots of our subject's hair and forehead of our subject but too little face, as in Figure 8.13.

Perspective makes near objects seem larger and far objects seem smaller. If we look down a row of people or out into a crowd with a short focal length lens, the peoples' body and head sizes will diminish more quickly than normal the farther away people are from the camera. There will not only seem to be more space between them, the entire physical space of the room or terrain they are in will appear to be larger than it actually is. Television studio cameras often use short focal length lenses. They provide depth to the set with their great depth of field and exaggerated perspective, often making limited space look more spacious.

David Letterman in his late night show, often plays the focal length with hand and arm gestures toward the camera. He has a good visual sense of how he affects his television image, as opposed to many talk show hosts who still perform for an audience as opposed to the camera.

The effect of exaggerating space with a short focal length can be made even more extreme if the camera is placed near the floor so that we seem to be looking out across a vast expanse, as in Figure 8.14. Gregg Toland used these low-angled, short focal length shots to make the interiors in *Citizen Kane* appear opulent and expansive.

Since the lens exaggerates real distance, objects increase in size more quickly as they approach the camera. Car-mounted cameras using short focal length lenses accentuate high-speed chase sequences. As mentioned in Chapter 5, pointing the camera down the street in the direction in which the

FIGURE 8.13
Shooting a sitting person from a standing position with a short focal length exaggerates camera height, making the subject seem far down and distant, and showing more hair and forehead, but less face.

FIGURE 8.14
Short focal length wide shots near ground level exaggerate the expanse of space in the frame.

car is traveling increases the apparent speed of the car. Drive a car toward a camera with a short focal length lens and the car appears to come toward the camera faster. Throw a fist toward a camera so that the end of the swing is only a foot or two from the lens and the sudden change in fist size makes the act seem much more abrupt and violent. (See Figures 8.15(a) and 8.15(b).)

Normal Focal Length

A "normal lens" is so named because it renders perspective similarly to the way our eyes see perspective. A normal lens *does not* take in an angle of view similar to our eyes, which have an angle of view of almost 180 degrees, an extremely wide angle of view in photography. Only a specialized ultra-short focal length lenses called "fisheye" lenses can duplicate this degree of angle.

The focal length of the normal lens varies from one format to another. For example, in 35mm still and motion picture film, the normal lens has a focal length of 50mm. In 16mm film and some video cameras, the normal focal length is 25mm. Other video cameras have normal focal lengths that are somewhat shorter.

Because a normal lens renders perspective the way our eyes see perspective, height, distance, speed, changes in apparent sizes of objects and people at different distances from the camera, and facial contours all look natural. Because of this lack of distortion, many directors prefer to use this lens or one near the "normal" focal length for most of their shots.

Normal lenses do not have extreme depth of field, and under usual lighting conditions, they cause the background behind a subject to be slightly out of focus. This is much the way the human eye recognizes background while

FIGURE 8.15(a)
Short focal length shots of something moving toward the camera, such as a hand or fist, exaggerate the physical force and speed of the action.

FIGURE 8.15(b)
Completion of the action begun in Figure 8.15(a), staged close to the camera and shot with a short focal length lens.

focusing on a foreground object or sees foreground objects in a blur when we shift our focus to objects at some distance from us. The somewhat restricted depth of field that a normal lens produces can be desirable for many shots—major architectural structures and large shapes remain recognizable, but the details are out of focus enough not to be distracting.

Because of the shallow depth of field, it becomes important to shift or fol-low-focus as the subject in the scene moves toward or away from the camera.

We do this by taking focus readings at the beginning and end positions between which the subject will be moving and shifting focus during the shot while the subject moves. Sometimes it's useful if an assistant puts a thin strip of white camera tape on the lens alongside the distance markings on the focus ring. Then the beginning and end points can be marked with a marker or pen, and the assistant can pull focus while the camera operator pays attention to the framing of the moving shot. With or without an assistant, it's important to rehearse pulling focus with the movement of the subject until it is a comfortable and well-choreographed action. The result should be that the subject remains sharp while various parts of the background drop in and out of focus. As the focus shifts, the moving subject can lead the audience's eye to various details within the scene.

Similarly we can produce a more pleasing move during a shot if we move the camera—dollying the camera in or out—rather than zooming in or out with a zoom lens. Zooming produces the effect of magnifying or shrinking the image, rather than the effect of moving through space.

Long Focal Length

Longer than normal focal lengths are extremely useful tools for a director. Long focal length lenses take in a narrow angle of view and magnify a small portion of the scene before the camera. At extended focal lengths, these "telephoto" lenses work exactly like telescopes—making distant objects seem closer and filling the frame with the details of a scene. Long focal lengths enable us to pick out details and isolate them, investing them with significance and enriching the context of a scene.

Depth of field in long focal lenses is very shallow, throwing backgrounds progressively out of focus as focal lengths increase. At about 100 millimeters in 16mm film (200 millimeters in 35mm film), depth of field is narrower than the thickness of the human head. If we focus on a subject's eyelashes in a close-up at this focal length, the nose and ears will be out of focus. In a three-quarter shot, focusing on the subject's eye on the side closest to the camera causes the eye farther from the camera to be a bit out of focus.

The depth of field in a long lens is far shallower than in the normal lens. This greatly increases the ability to selectively focus on subjects while keeping the background out of focus and less distracting. More than this, out-of-focus backgrounds resulting from shallow depth of field create a certain look—they set the focused subject like a cameo against soft, cloudlike diffusion, sometimes enhanced by sparkling highlights. (See Figure 8.16.) The effect can be quite romantic although, as with any pronounced effect, it can seem contrived if overused.

The shallow depth of field created by long focal lengths enhances the effect of rack-focusing. Rack-focusing is an effect in which we see a subject in the foreground with the background out of focus (or vice versa), and then, motivated by some significant moment within the scene, we shift the focus from the foreground subject to another subject in the background, coalescing the

FIGURE 8.16
Long focal length shots sets the subject against soft, diffused backgrounds and flatten features.

image of the background subject into sharp focus while throwing the previously focused foreground subject out of focus. In *Terminator 2*, for example, when the Terminator (Schwarzenegger) is first sent back to contemporary Los Angeles, he stands up, is given a close-up with a long lens, and then he shifts his eyes to camera left. There is a rack-focus, and what was a blur between the two trucks is now clearly the sign of The Corral, the biker bar where he goes to get clothes. Rack-focusing motivates the transition to the next sequence.

Although long lenses require more space in interiors, superior camera mounts for smooth camera moves, longer time in shot setups, and more critical focus control, they are often essential for quality production and an important element in polished professional work.

Distortion of perspective by long focal lengths is the reverse of the distortion produced by short focal lengths. This distortion is especially useful in treating dramatic action. Long focal lengths distort perspective lines so they appear to converge farther away than where our eyes normally expect to see them coming together. The effect causes an object to change size much more slowly than we anticipate as it approaches or moves away from the camera. Thus, in Mike Nichols's *The Graduate*, near the end of the movie when Benjamin (Dustin Hoffman) is running toward the camera, trying to reach the church before his girlfriend, Elaine (Katharine Ross), gets married, he appears almost suspended in space, running and running but getting nowhere.

Another excellent example of the use of the long lens to suspend an object rushing toward the camera is in David Lean's *Lawrence of Arabia*. The scene occurs near the beginning of the film when Lawrence (Peter O'Toole) is being led out to the desert by a guide to meet with the Arab tribal leaders. They stop at a well for water and, as the guide starts to draw water up from the well, a shot rings out. Lawrence spins around to look into the desert to see who fired the rifle. We are then treated to a magnificent shot of a robed figure on a draped camel racing toward us at full gallop, but suspended in some kind of perpetual motion, silhouetted against the desert sunset as a mythical Oriental figure of doom.

Another effect of the long lens is to compress space. This causes subjects and objects at varying distances from the camera to appear all crammed together at about the same distance from the camera. The long lens shot from center field of the pitcher in baseball games usually shows a batter nearly the same size and looking as if he were only a few feet away.

John Schlesinger used a short focal length lens in his film *Midnight Cowboy* to exaggerate perspective and emphasize wide open spaces of Oklahoma. Then, when Joe Buck (John Voight) arrives in New York City, there is a wonderful shot taken with a long lens looking up a crowded New York City sidewalk. The streets appear packed with people's heads and shoulders piled on top of each other. And there is Joe's cowboy hat compressed in the middle. The sense of the cowboy lost in New York's mass of humanity is intense.

If we look out across a room filled with people using a long focal length lens, heads and shoulders will diminish in size only slightly. Someone in the back of the room will appear almost as large as someone nearer to the camera. Because diminishment in size is a critical cue for distance, the result is that the distance from the front to the back of the room will seem compressed (just the opposite from the effect of the short focal length lens) and people will appear packed tightly on top of each other. Most of us are familiar with the long lens shot of rush hour traffic with what appears to be cars stacked up on top of one another. Long lens shots can create beautiful backdrops in films like *On Golden Pond*, when the subjects are next to the lake. Compressing distance with a long lens brings the water up as the background, out of focus, shimmering, and very pretty.

Although these examples show extreme uses of long focal length lenses to compress space, the most common use of the long lens for spatial compression can be found in almost any well-executed production. Directors often enhance dramatic tension in a dialogue scene by shooting over-the-shoulder shots of subjects with longer than normal focal lengths. Long focal lengths in these kinds of shots compress the space between characters, causing them to appear closer together, more face to face. Heightening the effect on dramatic interactions with long lenses can be very powerful.

We might expect to see this kind of manipulation in more stylized productions, but we also find it used in more realistic works as well. For example, in Martin Scorsese's *Raging Bull*, there is an extraordinary scene in the kitchen when Jake (Robert De Niro) commands his brother, Joey (Joe Pesci), to hit him in the face. The over-the-shoulder shots of the two men in the growing tension of the scene are all long focal length, compressing the space and the drama between them. Furthermore, as mentioned in Chapter 5, there is another use of focal length manipulation at the end of the scene. At this point, Scorsese switches to a short focal length shot of the brother just before they stand up and he throws the punch. The switch to the short focal length lens at this point exaggerates the foreshortening, emphasizing the violent motion of the fist.

Knowledgeable directors don't select focal lengths for their dramatic effect only occasionally—they do it all the time. But, as we have mentioned, long focal lengths require more space, better camera mounts, and more setup time. It is interesting to trace the evolution of a director's body of work. Often we see a pattern of increasing use of longer focal length treatment of dialogue and action as larger budgets make it accessible. We have noted this process of evolution in looking at Spike Lee's earlier film, *She's Gotta Have It* and comparing it to his later film, *Do the Right Thing*.

Focal Length and Portraiture

A powerful effect of short focal length on perspective is in the way it distorts the human face. If we shoot a frontal close-up of a subject with a short focal length lens, the exaggeration in perspective causes the nose to protrude forward, the forehead to slope back, the brow to jut outward, and the ears to be set farther back. We can create a gargoylelike, subhuman, Neanderthal look. This can be used to achieve a comic effect (Jim Varney's Ernest character), to exaggerate monstrousness (*The Shining*, when Jack beats down the bathroom door), or to emphasize a look of horror (Nancy, in *Nightmare on Elm Street*). If the shot is slightly higher, the head bulges at the top, leading away to a narrow chin and diminutive shoulders. From below, the jaw becomes more pronounced with the brow narrowed. Although we seldom use these exaggerations, it's important to recognize the distorting effect of a lens on the face. Differences in the way we shoot a face powerfully influence how a person looks. If the face shot is a medium close-up with a short focal length lens, as in Figure 8.17(b), it may be difficult to cut it with a shot taken with a normal or long focal length lens as in Figure 8.17(a) or 8.16.

A long focal length lens has the opposite effect. It flattens the subject's features. Noses become shorter, ears seem farther forward, and foreheads, cheeks, and jaws flatten and look more squared, flaring to the side rather than sloping back. (See Figure 8.16.)

This effect can alter the appearances of both women and men. A young actor who is supposed to play a tough character but is too round and open faced can be squared off and roughened by using longer than normal focal lengths.

If we shoot close-ups with long focal lengths, medium shots with a normal lens, and wide shots with short focal lengths, we can make a subject's face look different in each of the three shots. This haphazard distortion of facial features caused by changes in focal length to achieve differences in framing (CU, MS,

FIGURE 8.17(a)
A medium close-up
shot with a normal
lens.

FIGURE 8.17(b)
The same subject
shot with a short focal
length lens. Compare
these to the same
subject shot with a
long focal length lens
in Figure 8.16. Notice
how short, normal,
and long focal length
lenses dramatically
change the face of the
subject.

or WS) is a common disfigurement when we use zoom lenses without understanding the effect of focal length on perspective.

Because of this shifting distortion, many directors prefer to move the camera closer to the subject, shooting the close-ups with a normal lens, rather than staying where they were for the wide shot but using a longer lens. Although the members of the audience may not consciously be aware of the effect, they will know the camera is close to the action, not observing the action from a distance and magnified as if through a telescope.

Camera Movement

Moving camera shots can truly heighten the audience's experience of watching a production. Besides taking the audience into the action, a moving camera can draw the audience into the fantasy of the moment, involve them in the excitement of the drama, pull them into the dialogue, or float them through the action. Moving camera shots add to the dynamic treatment of the action in a scene. Many high-action scenes are worth studying to see how accomplished directors can use the moving camera to impart powerful movement to a scene. As mentioned earlier, the night the Viet Cong attack in *Platoon* is a *tour de force* use of moving camera technique to enhance physical action in a scene.

The types of camera moves are as follows:

- Pans, in which the camera rotates horizontally
- Tilts, in which the camera rotates vertically
- Dolly shots, in which the camera moves backward or forward
- Trucking shots, in which the camera moves sideways
- Pedestal or crane shots, in which the camera is raised or lowered
- Canting shots, in which the camera is rocked sideways

Also included within the inventory of moving camera shots, although they involve lens manipulation rather than camera movement, are the following camera moves:

- Zoom shots, in which the focal length of a zoom lens is lengthened or shortened
- Rack-focus shots, in which a shallow depth of field is shifted from foreground to background or vice versa by a shift in focus (also called follow-focus when a subject moving forward or away from the camera is kept in focus).

We can execute all these moves at varying speeds and with either mechanically smooth perfection, or a more imprecise, shakier hand-held camera look.

Sometimes several of these moves are orchestrated together, as when the camera is mounted on a dolly or a crane and the movements of the camera are choreographed with the action of the performers, giving a fluidity of motion to the audience's point of view in the scene.

The Moving Point of View

Because the camera's point of view often represents the eyes of the audience, moving camera shots are a little tricky. The human eye doesn't pan very well. Try it. It follows a moving object, or if given none, it looks at a spot and then shifts to another spot. The moment the eye focuses on a spot, it de-selects the rest of the scene. In effect, it cuts from place to place in the scene before it. Zooming is a particularly unnatural act. Although these movements are frequently appropriate ways to cover action, when we use them we risk making the audience too aware of the artificial contrivance.

Moving camera shots and zooms are also difficult to edit. Except in fast-paced action scenes, or in a cut from one moving camera shot to another, or in other stylized treatments, it seems very abrupt and awkward to the audience to cut into a shot that is already moving or cut out of one before the movement stops. There is very little an editor can do to increase or decrease the pace of the move so that it matches the pacing of the rest of the scene without using expensive optical or computerized effects. Thus, when faced with a moving camera shot, the editor is stuck unless other shots cover the action. Until our ability to previsualize the finished piece has matured, it's better to avoid zooming and panning the camera in an attempt to follow action.

Specific Compositions

Shots with camera moves need to be specific. As with wide-angle shots, the audience needs some sense of what is important in the frame. Long panning shots without structure or composition give the audience little or no information. Whether done by panning across or trucking through a location, such shots set up the audience's anticipation for an unexpected surprise at the end of the shot or some kind of rewarding payoff. The audience expects the shot to move from something important, a specific composition, to something else important in another composition. Random moves over a scene leave the audience feeling the cupboard is bare. (The same is true with a shot panning along the outline of an object in a slow reveal that doesn't end on a significant composition). For this reason, it is a common technique to establish some moving subject within the scene for the camera to follow as motivation for the camera move. An excellent example of this is in Howard Hawks's *His Girl Friday,* when the camera follows the man through the newsroom to the elevator for the entrance of Hildy (Rosalind Russell). A nearly three-minute trucking shot to establish the conditions of a large location occurs at the end of Kenneth Branagh's *Henry V,* as the camera follows Henry (Branagh) carrying the dead body of the page boy as he walks through the carnage of the Agincourt battlefield.

When there is a specific subject, let the audience look at it. Waving and bobbing the camera around from subject to subject and back again may emulate a home video look that is sometimes the desired treatment. Moving the camera is also a means of changing point of view and can substitute for cutting from one shot to another. When considering a camera move, remember that we should have some reason for choosing a move over a simple cut because the cut will appear far more natural to the audience.

Motivating the Move

Moves need to be motivated. If the audience feels naturally motivated to shift its gaze and the camera makes the move, the move will seem natural and uncontrived. A good practice is to let subjects motivate the move through their action. They can do this by suggesting that action is occurring in another part of the scene not within the frame, perhaps with a shift of the eyes or slight head gesture. This makes the audience want to see the off-screen action. The subject can also move to another part of the scene.

The motivation for most camera movement is to pan or truck with moving subjects. We often pan with subjects when they walk within a room or between rooms, run on the ground, or move about in cars, on motorcycles, astride horses, and so on. Though pan shots usually require some degree of follow-focusing, they are much easier to execute than trucking shots and are therefore more commonly used for following action. However, trucking shots physically move the point of view of the audience rather than simply rotating it from a fixed perspective. Therefore, this conveys the action with a treatment that is much more dynamic.

Panning and trucking shots with fast-moving subjects are often enhanced by placing the camera so that objects such as trees, fences, and brush are between the camera and the moving subjects. These foreground objects stream or flash through the frame as the camera moves with the subject.[7] Point-of-view traveling shots can be very exciting. Witness some of the helmet-mounted shots in documentaries featuring downhill skiing, luge, kayaking, or other fast-action sports. William Friedkin padded his Panavision camera and rolled it down the long flight of steps in Georgetown to give an exciting point-of-view shot to the priest's suicide in *The Exorcist*.

When the subject does not motivate the move, the audience assumes that it is motivated by the director, perhaps to reveal to the audience something of which the subject is unaware. The camera move suggests to an audience that it will reveal something else in the scene that is also significant and interesting. Through this we can isolate and draw the audience's attention to small objects in a scene by dollying in on them. Dollying back from a small portion of a larger scene can reveal context and location. In wide establishing shots, dollying in can carry an audience into the scene.

Action in the scene also motivates moves. Many shots require minor reframing as action changes composition. Subjects approaching the camera usually require an upward tilt of the camera to maintain proper headroom. A shot that begins with one person sitting but then introduces a second person walking into frame usually requires a tilt up to avoid cropping the head of the second person and an adjustment for the new two-person composition.

Every movement the subject makes should not motivate a camera move, however. It's important not to try to follow small actions by keeping a subject centered in the frame, but to hold a steady composition and let the action move through the frame. Panning around from one subject to another and chasing quick, random subject movement with the camera not only has an unsettling effect on the audience, but, as mentioned, also makes the pacing of the edit difficult to control.

Executing the Move

A well-executed moving camera shot usually has an opening framing held on the screen, a smoothly paced move, and a final composition also held on the screen. Usually, a camera move starts from one subject and goes to another subject. The shot should start on a well-framed subject. We then hold that frame for at least several beats. (We count beats at the rate of approximately one beat per second.) This pause before the move allows for some pad, extra footage, which lets the editor decide how long the shot needs to hold and when to start the move based on the pacing considerations of the sequence. When we frame a shot, we are telling the audience that there is something in that composition to see. At the beginning of a moving camera shot, the audience needs a few seconds minimum to recognize and absorb the content of the initial composition. If we start a shot and move the camera immediately, we are saying to the audience that really there was not anything to look at in the initial framing and where we really want it to look is someplace else. The content of the shot becomes the camera searching for the shot, instead of the shot itself.

The second stage of a moving camera shot is the move. To find the pace of a camera move, the directors, camerapersons, and crew often identify the number of beats it takes to achieve the move. A fast move might be a two-beat pan; a slow one, a five-beat pan. A fast or slow move should be choreographed with the pace of the action and the pace of the editing that will be created later. A slow move in a fast-cut, fast-moving scene can break the rhythm and be a disaster unless it is deliberately planned as a moment in which the pace of the scene is to be retarded. Conversely a fast pan in a slow-moving scene can disturb the calm and distract the audience awkwardly unless a jolt is the intended effect. If the vision of the finished production is still uncertain, it's always safe to shoot the move at several varying rates.

The third stage of a moving camera shot is the framing achieved at the end of the move. As with the framing at the beginning of a moving shot, when we arrive at the final composition something of significance should be in the frame. When we get to this framing, again, shoot a few beats of pad to give the audience a chance to see what has been revealed and to give the editor a chance to decide tempo and rhythm.

Sometimes moves are made that can't be used in the edit because they are the wrong pace, they pick up an unwanted object in the shot, or they have some other technical problem. Holding on those beginning and ending framings allows the editor to remove the footage of the camera move and work with the two steady frames at the beginning and end as two discrete shots.

Dollying in slightly and tightening the frame can heighten the dramatic tension in shots involving confrontation or intense interaction. Conversely, dollying back or a pedestal up can relieve tension and help bring an interaction or scene to closure. As with any move, these small adjustments need to be deliberately executed. A frame that creeps after a subject or is constantly adjusting to improve the composition is often more distracting for the audience then living with an awkward or unbalanced composition. It also seems amateurish.

Complex Moves

We briefly discussed moving the camera as a stylistic decision at the beginning of Chapter 7. Long-take styles, whether executed with deep focus and multiple planes of action or complex camera moves, involve true choreographed performance, which can lend elegance and grace to a production. Long-take styles enable us to treat the audience to such fascinating shots as the six-minute moving camera confection that opens Robert Altman's *The Player* or the famous opening in Orson Welles's *Touch of Evil*.

This style of production is only successful when the visualization of the final production is complete, accurate, and well communicated to cast and crew. For safety, a single, complex long take is often covered by individual shots of the same action. As much as a long take can enhance the style of a production, it can devastate the quality of the final piece if ill conceived or poorly executed.

Most camera moves follow (actually stay with or even lead) the action. One fairly simple, but effective move contradicts this generalization. It involves moving the camera in the opposite direction of the subject. Thus, if the subject were moving from screen left to screen right, the camera might truck left, against the movement of the subject, but pan right holding the subject in the frame, allowing us to see first where the person is coming from and then finally where the person is going. This is often executed with a medium shot that keeps us close to the character and the action while progressively revealing the space around them without going to a wider establishing shot. This move is a particularly effective way of avoiding wide shots where the action or character might get lost on a television screen.

Long involved shots require time to set up and, of course, the necessary equipment to create smooth camera movement. Their value to the production often has to be weighed against the time it takes to move and set up the camera and lights to cover the same action in several different shots. Furthermore, in film especially, they may contribute to higher shooting ratios because more things can go wrong in a long take. A long take that goes wrong near the end creates lots of useless footage. Thus long-take styles generally are limited by budget and resources.

Camera Mountings

Camerapersons sometimes fall asleep at night imagining new ways to mount a camera to achieve a combination of mobility and stability. The ideal camera mount would be an invisible skyhook that would enable the camera to float in midair and hold rock steady, yet move in any direction with agility and precision. The demands of moving-camera technique and long-lens cinematography make camera mounts a cameraperson's obsession.

At the simplest, we hold or mount the camera on something to make the shot steady. The longer the focal length, the steadier the mount needs to be because long focal lengths magnify any shaking of the camera. The more we want the camera to move, the more we rely on the mount to effect this movement smoothly, unobtrusively, and perhaps repeatedly with precision. The longer the shot needs to be held, the more important it becomes that the mount isn't subject to fatigue, breathing, or heartbeat.

The Hand-Held Camera

Cameras have become so reduced in size that most can be hand held or supported on the shoulder. The hand, arm, and shoulder are probably the most commonly used camera mounts. However, if we physically hold the camera in our hands, we soon discover that shooting steady shots, especially with long focal length lenses, moving smoothly, and avoiding unacceptable shakiness is difficult.

Shoulder-mounted cameras and cameras mounted on bodypods can be held steadier than cameras simply held in our hands and supported by our arms, but we still find that there is a maximum focal length beyond which we cannot hold a steady frame. Consequently, depending on the physical shape we are in, we are limited in the long focal lengths that we can use when we are trying to replicate the good hand-held and body-mounted camera technique such as we find in some documentaries, news, and certain forms of advertising and music videos.

Although it is possible to walk with a hand-held camera and produce a somewhat smooth movement by bending the knees and doing a kind of Groucho Marx glide, this is usually attempted only when it necessary to track a moving subject. Sometimes, when a subject is walking from one location to another, the person hand-holding the documentary camera must get in front of the subject and shoot the oncoming person in a frontal or three-quarter shot while glide-walking backwards. To accomplish this kind of move and produce a well-composed, acceptably steady shot is very difficult and takes practice. It's helpful at these times to have an assistant, soundperson, or reporter who can put a hand on the backward-walking cameraperson for guidance.

Although we might occasionally find the need to do a walking shot, the better technique with a hand-held camera is to treat our body as a mobile tripod and use our legs *between* shots to move rapidly from one shooting angle to another, but then stay in position during each shot. In other words, good hand-held camera technique may involve some panning, tilting, and zooming, but we only do walking shots when we must.

Even when staying in one place during a hand-held shot, however, it is still easy to shoot shaky footage, especially as muscles frozen in one position begin to fatigue. Another problem that often occurs when we support the camera with our bodies is that we can lose our sense of level and our shots can come out oddly canted, as shown in Figure 8.18.

For all the problems of hand-held shooting, however, it is probably the best way to learn camera angles and framing. The hand-held camera is fast, versatile, and uninhibited except by the cameraperson's physical limitations. It allows us to change camera positions easily for various shots, getting the audience into the action. However, when the shots on the screen are judged unacceptably shaky and unsatisfying, the need for steady shots and quality images will drive us to spend the time and energy necessary to wrestle a tripod into position.

Tripods

Though not as convenient as our shoulder, a tripod is much more stable for creating shots that are steady and level. Tripods come in an array of styles,

FIGURE 8.18
When hand-holding a camera, we can lose our sense of level and shoot takes that are awkwardly canted.

some that simplify the shooting of extreme low angles, some with heads on ball mounts that make it easy to get the camera level, and some with quick release mechanisms that allow us to mount and dismount the camera from the tripod quickly and easily. However, in a small production, they are an additional piece of equipment that someone must handle. And, even as it solves the problems of stability, it introduces new difficulties. If a tripod is not heavy enough for the camera, we will still get shaky shots. Not only that, but a light tripod made top heavy by too large a camera can easily fall over, causing hundreds or thousands of dollars in damage. Furthermore, a light or poorly constructed tripod head is incapable of delivering smooth pans and tilts, and it produces unacceptably jerky camera moves.

A good tripod—heavy enough to handle the camera with a head capable of delivering smooth movement—can be cumbersome, even if it is made of lightweight materials. Tripods take time to set up. At a minimum, for each shot we have to adjust the legs to the proper length so that the camera is at the desired height and is level when the legs are spread. Even making these adjustments correctly is time consuming. Setting the tripod properly for every shot is a chore and slows the production process. Once the tripod is in place, we tend to block action around it rather than move it into the heart of the action. Therefore, it can discourage breaking scenes into separate shots and, instead, encourage the blocking of action in front of the camera in long, wide takes, as if on a stage. The result is that we exclude the audience from the space in which the action takes place and relinquish one of the fundamental strengths of film and video.

Dollies

Less cumbersome than tripods are camera dollies. Again they increase the size of the crew because more people are necessary to transport and grip for a dolly. However, because they provide maneuverable mounts for the camera, they tend to encourage the camera's being inserted into the action. It takes time in production to plan for dolly moves and to rehearse and execute moves. However, it is often worth the extra crew and time necessary to pull off a camera shot which moves and flows with the action.

Wheelchairs make reasonably good dollies in low-budget productions. A cameraperson sits in the wheelchair holding the camera while being pushed or pulled along the floor by an assistant. Obviously this can work only if the floor is smooth. Also, we are limited by the cameraperson's ability to hold the camera steady.

Simple dollies can be built with a piece of plywood large enough to carry a tripod and wheels of a diameter large enough to even out irregularities in the floor. The usual tactic for executing camera moves over rough surfaces and irregular ground is to lay track over the surface and then mount a dolly with four sets of dual wheels that can ride on the track. It is even possible to build a low-budget version of a track dolly, using lightweight PVC pipe for the track and eight wheels mounted inward in four sets of two.

More elaborate camera mounts are usually rented. These include various types of dollies, pedestals, cranes, and booms, which can be expensive. A well-planned shot script might include several sophisticated camera moves, which would enhance the production value during one or two pivotal scenes. If the shots can all be executed in one or two days, equipment rental expense can be minimized.

Since the first *Rocky,* the Steadicam has become a mainstay in the arsenal of film and, more recently, video production. The Steadicam combines the stability of a tripod or dolly with the flexibility of hand-held camera technique. It is a spring-loaded, gyroscope-steadied contraption that straps onto a cameraperson and allows free movement while keeping the camera steady. It requires practice to use well, and many camerapersons sell their skills as specialists in its use. A small, lightweight version is also sold to the home video market that may be available in your area.

Composition

When framing a subject or when holding a subject in the frame during a moving shot, we want to compose shots that make use of the entire frame. Especially during moving camera shots, there is a tendency to mistakenly regard the frame as an aiming device and our camera as some kind of gun, constantly placing the subject in the center of the frame as a target lined up in our cross hairs. Always placing the subject in the middle of the frame creates repetitive, static, and even awkward compositions that undermine visual interest.

Dynamic Composition

A well-framed subject in a medium shot or a medium close-up should have a small amount, but not too much, space between the top of the head and the top of the frame. If there is too much space, the framing looks awkward. If we place the subject's head in the center of the frame, we usually create a composition with too much headroom. A related problem with compositions involves not providing any headroom at all, but instead placing the top of the frame directly on top of the subject's head, as shown in Figure 8.19.

The best framed shot, however, can get away from us as the camera or subject moves. A common problem is chopping off the top of the subject's head with the frame line. This often happens when a shot opens with a seated subject. Then a second person walks into the frame and the camera can't tilt up to accommodate the standing height of the second subject without losing the seated person. The resulting shot decapitates the unfortunate standing subject, and the audience watches the pathetic sight of a headless person walking around the frame. Our problem is that we did not anticipate the entrance. The camera shot of the first person needs to be low enough that the tilt up will keep both subjects in the frame.

FIGURE 8.19
No headroom.

Another consideration related to placing the subject in the frame is the amount of space we proportionally compose in front of and behind the subject when the subject is looking toward one side of the frame or the other. Seldom do we block action so that subjects are facing frontally toward the camera. Most of the time, we block subjects at an angle to the camera, not in profile, but in some form of three-quarter front shots. In a profile or three-quarter front shot, we find that we need to place the subject off-center for pleasing composition, providing more space in front of them (in the direction in which they are looking) and less space behind them. This is sometimes called *lead space* or *nose room* and is shown in Figure 8.20.

As the subject moves, we attempt to maintain this lead space so that the subject always appears to be moving into an empty area in the frame rather than running into the edge of the frame. This becomes very difficult in tight compositions. Even experienced actors in a rehearsed scene can make unrehearsed moves if it feels right to them during the moment of their performance. This is the case in the tight shot of Sigourney Weaver in *Ghostbusters* when she pulls Bill Murray down on the bed with her while under Gozer's influence. Her performance is terrific, and the camera operator loses her head during part of the shot. Not an uncommon or infrequent problem.

There is a major distinction between symmetrical compositions and dynamic compositions. We usually create symmetrical compositions when we place subjects in the middle of the frame, or when we carefully balance subjects so that they are of equal size and weight on each side of the center line. We can use symmetrical compositions to good effect. Ingmar Bergman often used them to reinforce the formal nature of a relationship. Also, confronta-

FIGURE 8.20
Lead space.

tions between adversaries or two people coming together in a romantic em-brace are sometimes treated by symmetrical CU profile shots of the two subjects facing each other nose to nose from each side of the frame.

Symmetrical compositions are static, having an enclosed quality that draws the eye away from the edges and toward the middle of the picture. Con-sequently they can be useful in conveying a sense of enclosure or imprison-ment. A symmetrical landscape shot of a mansion with a road leading to it and trees bordering it will impart a sense of stability—a self-contained world. There is an excellent use of symmetrical composition at the beginning of *Dead Poets Society* when the boys march into the hall framed in heavily symmetrical shots, conveying rigidity, immobility, and confinement—themes that are then well developed in the plot.

Dynamic compositions, on the other hand, balance uneven size and mass in the frame to lead the eye away from the center. A simple over-the-shoulder three-quarter shot of two people in dialogue, with the shoulder and back of the head of the foreground person large in the frame and the torso and head of the person facing the camera smaller in the frame, is a common example of dynamic composition. In this shot, we must place each character so that their uneven size and mass still balance the composition.

Several times in this book we have discussed the importance of creating the illusion of three-dimensional space by using foreground framing devices and angling shots so that perspective lines converge to the side of the frame. Shooting square into a wall or scene with no foreground framing device is al-most a sure formula for flat, uninteresting compositions. (See Figure 8.6.)

Rule of Thirds

One useful design tool that can aid in the creation of dynamic composition is the *rule of thirds*. This classic concept suggests that we divide the frame into thirds both horizontally and vertically. The points where the vertical and horizontal lines cross are aesthetically pleasing spots to place subjects or to have perspective lines converge. Similarly, we find it is usually best to avoid placing horizon lines exactly in the middle of a frame, but to place the horizon either above or below center, approximately one-third or two-thirds up the height of the frame. (See Figures 8.3 and 8.11.)

Another useful concept for the creation of dynamic compositions is the idea of balancing unequal weights on a teeter-totter (or, as expressed more formally in physics, a lever and fulcrum). Remember the idea? A lighter weight can counterbalance a heavier weight if it is placed farther away from the center fulcrum. We find the idea works in composition as well—lighter mass can counterbalance heavier mass if it is placed farther from the center of the frame. We are so familiar with this concept that if we frame a subject off-center so far to one side or the other that a "hole" is left in the frame, we are led to anticipate that the hole will soon be filled by the introduction of a new element such as the entrance of another person.

The Compositional Triangle

The compositional triangle is another helpful design idea. When framing subjects, we often find we are composing three principle elements rather than two. This may be three people, or two people and some significant object or piece of architecture. Obviously, under these circumstances, the simple idea of two objects of unequal size balanced on a fulcrum at different distances from the center requires some elaboration. The concept of balancing unequally sized objects at unequal distances still holds, but now we imagine the objects at the three points of a triangle, with their distance and placement proportional to their size. Thus we can compose two smaller objects to counterbalance one larger object, or arrange objects at different distances around a central point, as shown in Figure 8.21.

One simple rule of composition is to eliminate extraneous elements. If our composition includes parts of people, fragments of furniture, or little bits of ancillary objects that simply litter the frame, the best solution is to tighten the shot and frame out the distracting clutter. Related to this is the tendency to frame details of hand activity too loosely. Suppose we are shooting someone carving a small wooden figurine. We start with a medium shot showing the person, including the busy hands. An awkward but common transition we often see is a tilt down while staying in the medium shot so that the hands shift up near the center of the frame. (The bull's-eye framing we usually try to avoid!) The idea, of course, is that the cameraperson wants us to see what the hands are doing. However, we are still in a medium shot, which includes a large portion of the subject's body, so that tilting down to draw attention to the hands also has the sad effect of chopping off the subject's head. If the

FIGURE 8.21
We can compose three objects by clustering two nearer to the center and the third farther from the center of the frame.

hands are included in a medium shot, we will see their activity just as easily near the bottom of the frame. If the cameraperson wants us to see more detail, the better solution is to move in to a close-up of the hands so that the cropping of the full figure is acceptable and not ungraceful. (See Figures 8.22(a) and 8.22(b).)

FIGURE 8.22(a)
Tilting the camera down to draw attention to the hands in a medium shot can result in an awkward framing of the subject, cutting off the head.

FIGURE 8.22(b)
If we want to emphasize the action of the hands, we should go in to a tighter medium close-up of the hands.

A similar composition error we see often results from wanting to show details in the background and framing the shot to place these details more prominently in the frame, but in doing so, creating a very awkward framing of our main subjects. For example, suppose we want to shoot on a city street that has a strong international flavor. Along the street are many storefronts with signs over the doors written in foreign languages. We want to show this to our audience. If we simply take the shot from eye level out in the street or at the edge of the sidewalk and tilt the camera up to show the signs, we inadvertently cause people walking by to have their heads and shoulders sticking up from the bottom of the frame in a very awkward composition. The solution in this situation is to lower the camera point of view, framing both the signs above the shops and the passers-by. (See Figures 8.23(a) and 8.23(b).)

The most important point in these various examples is to avoid falling into the trap of concentrating on one element within the frame at the expense of badly composing other elements and the entire shot.

Good composition involves designing the whole frame, not just properly positioning our major subjects. Often, while learning camera technique, we first learn to place our main subjects in the frame but fail to see the entire composition. Besides badly framed backgrounds, we can, for example, inadvertently leave large portions in the background of our composition without any interesting elements. We can have distracting empty space, which draws the eye away from the action. As discussed in Chapter 7, we should use set dressings, props, and architecture as elements to create a fully composed frame.

FIGURE 8.23(a) Sometimes we awkwardly frame subjects by also trying to frame objects in the background. In this case, in trying to show the awning sign over the door, we have placed the subject too low in the frame.

FIGURE 8.23(b) We need to see the composition of all the elements in the frame and line up the camera to compose everything comfortably. In this case, lowering the camera shows the sign and brings the subject up higher into the frame.

The secret of good camera work is the ability to really see the frame. It is a skill that must be mastered. When we begin learning camera technique, we are aware of how the subject looks to our eyes—as a reality before us. When we first look into the viewfinder, we tend to see what we know is there, not what the camera is really shooting. Once we had a student who brought in a film of his wife having a picnic in a park and frolicking on a playground slide. The intended treatment was idyllic, but the student had shot all of the many close-up shots with a short focal length lens, making his wife look grotesque. We discovered that the student had truly intended a romantic treatment. What had happened? While the student was shooting and editing, he only saw his wife. He did not see the image.

Point of View

Camera technique—camera placement, framing and angles, lens selection, and composition—all contribute not only to how the audience's eyes will see the image, but what relationship the audience will have with the action. By means of camera technique, we place an audience in the scene, or just outside it, or far away from it. Deciding how far from or close to the action we want the audience, where we want the audience to be, and from what vantage point we want the audience to see can only be decided if we know what our purposes are.

We know, for example, that a close-up shot with a long lens is somehow recognized as taken from a distance, whereas a close-up with a normal or short lens is recognized as taken from close to the subject. In documentary or theatrical work, the difference in effect between two close-ups, one shot with a long lens, the other with a normal lens, can be remarkable. An audience feels and reacts to actions on a screen depending on the perceived distance. This is not thought about abstractly, but rather it works at a visceral level. If we place a camera near the floor so that figures tower over us, we have to react. If we are free, above our subjects going about their business below us, we have to look down on them, literally.

Camera technique, then, is not simply a matter of recording subjects and action on film or video, nor is it a matter of creating pretty pictures. Camera technique is the creation of an illusion of reality that exists on the screen, rendered and interpreted with all the photographic devices at our disposal.

Notes

1. In Hitchcock's *Rear Window,* our ability to see what is going on in the murderer's apartment is limited to what we can see through the window from a distance. Our point of view is confined with Jeff (Jimmy Stewart), immobilized by a broken leg, and moves from plot action in one window to subplot action in another as he watches events in the apartments he can see from his room. Much of the film deals with overcoming this limitation in point of view and discovering the nature of the crime being witnessed.

2. Some genres and dramatic conventions in film and video do recognize the presence of the camera. *Cinéma vérité,* for example, is a style of documentary production that makes no attempt to conceal the fact the scene is being filmed by a camera. In television news and some nontheatrical productions, direct address to the camera by a reporter or an on-camera narrator is common. Similarly, some dramatic directors such as Woody Allen will also recognize the existence of the camera. For example, in *Annie Hall,* Allen steps back from the drama

and breaks the fourth wall when he confides with the audience what a pleasure it is to have Marshall McCluhan personally confirm a philosophical point made while standing in line at a movie theater.

3. This may change as High Definition Television (HDTV), with its greater size and higher resolution, gradually replaces our present video format.

4. In this scene, Nicholson appears to be several inches taller than William Hootkins, the actor playing Eckhardt. This is in part due to the angle but probably also enhanced with a box for Nicholson to stand on.

5. It's interesting to note in *Home Alone* and *Home Alone 2* how often Macaulay Culkin is blocked above the bad guys so that he gets the low angles and they get the high ones.

6. A reflex viewfinder is an optical system we find on most film cameras that allows us to see the image directly through the taking lens. In video, monitors also provide us with a direct view of the shot as seen through the taking lens.

7. A beautiful example of this technique occurs in *Butch Cassidy and the Sundance Kid* in the bicycle interlude where Butch (Paul Newman) rides by with Etta on the handle bars as we truck along with a board fence between us and the riders, the slats of the fence flashing through the frame providing stroboscopic glimpses of the playful scene.

9

EDITING FOR INTERPRETATION

Salvaging the Production

To an editor, everything that happens during the production process is merely the creating and collecting of raw materials that the editor, with great skill and artistry, will make into a viable film or video. The editor is the one who ultimately creates the production. It should be pointed out that writers and directors don't necessarily hold this point of view! But, it's a good place for us to begin because it is the editor's job to put everything together into a coherent film or video production. The editor has to analyze the given material and make intellectual and aesthetic decisions that will result in the finished work.

Arthur Penn has told the story of screening the rushes to his film *Little Big Man* with Dede Allen, who was to edit the picture. After looking at the miles and miles of film, he was totally distraught. To him, there was little chance that the footage could be cut together coherently. It looked like his career was probably over and the studio left with a financial fiasco. He was depressed. He said he felt so hopeless he leaned against the building where the dailies had been screened and nearly wept. But Allen told him to take off for the islands for a couple of weeks and not to worry about it. He didn't, but in two weeks time, she had found the movie in all the footage he had shot. She saved him, the film, and perhaps the studio. He gives her almost full credit for the extraordinary film made from that footage.

Like many creative arts, visual media production involves two very different processes—first building up material, and then cutting and honing away until the work emerges in final polished form. If those involved in accumulating the material don't consider the next process, the honing away, the poor lonely honer likely will be left to resolve clumsy problems, albeit as creatively as possible.

Creating Materials to Edit

Editing is the manipulation of time. Shots do not follow one after another on the screen as discrete frames, like pictures hanging in a gallery. We cut them together creating seamless interpretations of reality or impressionistic compositions that unwind over time. Editing is like composing music or choreographing dance. Using the elements at hand, the editor crafts the production to move from moment to moment through artful transitions and juxtapositions interestingly and expressively. The editor manipulates time and defines meaning through the orchestrating of images. The process of editing interprets the subject and is a major creative stage in the total treatment of the piece.

The degree to which editing contributes to interpretation increases enormously when we plan the style of cutting while planning the other elements of production: *mise en scène,* cinematography, lighting, action, and direction. Planning an editing scheme involves answering basic questions: How will each shot cut to the preceding and successive shots? How will these combinations lead an audience through the unraveling of events and images?

The forms of editing are as infinite as variations in musical style, but it is useful to distinguish between two very different approaches to editing sequences of shots together. Continuity editing creates the illusion of continuous reality. Montage editing creates an abstract or impressionistic rendering of a theme or subject. Both require very different approaches to acquiring images for the editor.

Shooting for Continuity Editing

For both theatrical and documentary production, shooting is the gathering of material suitable for cutting on the editing bench. Beautiful, powerful shots or terrific performances that do not cut are useless. We shoot most scenes in film and video and edit them to create the illusion of ongoing, continuous reality as they progress from one shot to the next. Known as *continuity,* this form of editing enables us to invent a believable mirage on the screen in which the audience can become involved, watching what seems to be real people participating in real interactions and experiencing real events in what appears to be real time. Whether dramatic or documentary, a well-crafted film or video that is shot and edited to produce this illusion makes it easy for the audience to forget they are not watching events in a world but only pictures on a screen.

"Continuity" is a word that is also used in arts other than the visual media. Drama and literature, for example, talk about continuities of theme, motif, character, and place. However, in film and video, the word applies to an attribute that is unique to the moving image. Creating the illusion of continuous action as we cut from shot to shot is a defining aspect of film and video, setting these media apart from every other art form.

Editing changes in camera framings and angles are as important a part of film and video as the shots themselves. In 1948, Alfred Hitchcock experimented with choreographing the camera movement with the action of the drama in his film *Rope,* so that the entire piece was one continuous, real-time action from beginning to end. Characters would periodically block the lens, giving a black frame so the camera rolls of film could be changed and later cut together. It could hardly be called editing. The poor editor, William H. Zeigler, had his credits buried in a list of other production credits. For all of its intelligence in the effort, the film seems very artificial and the actions extraordinarily contrived.

It's not by accident that we can shoot separate shots and edit them into a sequence that gives the audience the illusion of uninterrupted time. Time, as they say, marches on and the camera captures only pieces of it. The ever-changing nature of the real world and the periodic nature of shooting precludes the off-handed taking of individual shots that can be cut together to convey the sense of continuous reality. Like the chances of arbitrarily dropping the needle on a phonograph record in several different places with the hope of playing something that might sound like a continuous song, random shots rarely cut together.

Jump-Cuts

Consider the situation of pointing a camera at a scene, any scene in which there is ongoing action, and starting the camera for a shot. Suppose the camera shows a simple wide shot of two people in a restaurant. As the couple talk and eat, people sitting behind them also shift around, waiters come and go, food and drink are served and consumed, candles burn down, and tables are cleaned and set. At some point, we cut and wait for another interesting incident. Several minutes later, we start the camera for a second shot without moving the camera or changing the framing. Of course, between shots, when the camera is not running, many changes have occurred in the scene.

When we screen our film or tape and the first shot cuts to the second one, we will notice many discontinuities—people suddenly change position; a waiter who was in the first shot abruptly disappears in the second shot; food and dishes magically appear, disappear, and change position; candles instantly change length; and so on. When seen together, these two shots do not produce the illusion of continuous reality and we know time has elapsed between the takes. We call this kind of discontinuity a *jump-cut,* and we should avoid it if we want to create continuity.[1]

On larger productions, someone is usually hired for the sole purpose of ensuring continuity from shot to shot. Not surprisingly, they are called Continuity Clerks or just plain Continuity. If we are shooting a small production, continuity is a matter of preproduction planning and paying close attention during each take. When it is no one's specific job, it generally falls to almost everyone to watch for potential continuity problems that would leave the editor out on a limb. Never leave a set or location without having a clear plan of how the shots will cut together.

Avoiding jump-cuts and creating scenes in which shots have continuity requires the knowledgeable application of very specific techniques. Shots can be cut together to avoid jump-cuts and produce continuity in only four ways:

- On-screen and off-screen action
- Cutaways or cross-cutting
- Cut-ins or inserts
- Match-cuts

As an exercise, use a VCR or laser disk player to closely watch a well-edited production. Scanning edits in slow motion proves that every continuity cut is one of the four listed above. It can be enormously instructive to look at a film this way, closely examining the editor's choices with the cutting material. Any film or video production, either theatrical or documentary, that has the appearance of continuity in its actions and events will probably serve to illustrate the points we are making here. For our purposes, we will look at some edits in the opening scenes of *Thelma & Louise*.

Thelma & Louise is a wonderful film to examine closely, providing excellent examples of good editing technique. Thom Noble, nominated for an Academy Award in the category of Best Editing for his work on *Thelma & Louise,* earned the Oscar in 1985 for his editing of *Witness*.

Off-Screen and On-Screen Action

Shooting action moving off-screen or shooting so that action moves on-screen is really quite simple. We set up the shot by resisting the urge to follow the action. Instead, we allow our subject to leave the frame at the end of a shot, or we start with an empty frame and let the subject enter the shot at the beginning of the take. The editor can cut from an empty frame to almost any shot or from almost any shot to an empty frame and maintain visual and temporal continuity. This capability is very powerful because it allows us to compress time, while keeping the audience's attention focused on the main subject and moving the story forward.

Off-screen and on-screen action can be used within a sequence to move characters efficiently from one setup or arena of action to another, or to make transitions from one scene to another. The opening shot of *Thelma & Louise* takes place in the diner where Louise works. The camera follows Louise (Susan Sarandon), armed with three plates of food, as she snags a syrup dispenser and crosses from the grill area to a booth where she deposits the food. The camera then continues as she picks up two pots at the coffee station and heads off-screen, ostensibly toward her next table of customers. As she turns her back to the camera and begins to move off-screen, the shot cuts. The next shot is an empty frame with only the Venetian blinds on the front window of the diner in the picture. The camera holds this shot for a few frames—not even a full second—and Louise enters the shot in a close-up, smiling at her next table of customers. The action at this table ends on a close shot of one of the customers as we see Louise's hand pouring coffee and then retreating from the frame. A fraction of a second after her hand has moved off-screen, there is a cut to Louise on-screen back in the kitchen area lighting up a cigarette and beginning her telephone call to Thelma.

There is a third example of off-screen/on-screen action a few moments later in the film. Thelma (Geena Davis), in her kitchen, has just finished talking to Louise at the diner and calls to her husband to hurry up. She is facing toward the kitchen door, her back to the camera. She turns and passes us screen right to leave the frame. In the next shot, we are in the dining area. Immediately Thelma enters the frame on our left, heading away from the camera to the table where she reaches to clear something. In this example, the off-screen shot is cut directly to the on-screen shot and the movement of Thelma from one shot to the next appears continuous because her rate of walking is the same in both shots.

On-screen and off-screen editing of necessity builds at least a momentary pause in the action. We usually cover this by having the momentum of the action on the screen continue through the two shots, as in the example of Thelma moving into the dining room, or by having dialogue overlap the cut.

On the other hand, as pointed out in Chapter 4, pauses in the relentless flow of the production are often used to let a salient point sink in for the audience. A pause can allow a "heavy" or menacing statement to hang in the air. The brief pause of an off-screen or on-screen action can tell the audience that a character is thinking and preparing a response to a challenging situation or perhaps is about to go off in a different direction with a new idea.

Often, we use off-screen and on-screen action to avoid a time-consuming movement from one area of the set or location to another. This allows our screen time to consist of significant action that moves the story forward. Otherwise, our scenes become filled with stupefying transitional material of people walking across rooms, up stairs, or down halls with no other purpose than to go someplace else.

In the theater, there is the tradition of breaking action of a scene into what are called *French scenes*. French scenes begin when a character enters the scene and end when a character exits. This works well because the reason for most entrances is to move the drama forward. Otherwise, there would be no reason for the entrance. Exits usually occur when whatever was going on between the character and the other(s) on the stage has come to a conclusion. Once a character's task has been accomplished in a scene, it makes sense for the actor to exit so we don't have superfluous characters hanging around the set with no real purpose. On-screen and off-screen transitions provide the same kind of delineation in film and video production by beginning and ending scenes. For example, the little four-shot scene of Louise with the two customers at the booth begins with an on-screen entrance and ends with an exit from the frame.

It only takes a few empty frames to move a character from one location to another. In the scene where Louise has poured coffee for the two women at the booth, the last shot of the scene is of the young woman as Louise's coffee pot retreats from the frame. We hold for a few frames on the woman's face and then cut to find Louise standing in the kitchen putting a match to her cigarette.[2] In real life, she would have had to return the coffee pots to the coffee station, walk back behind the counter to the rear of the kitchen, find her cigarettes, fish one out, put it in her mouth, and strike the match. But the few empty frames are enough for the audience to allow all that action to have occurred.

At the end of the scene with Thelma and Darryl, we are on a close shot of Darryl. The next cut is to an exterior of the house, and in a matter of a few frames, Darryl comes out the door heading for his car. Later, when Thelma and Louise are about to set off on their odyssey, they snap a self-portrait with a Polaroid and we hold on that two-shot for a beat then cut to an empty highway. In less than half a second, their car enters the middle of the frame, surfacing a small rise in the road, and we are into their traveling sequence. Moving action off-screen or on-screen is the primary transitional device used to define sequences of action. Nearly every sequence in *Thelma & Louise* is delineated by the on-screen or off-screen continuity device.

A double off-screen/on-screen cut, with a character leaving the frame, then entering the frame in the next shot, usually requires many empty frames and thus makes a very heavy transition. It acts as a kind of "curtain drop" and often suggests a significant passage of time or the end of an act in the drama. Such a transition may be appropriate when the preceding scene has been fraught with emotion and the lengthy pause seems necessary to calm the audience down a bit before going into the next sequence.

Besides providing pauses, shooting for an on-screen or off-screen edit permits confining action to small areas, which can be especially helpful in limiting the number of lighting instruments that need to be used and the amount of time needed to set them up. This is an advantage in very large spaces such as supermarkets, gymnasiums, or warehouses, where areas of action can be isolated with off-screen/on-screen movement because it may be impossible to light the entire location successfully. It can also be useful in tight areas such as kitchens or small bedrooms where it is difficult to light the entire space because the camera and crew may occupy half the room during any one shot.

In documentary work, allowing a subject to move out of or into the frame, as opposed to constantly following the action, gives the editor needed flexibility. Suppose we have a scene of a mechanic working on a car in a garage. The action is continuous, yet complex and confined within one space. Let's suppose the mechanic is adjusting the carburetor. We see her in a MS unscrewing the air filter, then slowly zoom in to a CU of her hands loosening the canister and lifting it off. Instead of panning with her hands holding the air filter as she removes it and takes it away, we resist the urge to constantly keep our camera on the subject and let her hands with the filter leave the frame. She is gone. Our next shot could be of her at the workbench having already put down the filter and picking up a screwdriver to adjust the carburetor valves or at the vending machine getting a soda to go with her lunch.

Because much of the sequencing of the action in documentary is usually unplanned in any detailed sense, shooting for the on-screen to off-screen edit allows the carburetor sequence to continue or gives the editor a transition to the next sequence, if appropriate. In the unpredictable realm of documentary photography, shooting for on-screen or off-screen continuity edits may make the difference between a tightly edited show and an editor's nightmare: no place to cut.

It's also worth pointing out in our auto mechanic example that when we are in the close-up of her hands lifting the filter, the mechanic only has to move a few inches to leave the frame. This is also true in the shot of Louise in which she enters the frame in a close shot in the second setup and also when she is exiting the frame after pouring the coffee. If these characters were shot in MWS, they would have to walk several feet, without our panning, for them to leave the frame. These several feet are lengthy, leaden seconds of time that is unrelated to moving the action forward.

It is usually preferable to move the action off-screen or on-screen in close-ups, in which the subject has to move very short distances, than in wider shots in which the character must move longer distances to clear the frame. Fortunately audiences are so used to the convention of characters moving off-screen to provide transition that when it is not possible to shoot the action in a close shot, the effect can still be achieved by starting a character's movement off-screen and cutting before the subject fully leaves the frame. At the end of the second telephone conversation in *Thelma & Louise,* as Thelma grabs her candy bar from the fridge and heads out the door, the film cuts to Louise already out the door of the diner and on her way. Thelma never gets off-screen and Louise's shot cuts a few frames into her entrance into the frame. The intention of off-screen to on-screen is clear to the audience and tightening the editing hurries up the action at a time when we need to feel the action is accelerating.

The off-screen and on-screen continuity device is an essential tool in the film or video photographer's bag of tricks. Without it, editors can use dissolves, wipes, freeze frames, and other effects that may sometimes work, but may be less satisfying and perhaps more expensive.

Cutaways and Cross-Cutting

Cutaways and cross-cutting are the most versatile of all continuity editing devices. Cutaways are shots that cut away from the principal action. Cross-cutting depends on having parallel action to intercut. As with on-screen and off-screen action, these devices can manipulate time and space. In these cases, it's not accomplished by giving the audience a few blank frames, but by allowing the audience to see other parts of the action or scene.

Cutaways direct the audience's attention away from the principal action, and cross-cutting directs the audience to look at parallel action. The audience expects that what we show is essential at this point in the production, not that we are resolving problems of discontinuity or manipulating time and space. Thus cutaways and cross-cuts should be to something that is essential and deserving of the audience's attention.

Shooting cutaways and directing action to allow cross-cutting are the essential trophies of any shooting expedition. Cutaways and cross-cutting move the drama forward, reveal emotion, and develop character. These are the devices that drive rising action and provide pacing and rhythm to the edit. Most editors feel that directors who don't shoot cutaways should themselves be shot!

Referring again to the opening of *Thelma & Louise,* the little four-shot sequence of Louise pouring coffee for the two women in the booth is built internally with cutaways. The first shot shows Louise entering the frame and looking down with a smile to screen right, then turning her head and looking screen left. There is no pause, but when her eyes have clearly focused on something off-screen to our left, we cut away from Louise to the dark-haired patron looking up off-screen to where Louise is still standing. We cut away from the woman back to a close shot of Louise who is now looking down as she ostensibly pours coffee while making a crack about smoking to the young women. She punctuates her remark by swinging her eyes back to screen left and that movement of her eyes again motivates the cut to the dark-haired woman. The woman reacts to Louise's comment and drops her eyes. We cut away from her to the blonde-haired woman. Louise's hand is extending from screen left into the frame pouring coffee. The blonde-haired woman is looking up at Louise. After Louise's off-screen line about the impact of smoking on sex, the blonde woman also looks away and drops her eyes as the coffee pot is pulled out of the frame giving us the off-screen cut. We have the feeling of continuous action throughout the little scene, yet we have never seen any of the three characters in the frame at the same time. The presence of random body parts creates the illusion, but it would have been possible to shoot all three actresses at different times with the help of a stand-in hand.

Eye movement often motivates cutaway edits. Someone on-screen looking at something off-screen makes us want to see what they are looking at. Cutting at the moment we want to see what the person is looking at makes the shift seem as natural as looking around a room.

Looking at how another character is reacting to the dialogue or the events of a story broadens our perspective and gives us, as an audience, guidance to interpretation. Reaction shots are like product endorsements. We become convinced of something because the person reacting is involved and convinced.

Reaction shots are the most common form of cutaway. They are used to provide flexibility in the editing of dialogue. Reaction shots allow us to share Louise's amusement at the ridiculous objects Thelma brings for their weekend away. Louise's reaction shot in the car while Thelma is pretending to smoke a cigarette is part of the fun in the scene. The two contrasting reactions to Harlan in the roadhouse when he approaches the protagonists are not only character defining, but they also kick off the event that will propel the rest of the narrative.

A reaction shot telegraphs emotion and makes us believe the person on the screen is feeling and thinking and not merely following direction, parroting lines, or delivering a prepared speech. Reaction shots suggest to an audience how to regard the action.

The reaction shot is used interestingly in *Thelma & Louise* when Harlan introduces himself at the roadhouse. The camera holds on him and plays his reactions to Thelma and Louise's dialogue rather than showing them as they speak. Letting the camera hold on him is a terrific way of giving him screen time and thus build importance in the drama for the role this otherwise minor character is about to play.

If we shoot dialogue between two people in a series of three-quarter front reverse angles, tight enough that we only see one person in each shot, then each person is a cutaway to the other. Any time we cut to one person, the other person can change position. Obviously, if the shots are wider over-the-shoulder shots that show the backs of heads and shoulders, then the body and head positions must match.

There is an interesting shot in *Thelma & Louise* right after Darryl has entered the kitchen in the opening. Thelma has been helping Darryl put on an ID bracelet in a medium two-shot. Action completed, the camera widens the shot and follows Thelma as she moves to the stove. We see Darryl moving off toward our left, and then he is out of the shot. The editor is then able to cut to Darryl's action a moment later without having to provide visual continuity to move Darryl around the room. Moving Thelma away from her husband into parallel action in the kitchen serves the drama with visual symbolism and sets up the cutaway continuity device. It's a neat piece of directing. When we block action to isolate one character from another on the set, we can handle the dialogue and action with simple cross-cutting. As with on-screen to off-screen action, it also allows the crew to work in a smaller area of the set and shoot the second character in a different setup.

In the scene after the murder, Thelma and Louise are sitting at a booth in a diner. In this scene, the characters are static, but the camera slowly moves in from a two-shot to a medium shot of Louise isolating her in the frame from Thelma. Again, the cropping in on Louise allows the editor the flexibility to use cross-cuts or play reaction shots as appropriate throughout the balance of the sequence.

Performances in dialogue scenes are often composites of various two-shots and reverse angles, each taken separately, so that the actual interchange between two people we see on the screen is wholly a construction created in editing. The technique of editing dialogue is so convincing that it is hard to believe that the interactions we see on the screen never happened but are only artifice. To create a believable illusion of an actual conversation taking place, our editing technique must be subtle and unobtrusive.

One editing technique we use to make our dialogue scenes flow smoothly is to avoid cutting only when one character stops talking and the other character begins talking. If we have a dialogue where the conversation goes back and forth, and if we cut back and forth always at the point where the delivery changes hands, after a few cuts the result is a kind of ping-pong oscillation that seems very artificial. It makes the dialogue sound like each statement is a mini-monologue spoken only for the camera rather than a response to what the other has just said.

To prevent the ping-pong effect, we employ a technique called an *overlapping edit,* or *split edit.* This simply means that we cut the picture from one person to the other at different places than where we cut the sound. On the screen, for example, we see one character talking and then cut to the other listening as we hear the first character finishing his or her lines. Because well-constructed sentences or sentence clusters build to an important point—a noun, a question, a phrase at the end—a good place to cut is just before the important point so the audience can see the impact of its delivery in a reaction shot. In *Thelma & Louise,* when the two women are in the car and Louise tells Thelma of her plans to go to Mexico, naturally we want to see how Thelma is reacting to the proposition. After Louise's statement, we cut to Thelma for her reaction while we continue to hear Louise's voice demanding that Thelma make a decision. We watch Thelma struggle with the choices.

A second variation is to have one character finish speaking, but then hold the shot and watch the reaction that follows with the other character responding off-frame. We then cut to the second character in mid-speech.

Cross-cutting dialogue becomes, then, a kind of adroit dance, slipping and sliding picture edits in front of, behind, and directly on sound cuts. Intelligent editing will use this technique to complement mood, speech rhythms, and dramatic content to create a seamless, credible portrayal of human conversation.

Cutaways and cross-cutting are the primary devices that editors use to condense time and mask physical changes in the scene. Recall the example of the two shots at the restaurant we used near the beginning of this chapter. Each shot showed various changes—patrons, waiters, dishes, candles, and so on. Suppose we take a third shot of someone *not* in the two wide shots, perhaps the restaurant owner talking to the cashier. If we insert this shot between the two wide shots of the patrons at the tables, the audience will believe that all of the changes that appear in the second wide shot occurred while they were momentarily watching the owner with the cashier.

Cutaways not only enable us to bring together two shots that would otherwise jump-cut, they also enable us to condense screen time devoted to an action. In *Thelma & Louise,* during the scenes at the roadhouse, cutaways of the singer get both Thelma and Louise on the dance floor. At the end of the attempted rape sequence, a cutaway to the now dead Harlan allows Thelma to get the car in a matter of seconds so that they can make their getaway. Primarily the use of cutaways to condense time is not to make major time shifts, but minor adjustments that appear natural and go unnoticed by the audience.

Cutaways are especially important in documentary production where we can't always plan our strategy for editing shots together for continuity. To take a simple example, suppose we have a MCU shot of a person explaining something at great length to another person. Sensing redundancy, on completion of the diatribe, we shoot a reaction shot of the person who is listening. During editing if we cut out the repetitive middle and insert our reaction shot we can create the illusion of continuous yet concise dialogue.

In documentary situations, one simplistic strategy to avoid jump-cuts is to make sure we never take more than one shot of the same thing. Each shot at a different location is a cutaway to every other shot, preserving our continuity. For example, suppose we are shooting documentary footage at a county fair. If we take one shot at the pie counter, one shot at the cow competition, one shot at the loop-the-loop, and so on and if the same people are not seen or recognizable in any two shots in sequence, we can cut the shots together in any order. The problem with limiting ourselves to one shot per action is that we have no material with which to build sequences of continuous action that involve more than one shot. The rendition of the fair will seem very episodic and fragmented, like a slide show with moving images. We can't create a sense of any ongoing actions and events over several shots. Obviously we must learn to complement this type of cutaway strategy with other techniques.

Cutaways may be of inanimate objects pertinent to the plot—the bottle of whiskey in the apartment of the alcoholic who professes to be on the wagon, the eyeglasses of the victim lying inconspicuously in the grass, the keys to the car left in the ignition. A cutaway may provide details of environment that reflect on a subject's personality and character—the teenager's childhood toy, the widow's companion cat, the soldier's family snapshot. We must exercise some care when shooting inanimate cutaways so they don't look artificially intrusive in the flow of the production. One solution is to shoot cutaways of inanimate objects near the camera position for the previous shot, or from a character's point of view. Maintaining the point of view, either of the objective camera or of a character, helps weave these shots into the action inconspicuously.

Directors frequently create cutaway material by setting up parallel action. Parallel action is an efficient way of storytelling that systematically enables cross-cutting and time compression. Parallel action is a familiar device in which we show two actions taking place more or less simultaneously and cut back and forth between the scenes. The most obvious examples of this in *Thelma & Louise* are the phone calls between Thelma and Louise and later between Louise and Jimmy as we also watch Thelma at the pool. Each of these sequences contain two separate scenes and we cross-cut between them. In parallel action, each scene acts as a cutaway to the other. When we cut from a scene and back again, the action can be far advanced, and we gain the powerful advantages of dynamic time compression, the dramatic possibilities of heightened tension, and the comparison of analogous actions between the two scenes.

Sometimes our scenes involve characters doing actions in solitude. This provides less opportunity for cross-cutting because there is no other character or group with which to establish cutaways or parallel action. If we have someone painting a picture, writing a love letter, or chopping lettuce with no one else there, we can perhaps cutaway once or twice to an inanimate object—the brushes and palette, a picture of the beloved, or a tomato—but the possibilities are limited. The solution is to divide the person into two sections—the head and the hands. We show the hands doing the action without showing the head, then we cut away to a MCU or CU of the person looking at what they're doing, concentrating, thinking, being careful. The subject's face, their reaction shot, cross-cuts with the action progressing in their hands. This is especially useful in a documentary in which following complicated hand movement may be essential.

Cutaways are very useful for condensing the time it takes to render action on the screen. For example, suppose we want to create a scene of someone chopping down a tree with an axe. The actual time it takes to chop down a hardwood tree a foot in diameter may be a half hour or more. If constrained to showing the action in real time, we could devote half an hour to the action and the scene will be long and tedious. What can we cut away to? The answer may be in the nature of the sequence itself. If this production is about the impact of deforestation on the local flora and fauna, a cutaway could perhaps be a squirrel running along the ground and up another tree. We could cut away to the neighbors looking over the fence with alarm, worried that the tree will fall on their house. We can also divide the action into two or more areas for photography: the woodcutter's face in a CU, another CU or MCU of the cut in the tree with each stroke of the blade making it deeper, and perhaps a MS or MWS of the lumberjack from a frontal angle where it is impossible to see the progress of the cutting. We can start the scene with our subject swinging the axe into the tree for the first few bites, then cut away to the frontal shot for a blow or two. When we cut back to the person cutting the tree, the action can have progressed by five minutes or so, although the cutaway was less than a few seconds. Now in the MCU we see that a clean, deep wedge has been cut and the axe buries itself with every stroke. Another cutaway, of the neighbors, the squirrel, or of the woodsman's determined face, and we can return to a tree nearly cut through. Thus, with a few cutaways lasting only seconds, we can cover and compress action lasting minutes.

The cutaway directs the eyes of the audience away from the main action into space not occupied by the subject. Cutaways may involve more than one shot, but during the cutaway, we are causing the audience to turn away from the space where the subject is and look at something or someone else. Ideally what we select for the audience should advance the action, explicate the drama, or expand our awareness of the character.

Cutaways that are irrelevant to the action, but look like they mean something—death, repressed sexual desire, on-looking nature, spiritual witness (especially with trees if the sun is seen through the branches), or the eye of God—slow the development of the production and create confusion rather than understanding. In fact, unless we develop the cutaway as a symbol internally within the action (as is the forest in Kurosawa's *Rashomon,* or the spider in Bergman's *Through a Glass Darkly*), their use is often fairly silly.

The challenge in shooting and editing cutaways is to find shots that provide both continuity and dramatic texture. A classic example of the problem might involve a scene in which kids are getting on a bus to take a field trip. We have shots of kids in line single-file climbing on board, while teachers and perhaps a few parents provide assistance. If this is a documentary, the next shot we are likely to take is looking down the aisle of the bus after all the kids have gotten on, probably with the bus moving and scenery passing outside the windows. Obviously the transition from kids getting on the stationary bus to the same kids in their seats with the bus moving is a jump-cut. Is there a cutaway we can use to cover the transition? A very poor but too often used cutaway is a close-up of the bus tire starting to roll. Although it bridges the transition, such a shot makes no sense dramatically. Here we are watching kids and teachers, when suddenly our nose gets jammed in front of a bus wheel. Far better to show a teacher or parent waving goodbye, or show an interior shot of the bus—a kid hiding behind a seat perhaps—which doesn't show whether or not the bus is moving.

Cut-Ins or Inserts

Sometimes we don't want to redirect the audience's attention away from the main scene, but still need to momentarily conceal the subject from the audience for purposes of continuity, time compression, or dramatic emphasis. A third continuity device that serves this need is the cut-in, or *insert*.

Like the cutaway, the cut-in or insert diverts the audience's attention away from the main subject. The difference is that the cut-in narrows our view to a small portion of a larger scene, forcing us to look at someone or something in close-up or greater detail and preventing us from seeing changes that may be occurring in the larger surroundings beyond the frame line. It's a bit like putting blinders on the audience, confining and directing their attention, and obscuring the activities going on around them. The intent is for the audience to believe that something in the scene is essential and deserves close attention at this point in the production and not that we are resolving problems of discontinuity or manipulating time and space. Thus cut-ins *should* be of shots that *do* deserve emphasis.

Most of the cut-ins in *Thelma & Louise* clearly deserve emphasis: the shots of Harlan's hands as he attempts to remove Thelma's clothes, the close-up of the gun when Louise shoots Harlan, the cut-in after the pan to the police computer screen listing automobiles registered by the Arkansas Department of Motor Vehicles. Each of these shots deserves the dramatic impact of a close-up.

Beyond the dramatic emphasis of the close-up, there are times when we wish to shift time or space, remove redundant material, or cover discontinuities during the cut-in. In these cases, the cut-in works similarly to the cutaway. The important difference is that the cut-in shows a smaller portion of the larger scene. Thus, although cut-ins conceal changes in the wider scene that would otherwise jump-cut, the small portion of the scene that they do show must match with what we saw of that same area in the wider scene.

Suppose we have a scene of a woman entering a room and putting a recently received, but as yet unopened, letter on a table. We clearly see the letter as a detail within this wider shot. We cut to a close-up of the letter to see that it has a postmark that bears significantly on the story. When we make this cut to the close-up, the details of the letter on the table must match what we have just seen in the wider shot. If we see her put down the letter diagonally near the corner of the table, but then we see the letter placed more squarely in the center of the table in the close-up, there will be a jump-cut. As with a cutaway, when we cut back to the wider scene, our character may have moved so that she is now about to sit in a chair and pick up the phone to call a number she is reading from a phone book. As an audience, we will believe that while we were looking at the close-up of the letter, the woman crossed the room and opened the phone book. The cut-in close-up of the letter, inserted between the two wider shots, creates the illusion of the woman's continuous action while condensing the action and time.

Cut-ins often look a little artificial and contrived for the camera. As with the cutaway, one solution is to shoot the cut-in from near the camera position of the outgoing shot. In addition, it often helps if the cut-in serves as a transitional shot to another camera angle or even as the last shot before a transition to a new sequence. Returning to the continuation of the shot before the cut-in sometimes contributes to a self-conscious feel because the audience understands that cut-ins cover an ellipsis in time and expect it.

The most common cut-in is probably a reaction shot MCU inserted after a wider two-shot. When two people are in dialogue, we usually see the two characters together in the same shot, at least at the beginning. Usually such a shot favors the speaker, who is shown in some version of a three-quarter front, and we shoot the listener from behind, over the shoulder in a three-quarter rear angle. An experienced director for such a scene, both in documentary and in theatrical production, invariably shoots one or several reverse reaction shots—a MCU of the person listening. The cut-in of the listener prevents us from seeing the speaker so that changes in head position and posture can occur unnoticed. This shot works the same as a cutaway reverse, allowing the editor to cut lines of dialogue in the speaker's performance, if necessary, or cover any other discontinuity.

Documentary directors and camerapersons develop an observant eye for unchanging but relevant details in a scene that can be used for cut-ins. The easiest subjects to find in a location for cut-ins are inanimate objects because they do not move unless picked up. It is often helpful to have a character glance at the object so that the eye movement can help motivate the cut-in to the object. A cut-in to a typewriter sitting on an author's desk, an open suitcase of a teenager preparing to leave home, or a cutting board with chopped onions in the kitchen of a cook preparing dinner—these are natural cut-ins that can build texture and relevant detail in a scene and provide continuity to cover potential jump-cuts.

Directors also keep an eye out for animate subjects that are temporarily motionless, for example, a student in a class who does not change position and whose eyes remain directed toward the teacher. With such a shot for a cut-in, we can condense the action in the scene shown in the wider shots of the class. The audience assumes the changes took place in the wider scene, while they were looking closely at the one student. Only the position of the student we cut in to has to match to the wider shots. The student reaction shot serves the "classroom sequence," providing interest and meaningful commentary, while giving the editor flexibility for structuring the scene.

Like the cutaway, cut-ins enable us to condense screen time, shortening the time it takes us to show a complete action or process. Unlike cutaways, however, cut-ins not only keep the focus on the principal action but emphasize it due to their close-up characteristic. They are as important for intensifying the drama as for providing a continuity cutting device.

The Match-Cut

The match-cut is the most obvious continuity edit. It conveys the illusion that there has been no elapsed time and that although the camera position may have changed, there has been no physical change from the previous shot. Everything matches. Therefore, it's one of the most difficult and thus less frequently used techniques.

In fact, if you have examined closely the opening scene of *Thelma & Louise,* you may have realized that the first cutaway sequence of Louise pouring coffee for the two women in the booth in the restaurant has jump-cuts in it. It appears from her body movement that Louise pours coffee for the blonde woman twice, and there is also a mismatch of Sarandon's arm in the cut to the blonde woman from the previous shot. Perhaps you may have also noticed that the level of Louise's drink at the roadhouse is inconsistent from shot to shot.

These examples clearly point out the difficulties in making match cuts, but this is no reason to shy away from using them as a continuity device. Obviously small discontinuities do pass unnoticed when the dramatic action is strong enough, or when the audience is clearly looking at a character's eyes and face during a scene and a mismatch is inconspicuous enough to go unnoticed. What is important is that the shots *appear* to match.

Executing a match-cut is very simple, but we need to watch three points. First, the action and position of everything the audience sees in the scene at the end of one shot obviously should match closely with the action and position of everything they can see within the frame at the beginning of the next shot. Second, it helps if there is movement in the first shot that matches to movement in the second shot. Finally, the framing of the image should change a full size from, say, a medium shot to a close-up or a medium wide shot to a medium close shot or the camera angle should shift at least thirty degrees of arc around the subject. Then the cut should pass by the audience unnoticed.

Providing action for the editor to cut on is very important. Suppose we take a medium wide shot of a person strolling along on a city street. Then suppose we take a second shot, a medium close-up of the person's feet walking on the sidewalk. If the shots are done correctly, we can edit these two shots together so that, in mid-stride, we can cut the two shots together and see the person walking as one continuous action.

Of course, everything else the audience can see in the frame should be the same for the match-cut to be successful. For example, if we saw the person in the medium wide shot on a sidewalk, but then cut to the feet walking on grass, we would have a jump-cut. Or, if our character were wearing a different pair of shoes, the shots would not match, although the audience may not notice if the shoes were not obvious in the wider shot, or if other elements of the *mise en scène* or drama were distracting them. Also, if the person is walking quickly in the medium wide shot, but slowly in the medium close-up, we would have an instantaneous change of pace that would ruin the match-cut. Naturally, if the person is about to step on the right foot in the medium wide shot, but then the left foot comes down after the edit, we would have a major mismatch of action.

If we achieved continuity of the action but still had discontinuity in lighting or sound, the match would be ruined. For instance, if the first shot were shot when the sun was out and the next when a cloud had passed in front of the sun or if shadows had shifted drastically due to a later time of day, it could be a very noticeable jump-cut. The light, especially the foreground and background levels, needs to match. Everything has to work!

When there is fluidity of movement through the cut, the cut goes by unnoticed because the eye is following the action. Walking is typical of the kind of action in which we make match-cuts. It is a cyclical movement with periods of acceleration and deceleration. One foot, then the other is raised, swung forward, and set down. If we have a medium wide shot and a medium close-up of this action, we theoretically can choose any number of points where we can make the shots match. We may cut, for example, as the foot rises from behind, at the top of the arc as a foot swings forward, as the foot descends to the ground, or immediately after it touches the ground.

However, when a foot is at the top of the arc and when both feet are planted, the body shifts weight, momentarily making two almost imperceptible pauses in the cycle. We find that match-cuts are smoother, most transparent, and least obvious when we avoid these pauses and make them during the moments of smooth action—right after the foot passes the top of the arc and is swinging forward and down, for example.

Although not a "rule," if about one-third of the action of the foot leaving the ground is in the first shot and two-thirds of the movement—the foot swinging forward and hitting the ground—is in the second shot, the edit will feel more natural and it seems as if the action is moving us forward in the story. Cutting a third of the way into the action ensures you are cutting as the action is speeding up and not slowing toward the pause.

Many actions, such as hammering a nail or sawing wood, have this pattern of action and momentary pause, like walking. As with walking, we find that we can make the smoothest match-cut on accelerating action, after the hammer has begun to descend about one-third the distance toward the nail or after the saw has been pushed one-third of the way through the stroke.

In the opening of *Thelma & Louise,* the first real match-cut is of Louise, on the phone to Thelma, as she pushes through the swinging door to the back room of the diner. As she hits the door with her back to the camera, there is a brief pause. Then she pushes the door about one-third of the way open. The editor then cuts to the interior of the back room as the action continues, and Louise makes her entrance in one fluid movement. This first match-cut with the reversal of action follows the "rule" of changing angles at least thirty degrees. In fact, because it is a reverse in the angle as the action passes through, it is interesting that the angles are matching mirror reverse angles. The first shot from the kitchen is a chest-high medium shot from about Sarandon's seven o'clock. The back room shot is the same framing, but this time it's from Sarandon's eleven o'clock. Matching reverse angles contribute to the fluidity of the movement. In the shot of Thelma passing by the camera on her way to the dining room we discussed earlier, the size of both shots is identical and the angles are again mirror images of each other.

Many times an action that at first glance appears continuous, such as walking through a door or picking up a pen, is actually a series of movements with brief hesitations between each. Reaching for and turning a doorknob is an example. The hand reaches for the knob, and then pauses after it grasps it before turning or pulling. As expected, we find the smoothest match-cut from a medium shot to a close-up of the hand is on the action as the hand is moving toward the doorknob. When staging action or following action in a documentary, it may seem normal to cut the camera on one of these completed actions. But, unless this shot ends the scene or sequence and thus you really want this pause, it is better to let the camera roll until the next action has begun, and then repeat or overlap the action in the next take.

In the shot of Louise going through the door, Thom Noble could have made the cut on that brief pause as Sarandon gathers her muscles for the push on the door. Instead he let the action of the push through the door begin before the cut. During production, we assume that Sarandon went through the door at least twice—once from the camera angle in the kitchen and once from the camera angle in the back room. In other words, to make the match perfectly, she repeated the action identically—the same hand in the same place on the door and at the same rate of speed.

Repeating action in precisely the same way is one of the most important abilities film and television actors have over their colleagues on the stage. The traditions of the theater dictate that each performance is at least somewhat a reinterpretation of the role. In addition, missing a mark on the stage may mean the actor isn't standing as directly in a light as the director blocked for that scene, but the audience probably won't notice. In film and television, because of the critical nature of focus and because we need to match actions from one shot to the next, hitting marks and repeating actions are important skills that we look for in our performers.

For a match-cut to work, overlapping action *must* be repeated. Simply stopping action midway through, reframing a new shot, and then completing the action won't work. We can't have someone reaching for the doorknob, or starting the glass to their lips, or whatever the action is, in a medium shot and then ask the talent to stop and wait for us to reframe a close-up before completing the action. If we direct action in this way, we will see the hand slow and come to a momentary rest in the medium shot and then move away from the stationary pause in the close-up. No matter how tightly we try to cut these shots, we will never get rid of the awkward change in pace or momentary hesitation of the action emphasized by the cut. It will feel as though the film or video paused and then lurched forward.

In some situations, action does halt for something significant to take place. Consider the action of someone looking at their watch when the pressure of time is important, or picking up and reading a note that is vital to the plot. Suppose we want to cut from a medium shot to an over-the-shoulder close-up of the watch or of the hand holding the note. Showing the move in a medium shot and then shooting a static close-up of the posed hand usually looks stilted and contrived when the shots are edited together. A more successful alternative is to shoot the move of the hand moving into position twice, both in the medium shot and in the close-up. Then, in editing, we can cut on the action so that we see the hand begin to move into position in the medium shot and complete the move and come to rest in the close-up. This avoids the sense of a pose, and the effect is more natural and seamless.

Another situation in which directors sometimes neglect shooting for a match-cut on action is when a character first notices and then looks at something intently, perhaps setting up a point-of-view shot. The person turns the head or looks up in a medium shot, and then there is a cut to a static close-up of the character's head, posed in an intent look. Again, the effect of these shots when edited together will be very unconvincing. It will have the appearance of double action. It's far better to shoot the glance and head move in both a medium shot and a close-up, then cut into the close-up on movement as the character turns the head and reacts.

The next match in *Thelma & Louise* is when Thelma takes the gun from the drawer. This is an ideal example of where a novice might have the talent open the drawer and then cut to the gun. But, in the movie, the match-cut follows the technique we have described. There is a shift in camera angle as well as in image size. It takes place on the action as Davis begins to open the drawer to the night table. About one-third the way through the action, we cut from the medium shot of Davis to the close-up of the drawer that shows the gun.

To cut on action, we must shoot our shots so that they overlap. In shooting theatrical work, we direct shots so that there is action before the beginning and after the end of the desired shot. For example, suppose we are shooting shots three, four, and five of a shot script for a drama. When we take shot four, we do not begin the action right at the beginning of shot four, but somewhere before the last complete action in shot three. Also, we do not stop shooting at the end of shot four, but we continue into the action of the first part of shot five. That way, when editing, shot four will not start from a pose and end in a pose, but will be in full movement from beginning to end. Even when we aren't anticipating a match-cut, this gives the editor the flexibility to find the best edit for continuity, rhythm, and dramatic emphasis. Not remarkably, even perfectly preplanned scenes often need a different approach by the editor than the one envisioned by the writer or director.

Given the fact that match-cutting depends on repeatable action, it might seem that the technique is rarely possible in documentary and can only be accomplished in theatrical or industrial productions in which we can ask talent to repeat actions to provide overlaps for cutting on movement. Actually we find that match-cutting is easy in documentary because many actions that people do naturally are repetitive.

Consider a documentary scene of someone doing the dishes by hand, without the assistance of a dishwasher. (As with all film and video scenes, we make choices because of photographic opportunities as well as dramatic logic and potential.) The actions of picking up a dirty dish, inserting it into the suds, scrubbing, rinsing the dish under running water, and stacking it into a dish drainer are done repeatedly. It is easy to shoot a MWS of our character picking up a dish and putting it into the suds, reframe and take a close-up of the hands scrubbing another but similar dish not distinguishable from the one seen in the MWS, and then take a third MS of the character removing yet another but similar dish from the suds to rinse under the water and stack. The subject of the documentary washes three different dishes, but we shoot and edit the scene to give the illusion of washing one dish in a continuous flow of action.

This may seem like a special case, but it's not. The world is full of repetitive actions. Many activities involve such repetition, and documentary film and video makers develop a high level of awareness and sensitivity to repeated actions and gestures.

Differences in framing between shots is the third consideration when shooting for a match-cut. If shots to be match-cut are too similar in composition, we will not see a clean match-cut, but two shots that "pop" on the screen or give the audience the feeling they have lurched toward or away from the subject. For example, if we have a shot of a character in a close-up and then a second shot in a medium close-up, we will see the figure appear to hop away from us across the cut rather than having a clear sense of a new point of view.

At the opposite extreme, if the change in framing is too great—if we cut from a wide shot to a close-up, for example—the effect is quite jolting and can seem crude, uncontrolled, or dramatically overstated unless there is justification for a "shock-cut." Generally, as stated earlier, seamless editing takes place over shots that change a complete "size" from ECU to MCU, CU to MS, MCU to MWS, or MS to WS.

Another consideration when shooting shots intended for match-cutting is the transition in angle. For example, if we intend to cut from a three-quarter front medium shot to a three-quarter front close-up, we find that the cut usually works best if we shoot the close-up a little more frontally, showing more face to the audience, than in the medium shot. Also, if we are looking at a person from a high angle in the medium shot and we want to maintain that perspective as we cut to the close-up, we should drop the camera down as we move it closer to the subject. If we mount the camera on a tripod and simply keep it at the same height as we move in on the subject for the close-up, our final angle will be higher.

Generally we want to avoid having our angles seem arbitrary as we match-cut from one shot to another. If we cut from a three-quarter front to a three-quarter rear, the angles should be complementary. If we take the front shot from the position of one o'clock, the rear should be from five o'clock. If the three-quarter front shot is more of a profile at the position of two o'clock, the three-quarter rear should be from the position of four o'clock. Changing both angles and image size is often an effective transition over a match-cut.

Intentional Jump-Cuts

Audiences are pretty smart. They know that a jump-cut means time has jumped—that an editor has removed material from the production. Thus we can use jump-cuts for precisely those reasons to convey discontinuous time or space.

There are several jump-cuts in *Thelma & Louise,* but the most interesting, perhaps, is in the roadhouse sequence. Both Thelma and Louise have gotten up to dance. It is now important that time has passed. Thelma is drunker and has gotten far too friendly with Harlan. It's handled with a jump-cut. People are dancing to one song, and then there is a jump cut to another song with a different rhythm and the people on the floor doing a different kind of dance. The effect is the same as if they'd cut to a clock and shown the hands spinning around. Time has passed. Things have changed.

Television interviews use this technique to indicate an ellipsis in an interview. It is a way of telling an audience that it is seeing excerpts and not a complete interview. It is like the three dots (...) in quoted material. And, because it represents a form of honesty by the editor to communicate that the work has been manipulated, advertisers use the same technique to suggest that the staged testimonial being presented is part of a lengthier, testimonial-type interview. It creates a pretense of honesty in their visual presentation.

Orchestrating Continuity

From our descriptions and examples of these different continuity techniques, it should be obvious that they have different qualities and can serve different purposes. It also should be clear that it is essential to plan in order for the editor to have cutting material. The way we plan our continuity in scenes and sequences also affects the "feel" of our scenes, as influential and expressive as *mise en scène,* camera, and lighting technique.

One lesson we learn early is not to use the same technique again and again, too many times in a row. Repetition of the same continuity technique over many cuts becomes obvious and artificial. The artifice becomes apparent, and the illusion of reality on the screen is broken. Selecting and varying the continuity cuts we use as we proceed from shot to shot in a scene or sequence is like playing a five-string guitar, with each cut—match-cut, cutaway, cut-in, off-screen action, and even the intentional jump-cut—having its own tone.

Shooting Strategies for Editing

There are two distinct strategies for shooting and editing continuity—the *master scene* approach and the *shot-by-shot,* which is sometimes called the *by-three's* approach. Multiple camera strategies and combinations of the two basic approaches are available to the director for various styles of continuity scene construction.

Master Scene

The classic, Hollywood master scene method of continuity involves shooting complete setups, whole scenes, or large portions of scenes in wide shots that cover extended sequences of action. Then the camera is moved to various angles and framings—medium shots, close-ups, reverse angles—repeating all or part of the actions covered in the master shots and shooting from these different positions. An editor then builds scenes by selecting from several shots of the same action. This method provides enormous flexibility in editing, enabling the editor to modulate nuances of performance and tightly control the pace, rhythms, and screen time of a scene by the wide selection of shots available and the many opportunities for cut-ins, cutaways, and match-cuts. In addition, the coverage of a scene by the master shot assures the director and editor that there will always be usable footage of the action without jump-cuts.

The drawback of the master scene method is a formulaic style of editing and a certain lack of fluidity on the screen. In addition, the talent must make repeated performances, sometimes out of sequence, and these can sometimes get wooden. However, the benefits afforded by the ability to control pacing may outweigh these problems if the talent can maintain a high quality of performance over many repetitions and there is photographic variety among the scenes.

From a director's point of view, an enormous amount of control is given to the editor, not only in structuring the scene, but in the ability to play dialogue in close-up, medium, or wide shots, or even in three-quarter rear and reaction shots. The editor can diminish or enhance a character's role in a production in ways the director did not intend. Imagine the change in the emphasis of a scene if, instead of ending the sequence on the hero's forceful close-up, it ends on the heroine's skeptical reaction shot! There is great power in this kind of editing to interpret or reinterpret the treatment of the production. It is interesting when watching films to see if there is a master camera angle and framing that the editor returns to in the construction of the scene.

By-Threes

The shot-by-shot, or by-threes, method is very different. It involves shooting each shot with three shots in mind—the shot we are taking, the shot that will precede it, and the shot that will follow it. Each shot is a link in a chain connecting to two other shots, and we plan the continuity transitions at the beginning and end of each shot ahead of time or at least on the fly as we shoot sequences.

Characteristically, when photographing the shot-by-shot method, the camera follows action. Rather than having actors moving in the proscenium arch of the wide shot, a moving medium shot brings the audience closer to the action and draws them into the set. We choreograph the camera work in coordination with talent and other movement so that one lengthy shot encompasses large portions of the action in a scene. This is a great help to many actors who prefer the longer take to develop their performance. The talent and the director can work for best performance and move on without having to repeat it again and again. This is especially good where emotional build is essential to the scene. Thus long takes and the *mise en scène* styles of scene construction are characteristic of this style of photography and editing.

Because each take involves complete action for a particular setup or scene, on-screen and off-screen action, and cutaway continuity techniques are another characteristic of the by-threes method. Matching action is less frequently used. Altman's work, such as *The Player, M*A*S*H*, and *McCabe and Mrs. Miller* provide good examples of this style.

Although some shots may overlap at the beginning and end, there is less coverage of action from multiple angles and essentially the editor must make predetermined edits. Obviously, without a master shot and with less coverage of action, we increase the possibility of inadvertent jump-cuts. Also, the editor's control of timing, pacing, and rhythm is less flexible. The creative decisions are made ahead of time, during scripting and shooting. If we make a miscalculation in the frenzied atmosphere of a production, the editor has limited ability to fix the problem in post-production. The editor has very little chance to shift emphasis or alter pacing. In addition, because there is a tendency to encompass all action in one long take, the production can get episodic in nature unless the editor takes great care to provide visual interest, usually by camera movement and cutaways. The director must concentrate on strong visual compositions of individual shots.

Documentary production is shot and edited in a by-threes approach because in most real, ongoing situations it is not possible to shoot a master scene and then go back and repeat the action for various other angles unless we are shooting repeatable action. Similarly, shooting by-three's does not depend on a person's ability to repeat lines and actions exactly as shooting a master scene approach requires. Finally, because there is less redundancy of covering the same action by many different shots, the by-three's approach consumes less footage—an important consideration in low-budget productions, especially in film.

Multiple Camera

Television, with its ability to switch or edit between several mobile multiple-camera positions, has given us an interesting version of the master scene style of production. With one or all cameras simultaneously recording during a performance, there is always real-time coverage of the production with plenty of opportunities for cutaway, cut-in, or off-screen and on-screen continuity. Actors have the luxury of rendering fairly long, uninterrupted scenes. Multiple camera strategies allow combinations of master scene and by-three styles of production. Because television is a smaller screen and a more intimate presentation, we can use tighter framing coupled with deep focus photography to establish locations and create spatial relationships. Thus we can orient the audience to a location's space by the depth of a medium or medium wide shot, as opposed to using the wider framings designed to play in movie houses.

A Marriage of Styles

The impact of television-style production and the recognition that the ultimate distribution medium for most feature films is video have contributed to the style of photography in many contemporary films such as *Thelma & Louise*. The technique is predominantly a by-threes style. It is characterized by long, beautifully choreographed camera moves such as the opening shot in the diner as Louise moves through, serving her customers, or later when she receives the phone call from Thelma and the cook picks up the phone and Louise takes it from him. However, although the editor may never use the master shot, or wide shot that covers all the action, directors still employ master scene strategy in scenes that involve dialogue or complicated action. They will have the actors repeat the action from two or more camera positions in medium shots or medium close-ups, and then restage portions for close-up for cut-ins.

A good example of this technique is in the scene where Harlan is attempting to rape Thelma. There are two "master" angles, one left of Harlan's shoulder and the other to the right and behind Thelma. The editor then intercut both angles and included the cut-ins, as mentioned earlier, to create the sequence. This gives flexibility to both the editor and performer, keeps most of the control with the director, and gives the audience a closer style of photography that is more intimate for ultimate television viewing. A good way to understand this camera and editing technique is to compare films such as the older and newer versions of *Henry V* or *Cape Fear*.

Shooting for Montage Editing

Although the desire to create believable scenes and sequences causes continuity editing techniques to dominate most film and video productions, it is not the only way to structure shots. Montage editing is the second method of organizing a shot sequence. "Montage" is a French word meaning editing, and it refers to cutting for continuity and also to every other form of shot sequencing. However, in current parlance, we associate montage with the juxtaposition of noncontinuous shots that are coherent and form sequences, yet are very different from continuity editing, serving very different purposes.

Montage Theory

When discussing montage, a distinction must be made between the use of the word as it is used in contemporary production and the use of the word as it refers to the classic theory of film formulated by the great Russian director and theorist, Sergei Eisenstein. For Eisenstein, film editing created meaning by means of the dynamic juxtaposition of images. Borrowing from the Hegelian philosophic foundations of communism, Eisenstein theorized that ideas could be synthesized in film by fusing dissimilar elements (thesis and antithesis). Although this may sound superficial or too abstract, Eisenstein elaborated his concepts to a highly refined state and created at least one great film, *Potemkin*, based on the principles derived from his theory. Ultimately, however, he did find the theory limiting and, as one of the original inventors of film form, expanded his repertoire of technique to achieve more dramatically fluid, less formulaic work.

All students of film and video should become familiar with Eisenstein's theories, but they should also realize that in professional production today, the term "montage" has quite a different meaning than Eisenstein's classical definition.

Montage Editing

Montage editing is a technique that composes shots associated by subject or theme in a way that conveys mood and ideas. Rather than ordering shots to create an illusion of chronological continuity, montage editing arranges shots by association to create an impression of the subject. If continuity editing attempts to convey a sense of real events taking place, montage editing attempts to express impressions and ideas through the composition of images and sound. Montage editing is like musical arranging. It is principally evocative and depends heavily on rhythm and visual design for formal structure. It is the method of many commercials, music videos, and opening title sequences in films.

In *Thelma & Louise,* the packing scene is an excellent example of montage editing. Packing to go is not essential to moving the story along. Its purpose is more to develop the differences in the two characters. Louise is neat and prim in her packing, suggesting that her life may be structured but drab. Thelma, the exact opposite, suggests a character who has no control over the chaos of her life. This is essential to the characterization as we see Louise later in the film become less "uptight" and Thelma begin to take more charge. Thus each shot supports the theme of the sequence. The montage also serves to introduce Jimmy, by his photograph on Louise's dresser, and the gun that Thelma puts in her purse.

To accomplish the sequence, Callie Khouri clearly indicated the parallel action between the two different locations in her screenplay. The shots were carefully planned during preproduction with each incoming and outgoing shot composition designed to relate the design elements and the action and movements within the shots while developing the thematic counterpoint. In the first shot of the montage, Thelma, her hair in rollers, walks down-screen from the bed leaving her suitcase opened. Standing screen left, she opens a closet. The cross-cut to Louise has her in the same position as Thelma, with her hair tightly pinned to her head. She moves forward and snaps open a plastic bag and, in a cut, puts shoes in it and places the bag in her suitcase. The cut to Thelma has her picking up dresses, the exact opposite of Louise's action. Cut to Louise, camera left as she is placing neatly folded shirts in her case. Back to Thelma as she, camera right with an opened drawer matching the location of the suitcase, drops something in and then pulls out the entire drawer, which we follow in a CU as it swings screen right, getting dumped into the suitcase. Next, there is a medium shot of Louise, center frame, looking in a mirror as she puts on her jacket. Then, in an intentional jump-cut, she is still center frame, but now in a three-quarter rear shot, facing screen left, on the telephone. The next cut is to Thelma, center frame in a medium shot, who swings screen left to pull open the drawer of the night table. This is followed by the CU shot of her retrieving the gun, as mentioned earlier. It is a wonderfully planned and edited sequence with each action, movement, and camera shot carefully planned to lead the audience's eye through the sequence. Although the actions are parallel, they differ from the parallel action cutting mentioned earlier. This sequence was clearly planned to support theme and characterization in a montage edited sequence.

In both theatrical and documentary productions, we often find we can effectively set a scene, define a theme, and establish a mood by abandoning continuity editing in favor of a montage sequence. For many producers, creating a montage sequence is a little like being let out of jail. The technique is so flexible and expressive compared to the more restrictive structures of continuity that it seems a more pure artistic form.

Montage sequences are designed to have expressive impact and can stand out in a production as especially memorable. The opening of *Apocalypse Now* in the Saigon hotel room, the weapons-making sequence in *Taxi Driver,* the sightseeing plane ride in *Out of Africa,* the steam bath scene in *McCabe and Mrs. Miller,* the wedding scene in *The Deer Hunter,* and Lee Marvin's wonderful regeneration from drunkard back to gunslinger in *Cat Ballou* are just some montage compositions that come to mind as memorable cinematic moments.

American Montage

There is a special type of montage so identified with classic Hollywood films that it is known as *American montage.* This form of montage cuts shots together of similar actions showing transition over time. Often, clocks or calendars are included to tell the audience how much time has elapsed between each shot. Welles used the technique in *Citizen Kane,* without timekeepers, in a sequence showing Charles Foster Kane at the breakfast table with his wife. Each shot represents a step in their growing estrangement and the deterioration of their marriage. As we precede from shot to shot, we see them age, and we see the interaction between them disintegrate from pleasant conversation, through curt business references, to silence, and finally to Kane hiding behind a newspaper.

Another example of American montage showing the passage of time occurs in *The Hustler,* where a marathon pool game is presented progressing through the night and into the next day in a series of shots of pool breaks, balls being sunk, whiskey glasses, and the ever-advancing clock.

Montage editing depends on coherent theme and treatment as well as coordinated visual design. Once we have decided to treat a subject with montage, we must ask ourselves what themes we want to convey. We must decide the *treatment.* In Chapter 5, we described possible variations in a fall season montage. For a second example, suppose we want to create a montage sequence about a couple preparing for a lavish dinner party they are throwing for business associates. The construction of such a sequence begins with a clear sense of the theme we want to convey. We could make the sequence emphasize hectic and exhausting preparation, or the creation of an elegant and elaborate setting, or inexperienced inadequacy, or any other treatment that may be appropriate to the dramatic context of the action.

For our example, let us assume that we want to convey themes of elaborate embellishment and transformation from the ordinary to the elegant. The next step is to brainstorm the possibilities. We list as many types of actions and shots as we can imagine. We should think of more ideas than we will ever use; we will select the best and most mutually complementary from the list and leave the rest. Here is a beginning, a short list from what would be a much longer list of possibilities:

- Polishing silver, setting out silver
- Buying good wine, reading labels carefully
- Setting out good china and crystal
- Dusting and waxing the furniture
- Cleaning the mirrors and windows
- Ironing, spreading the tablecloth
- Buying long candles, putting them in candle holders
- Lighting candles
- Arranging fine appetizers (caviar, lox, cheeses) on a platter
- Selecting specialty items at the supermarket
- Cooking a variety of special dishes, duck perhaps (all selected for photographic opportunities)
- Setting out flowers throughout the house

This list would naturally be quite different if we were to emphasize hectic and exhausting hard work for the sequence. Now, we begin considering how to shoot these actions so that we can edit together sequences of shots that provide interesting comparisons and contrasts. This is when we begin to visualize the design elements in the shots that will make the montage sequence a visually choreographed composition.

Subject and theme may provide meaning and conceptual coherence in a montage sequence, but design and rhythm provide the formal elements of composition. For example, we may decide that our montage of preparing for the dinner party should evolve from flat, lusterless monochromes to sparkling contrasts of amber and blue. Lighting candles and putting out silver and crystal glassware with lots of highlights will come toward the end of the sequence, but we might shoot ironing tablecloths and picking out wine with flatter lighting and more drab colors near the beginning. Perhaps polishing the furniture and cleaning the mirrors can provide transition to actions where colors start to brighten and objects begin to shine.

After fully imagining and developing the general structural patterns in line with the kind of possibilities we have begun to explore, the next step is to consider promising shot-to-shot design relationships. For example, a close-up of a hand placing the vertical line of a silver dinner knife next to the partial circle of a dish can be shot to create a frame similar to a close-up of a hand lighting a candle, with the vertical line of the candle next to the curved line of a flower bowl. Perhaps, we may want to reverse the design, with the curved line of the plate on screen left and the knife on the right, cut against the curved line of the flower bowl on screen right and the candle to the left.

In the preceding example, we have imagined similar designs we can create through shape. However, as we have discussed in an earlier chapter, design is more than just shape, and it can involve other elements such as color, shade, texture, and line. The finely textured filigree of the lace tablecloth might cut nicely to the similar finely textured filigree of decorative fern leaves that someone is placing in a flower arrangement.

Techniques at our disposal in montage editing include not only cutting shots together with comparable designs, but also cutting shots with contrasting designs. Movement within the frame can transform the design. Editors often cut montage sequences to music, sometimes integrated with other carefully composed sound effects. Dissolves and superimpositions often create juxtapositions and overlays of images and modulate rhythms.

Montage is an art of endless variation. A study of well-constructed montage sequences—in feature films, in commercials, in music videos, and in art film and video—is the best way to learn the possibilities and techniques of this most pure and expressive form in the visual media.

Rhythm

Rhythm is a critical element in both montage and continuity editing. In a very real way, editing is a musical form that depends on rhythm. Curiously, perhaps because of the emphasis students and teachers alike commonly place on narrative and visual forms, the foundation of rhythm in editing is often the last fundamental technique a person discovers when learning production.

Every action imparts rhythm to a shot. Walking, running, the jostling of a crowd, the movement of a hand, a kiss, the flow of every physical action, and the cadences of speech all establish rhythms within our shots that must be sensed and complemented in the editing if our scenes are to cut smoothly. Cutting on beats moves audiences unconsciously through the action and the cuts with the anticipation that comes from the subtle, rhythmic beats of a scene. A scene that is cut without beats and indifferent to the rhythms of the action seems awkward, fragmented, and arbitrary.

The rhythms of editing—either continuity or montage—are most obvious when we cut sequences to music. But even when there is no music, an editor still cuts to beats. If we walk into a professional editing room and watch a scene being cut, we often see the editor tapping one foot while pacing the rhythm of the actions and timing the cuts. As an exercise, pick a scene in any well-produced movie and practice tapping out the beats of action and where the cuts fall. A good editor will use this subtle form of audience anticipation both to satisfy and to surprise. For example, in *Psycho,* the cuts and the movement of the detective's entry into the Bates Motel and cautious climb up the stairs are edited on clear beat. However, when the mysterious, knife-wielding figure bursts from the door in the high overhead shot, it catches us by surprise on an unexpected upbeat.

As with music, the rhythms of editing in a scene can be very subtle and can include variations in measure (such as three-four, or four-four), pace (for example, fast, slow, or accelerating), and accent (on the beat, syncopation, and so on).

Patterns of Three

Analogous to the basic function of rhythm in editing is the repetition of the actions, words, and objects we establish to create patterns and motifs. Our brain seeks patterns and interprets movement rhythmically. We recognize a pattern when we see the same thing not once or twice, but three times. "Once is an accident, twice is coincidence, three times is a pattern." This phrase sounds so simplistic that to suggest it is a meaningful rule in editing probably seems silly. But it's not.

As we pointed out in Chapter 4, the use of threes is an important tool in structuring a production. Thus it is essential to the techniques of editing. We can find the use of threes in practically any good production and see it in many forms. It occurs in the repetition of three shots of the same subject to form a sequence with a sense of completion. It occurs when the same statement or observation is made three times, perhaps by three different characters, and we know something is either true or inevitable. The triad is such a natural form that we automatically use it to interpret the significance of things.

POV and Other Setups

Editing often involves planting cues, both visual and aural, which establish strong anticipations in an audience. If we follow through and deliver what the audience expects, they are usually satisfied. (Obviously, especially in narrative, if all we deliver is the expected so that the audience can predict the action and the outcomes, our work will probably be hackneyed and boring.) If we do not follow through with the expectations we set up, but offer interesting or ingenious alternatives that are of equal or greater value to the audience, we delight the audience with the unexpected developments. If, however, we establish anticipations, perhaps unintentionally, then ignore the expectations and do not deliver and have no good reason, we confuse and disappoint the audience. The impression will be that the production is incoherent, out of control, and constructed by inexperienced hands.

A sequence for a point-of-view (POV) shot, for example, begins with a character's glance—a reaction on the face as the eyes look in some direction. If we include such a shot in our editing, but then do not follow up with a POV shot of what the character is seeing, we bewilder the audience. Similarly, if we cut to a POV shot without the setup shot of a character looking, we frustrate the audience. They will not know how the shot is motivated.[3]

When we cut in to a close-up of an action or an object, we are signaling the audience that what we are seeing is important. If someone pours a glass of wine and we cut to a close-up of the glass, we are telling the audience that this wine somehow bears on the plot. If our cut to the close-up is pointless, we have led the audience to believe that the glass of wine is important, but then we betray them. The close-up is gratuitous. Throughout Danny DeVito's *Hoffa*, the camera cuts in on an object or form and uses the shape, color, or some design element to make a transition to the next sequence. The effect is like pointing to something and saying, "Made you look!" Because the object is not important, its only purpose is as a mechanical transition device. From an audience point of view, it is distracting, self-conscious, and annoying.

Editing is, above all, a matter of judgment. We must go beyond what we know we mean when we are editing, to put ourselves in the position of the audience and understand what meaning they can interpret from our presentation. When an audience surprises us by not understanding our work or by interpreting our work in an unexpected way, it's usually because we did not include the audience in our assumptions. When editing, we must see our work as the audience sees it. We structure our work in sequences that convey our meaning and make our intentions understood.

Confusion Versus Mystery

Editing, like all arts in the visual media, can be learned at the basic level in a short time, but it then takes years to master. Keeping our audience's interest during the steady revelation of new and unexpected information and withholding information until a dramatically effective moment without frustrating the audience are sophisticated skills.

Work that is intentionally incomprehensible or created to be "open to interpretation," mysterious, or paradoxical is more often annoying in its pretentious self-indulgence. Its message to the audience is that they may be too stupid to figure it out. Although the instincts to take a work beyond the obvious and touch the ambiguities of life is at the heart of serious artistic enterprise, attempting this without acknowledging the experience of the audience is naive and may rob the production of its meaning, significance, and richness of possible meanings.

Notes

1. Actually, jump-cuts can occur in scenes without breaking the flow of the narrative. However, jump-cuts that are deliberate and artfully done are the result of a controlled use of the technique. Jump-cuts that result from not knowing how to avoid them indicate a fundamental lack of skill.

2. Note that in the final shot of the scene where Louise is pouring coffee, as the coffee pot is being retracted from the scene, the woman turns her head away from Louise and drops her eyes. This dropping the eyes acts almost as a curtain coming down on the end of that scene, helping in the transition to the kitchen shot.

3. Again, it is worth noting that every technique is subject to manipulation. It is not unusual in horror movies to cut in POV shots without immediately revealing the character from whose perspective we are seeing the scene. The audience wants to see the monster through whose eyes we are seeing, but is titillated by having the information withheld until later. *Predator* uses this technique very effectively.

10

LIGHTING FOR INTERPRETATION

Film and video inherit directly from photography. Some film theorists, most notably Sigfried Kracauer,[1] have argued that photography forms the very essence of film art. Whether or not photography is the foundation of film and video aesthetics, it is true that creating and recording images made by patterns of light are fundamental to these media.

Film and video interpret subjects and scenes as images of light and shade. Of the three principal elements of cinematography—camera placement and composition, lens focal length, and lighting—DPs (Directors of Photography) usually consider lighting their greatest artistic challenge and most important responsibility. They find lighting a craft of endless elaboration and variation demanding high skill and subtlety, which can occupy a lifetime of professional development and expertise.

Lighting creates a reality for the audience. If the lighting is artificial and calls attention to itself, it breaks the illusion of reality. Lighting needs to be believable. We can destroy the believability of a well-scripted scene acted by able talent if we have lit the scene badly.

For the beginner, lighting can be a frustrating experience. Without adequate knowledge, setting up and plugging in high-wattage lighting instruments on location can blow electrical circuits, as well as the patience of talent and crew. To make matters worse, the results can look extremely artificial—hard lights harshly illuminating subjects with hot spots, glaring backgrounds, and deep, unwanted shadows. Sometimes, the outcome is brightly lit subjects in rooms that supposedly look illuminated but, instead, appear so dark that the action looks as though it is taking place in a coal mine. If an attempt is made to avoid these problems by bouncing light off the ceiling or walls, the reward can be flat, featureless light illuminating subjects and background so uniformly that the image is washed out and lacks definition and separation.

Creating setups for lighting designs that expose our scenes, characters, and actions credibly is not mysterious nor a particularly difficult process. It can be, however, quite time consuming and requires attention to the details of each setup.

Lighting often involves using instruments that draw a lot of power. When lighting on location, it is important for us to know how to tap into and control large amounts of electrical current safely and conveniently. For a thorough discussion of electricity and its use, refer to Appendix A.

Lighting Designs Versus Lighting Setups

In production, we make a distinction between *lighting designs* and *lighting setups*. Lighting designs are the way the frame looks, the patterns of light and dark in a scene filmed by the camera and projected on the screen. Lighting setups are the placement of lights we use to achieve lighting designs. They are the types of instruments we use and where we put them.

High-Key and Low-Key Lighting Designs

We commonly divide lighting designs into two major types—*high-key lighting* and *low-key lighting*. Bright, often shadowless scenes in which the frame is predominantly lighter than medium gray are high-key lighting designs. Shadow-filled scenes in which the frame is predominantly darker than medium gray are low-key lighting designs. Naturally these are simply convenient terms to describe some common designs or "looks." There are infinite variations between the two, and there are designs that do not fit into either category.

One kind of lighting design, for example, sets everything in the medium gray zone—a kind of bleak, foggy look. Roman Polanski used it at the beginning of *Tess* when showing peasants digging potatoes out of the muck on a cold and murky day.

Lighting designs are usually products of set design and costume, as well as lighting. High-key designs often emphasize color, shape, and lines within the *mise en scène*. This may involve using light-colored walls, furniture, and costumes, and then lighting these objects so there are few shadows. We generally don't allow the shadows that do exist to go dark. Traditionally we associate high-key lighting designs with television comedy, news and information, and lighthearted dramatic productions.

Low-key designs use shadow and texture in designing the *mise en scène*. We can create them through a combination of dark walls, furniture, and clothing lit to create large areas of deep shadow in the frame. Traditionally we associate low-key lighting designs with more serious drama, mystery, or even horror. Naturally almost any film will have some scenes that are high key and other scenes that are low key. However, we often find one kind of lighting design more prevalent in a film than another. For example, as mentioned in Chapter 5, the term *film noir,* or dark film, takes its name, in part, from the highly stylized low-key lighting designs that are used so frequently in the genre.

Lighting Instruments and Shading Devices

When lighting a scene, we use several different types of light sources. A small, bright light source with a tightly focused beam forms a hard light. Appropriately we call this kind of light a *spot*. Hard light can travel long distances with little falloff, and it creates sharply defined shadows. Spots are focused lights. Some are *open faced* using the reflectivity of their parabolic receptacles to condense the beam. Others use a lens on the front called a *fresnel* (from the Frenchman, who invented the design, and pronounced frā-nel′) to help focus the beam. We can focus the light from some spots or spread it out over a larger area. To do this, we move the bulb in relation to the parabolic receptacle or the lens on the front. (See Figures 10.1(a) and 10.1(b).)

We shade hard light from various parts of the set (or from the camera lens) by black metal shields, called *barndoors,* mounted at the front of the light. We can also place shadowing devices mounted on their own stands at any distance from the light. If these shading devices are rectangular in shape, we call them *flags;* if they are circular, we call them *dots*. Sometimes we want to deliberately throw a specific or irregular pattern of shadow on a scene, and we will use a specially shaped shadowing device called a *cukaloris,* or *cookie*.

The closer a shadowing device is to a light source, the softer the edges of the shadow it produces. Barndoors, mounted on the light instrument itself, produce shadows with soft, feathered edges. Because the shadow edge of a barndoor changes so gradually from light to dark, we sometimes control the intensity of our illumination from a hard key not by lighting our subject directly, but by carefully adjusting the barndoor so that the reduced lighting of

FIGURE 10.1(a)
By adjusting a focusing spot, we can cast a light that is flat and covers a wide area.

FIGURE 10.1(b)
Or, we can make the
light harder and
brighter, and cover a
smaller area.

the feathered shadow falls on the subject. Because we place flags, dots, and
cookies farther away from the light, they create harder edged shadows.

Light that emanates from a large area has a completely different character
than light from a small, bright light source. The light is much softer, falls off
more quickly, and produces soft shadows or almost no shadows at all. (See Figure 10.2.)

FIGURE 10.2
Light from a large area,
bounced off of foam-
core in this case,
creates a soft light key
which looks very
different from a
hard light key. (Also
see Figure 7.9.)

Hard Light and Soft Light

The difference between hard light and soft light can be thought of as the difference between the following:

1. A sunny day when the sun (a small, but brilliant light source) brightly lights our subject or scene with directional light creating deep, hard-edged shadows.
2. A hazy or slightly cloudy day when the sun's light is diffused and our subject and scene are more evenly lit and softly shadowed by light coming from all directions of the larger area of the sky.

Often, we use hard light for our keys and soft light for fill. This is hardly an absolute rule, however, and we can achieve some attractive lighting, especially in close-ups, by keying with a soft light.

Hard lighting produces sharper edged shadows that can be used to emphasize skin texture and accentuate such features as cheekbones, clothing textures, furniture carvings, set moldings and decorations, and drapery folds. Soft lighting diminishes this three-dimensional rendering of texture.

Most location lighting instruments are small and bright to make them easy to carry, but this makes them hard lights by nature. Creating soft light with them requires some deliberate modifications. Most major lighting manufacturers produce a type of instrument called a *soft light*. These lights follow the same principle as the photographer's umbrella, a device for creating soft light by bouncing light off the large reflective umbrella's interior. Manufactured soft lights are large metal or canvas reflective half-barrels containing one or two lamps that are placed so that the light reflects off the white or silver interior. They are about three feet wide by two feet high so, as a source of illumination, their area is large enough to provide a fairly soft light.

Another way of creating soft light is to hang diffusion material in front of a lighting instrument, creating an effect similar to the softening of sunlight by light cloud cover. We usually clip diffusion material directly onto the front of a lighting instrument's barndoors. This must be done carefully, because location lights are very hot. We want to use diffusion material that will not ignite from the heat of the lamp. Several types of heat-resistant diffusion material of various weights and thicknesses are available, including frosted plastics and woven fiberglasslike fabrics. Metal clips are best for securing the diffusion onto the barndoors because wooden clothespins may catch fire. Take care not to burn yourself as well. A good, heavy work glove or oven mitt is a handy addition to a gaffer kit.

A third way of creating soft light is to bounce light off a wall, the ceiling, or a portable reflector. White posterboard or, even better, an inexpensive Styrofoam sheet material called *foamcore* is readily available at art or office supply stores and ideal for this purpose. Because soft light falls off very quickly, to be effective at more than a few feet from a subject, we have to bounce a large amount of light off the wall or the foamcore. Powerful HMI (Halogen-Metal-

Iodide) lights that provide enormous amounts of illumination for their size make this technique of creating soft light quite common.

Scrims are another kind of screening device that we can mount directly at the front of the lighting instrument. They are wire mesh screens of different gauges used to cut down the amount of light coming from an instrument. Scrims do not diffuse light; they only reduce it. Full-scrims shield the entire front of the light, whereas half-scrims shield only half the face of the light. Half-scrims are useful when one subject is nearer to a key than another subject, or when a subject moves toward or away from a key light in a shot. We can place the half-scrim on the light to reduce the light falling on the subject near the light source, while the light falling on the subject farther away is undiminished. This compensates for the greater intensity of light falling on subjects closer to the instrument and creates a more even illumination throughout the depth of the frame.

Lighting and Contrast

Contrast Ratios

In executing lighting setups, we distinguish between the *key light,* which is the main lighting source illuminating our subject, and *fill light,* which we use to lighten dark shadows created by the key light. As stated earlier, we often use hard light for our key and soft light for fill.

Comparing a measurement of the shadow depth on the dark side of our subject and with the brightness on the key-lit side gives us a *contrast ratio.* We add fill light to the subject's darker side to lighten the shadow, creating the contrast ratio we want. Both film and video exaggerate contrasts compared to the way our eyes see contrast. Therefore, except in the most stark scenes, we normally find we must add fill light (usually a surprising amount) to achieve the desired look in the frame. One advantage of video, by the way, is that we can see the effect of the fill light we have added by viewing the results in the monitor (if the monitor is properly adjusted). With film, we have to learn how the film responds to various contrast ratios so we can get the look we want when it comes out of the lab.

Contrast ratios are differences in *f stops,* or comparisons of light intensity. An increase in one f stop is the result of twice as much light falling on the subject, so we can describe contrast in terms of ratios. (See Figures 10.3 through 10.7.)

Generally in film, depending on the stock we use, 8:1 or 16:1 is as high a contrast ratio as we can shoot and still show some detail in the shadow areas. In video, the range is narrower, and to achieve the same effects in contrast, the lighting has to be flatter with smaller contrast ratios.

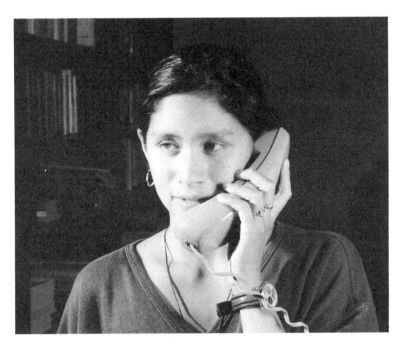

FIGURE 10.3
The key side of a subject's face is one f stop brighter than the fill side, which means that twice as much light is falling on the key side.

FIGURE 10.4
The key side is two f stops brighter than the fill, which means there is four times (2×2) as much light.

FIGURE 10.5
The key side is three
f stops brighter; the
ratio is 8:1 (2×2×2).

Lighting Ratios

We also measure differences in lighting intensities between foreground and background. We call these *lighting ratios*. Obviously, low-key lighting designs have high lighting ratios, whereas high-key designs have low lighting ratios.

We set the contrast ratios and lighting ratios to give us the effect, look, and mood we want. (Again, it's usually surprising how much fill and set lighting our scenes require.) Although the eye can see detail in a setting that includes a very wide range of contrast (a range of approximately 10 f stops, or about 1000:1), film stocks and video systems are only capable of rendering detail in a more limited range of contrast and lighting ratios. Consequently a contrast ratio of 2:1 (one f stop difference between key and fill) is barely noticeable to the eye, yet it reproduces as prominent modeling with clearly defined shadows in a film or video image. Ratios of 4:1 (two f stops difference), which are noticeable to the eye but not extreme, produce strong shadows and bold modeling; whereas 8:1 ratios (three f stops difference) produce stark effects and plunge the shadows deep down into gray scale, well toward black. Ratios of approximately 8:1 are commonly found in low-key lighting designs of the *film noir* look. At this level, the shadows are very deep, but there is still enough light in the shadow area of the face and background to see some detail.

Lighting ratios (foreground to background) follow a similar pattern. In the same way that a bright key light causes the shadow side of the subject to ap-

FIGURE 10.6
The key side is four
f stops brighter; the
ratio is 16:1 (2×2×2×2).

FIGURE 10.7
The five f stops differ-
ence between the key
side and the fill side
means that the ratio is
32:1 (2×2×2×2×2).

pear dark and requires the addition of fill to lighten the shadow area, a brightly illuminated foreground subject can cause a background to look quite dark and will need the addition of lighting to create the intended effect and mood. Of course, in some low-key scenes, we might not use any set lighting to keep the background as dark as possible. In most low-key scenes, however, we use some set lighting to see the detail needed for dramatics and pictorial composition.

The instructions that come with a light meter provide the basic information regarding its proper use. We recommend reading the instructions. Control of the photographic rendering of a scene requires a knowledge of the basic principles of exposure and contrast. Refer to Appendix B for a discussion of light measurement.

Lighting Setups

We define lighting setups by how we place the key light. The two most common types of lighting setups used to create most lighting designs are the *narrow lighting setup* and the *broad lighting setup*. A third type, the *cross-lighting setup*, is used occasionally to achieve certain effects and solve some interesting problems.

Besides the key and fill lights, a lighting setup often includes *backlights*, also known as hair lights and kickers, to create a rim of light along the top and side of a subject's head and shoulder. *Eyelights* can put sparkle in the person's eye. *Set lighting* illuminates and creates shadow effects on the set and background.

Narrow Lighting Setups

The lighting setup most often used to create tonalities in the medium to dark range—a low-key frame—is the narrow lighting setup. In narrow lighting, we place the key light on the side of the subject opposite the camera. Spill light from the key falls off-frame, leaving the background without illumination. We can then place fill light on the side of the subject near the camera, reducing the contrast ratio between the key and fill sides of the subject. Fill light in a narrow lighting setup does fall in the direction of the background within the camera frame, but because fill light is soft and because soft light falls off in intensity very quickly, light spilling onto the background from the fill light is usually of low intensity and not visible to the film stock or video system unless the subject is close to the wall (see Figures 10.3 through 10.7, and 7.4(a) and 7.5).

Theatrical filmmakers use narrow lighting extensively. As mentioned in previous chapters, it is an important technique to create both mood and character. Narrow lighting puts the modeling of the face on the camera side. With this type of lighting, even subtle changes in facial expression register with an audience. This allows revealing portraiture and, in narrative productions, gives talent a wider range of subtle expressions with which to work.

It is very difficult to create a low-key lighting design using a narrow lighting setup in a small room with white walls and ceiling. Although the spill from the key light falls off-frame, if it bounces off a wall too close to the action, it lightens up the background of the shot. If possible, restage the action to a larger room.

When it is absolutely necessary to create a low-key design in a small space, we can hang dark fabric or black background paper off the side walls to absorb the light or use a softlight as a key close to the subject. Soft light falls off rapidly and hits the background with its intensity greatly diminished. Very little light bounces off the side walls or ceiling.

A soft light key has an interesting effect. In relatively close shots, if we can place the soft light source close to the subject, we may not need any additional fill light because of the "wraparound" quality of the light. A closely placed soft light as a key causes very soft modeling with soft-edged shadowing that deepens on the side of the subject opposite the key and with lustrous, glowing light on the key side.

When creating a low-key lighting design, we can create stark contrasts with black or near-black shadows by simply using one or two key lights in a narrow lighting setup without fill. This is why some of the most dramatic lighting effects are the simplest to produce. On the other hand, usually we want to see some detail on the shadow side of the subject—facial expressions, especially—so it is necessary to add fill light to reduce shadow. Whichever fill technique we use—whether a soft light, bounce light off foamcore, or diffusion—the goal is to add fill to produce the depth of shadow we want, considering the way the film stock or video system sees contrasts.

Fill light does not significantly add light to the background unless a subject is positioned right in front of a wall. Moving the subject a few feet from the wall greatly affects the intensity of the light on the background. After a few yards, the falloff from a not-too-bright soft light can be so great that the background drops effectively into black. (See Figure 10.8.)

With a narrow lighting setup, we generally block action away from walls. The background then can be left black or near-black, or we can light it separately. This technique keeps the talent's shadow out of the scene and gives enormous control over the lighting of a scene and the subtle establishment of mood. For example, we can throw a diagonal of light up the back wall, creating a design element in our *mise en scène*. A splash of light can produce a "halo" on the background behind the subject, falling off toward the edges of the frame. A darker background behind the subject can provide contrast, setting off the backlit subject. We can then brighten other areas of the background counterbalancing the lit foreground subject in our composition. We can also splay shadows from cookies or even shadows of recognizable objects, or project colored light as from a stained glass window, across a back wall. All these lighting effects are possible with the key placed in a narrow lighting setup, allowing us to light the background separately.

Narrow lighting setups can also be used for high-key designs just to give us this ability to light the background separately from the subject. In these cases, we light the background brightly, so that we produce a high-key lighting de-

FIGURE 10.8
A narrow lighting
setup, with fill added
to see detail on the
shadow side. Even
though the subject is
only about four feet
from the wall, the key
is thrown off-frame
and the background is
kept relatively dark,
illuminated only by
the spill from the fill
light.

sign in which the frame is predominantly brighter than medium gray. Narrow lighting sculpts the subject more three-dimensionally than broad lighting set-ups and is often used for this effect, even in high-key lighting designs. Also, narrow lighting setups are often used in high-key lighting designs simply because we have established a practical window or another motivated lighting source that dictates the light coming from a direction opposite the camera.

Broad Lighting Setups

Broad lighting setups, in which the key light is on the same side of the subject as the camera, cause light from the key to spill onto the background in frame. Thus we usually associate broad lighting setups with high-key lighting designs. (See Figure 10.9.)

There are various high-key "looks," which are the products of key light placement, hard versus soft lighting sources, contrast and lighting ratios, and amount of backlight used.

As with narrow lighting, an important design consideration in broad lighting is the degree of contrast to set between the key and fill side of a subject's face. We can use little or no fill and leave the shadow area dark, creating a stark lighting effect, or we can add large amounts of fill so that the shadow side is well lit and we can easily see the details of facial features and expressions.

Because the eye of the audience seeks detail and facial expression in a close-up, we usually reduce the contrast ratio as we move from wide and medium shots to close-ups. For example, if we show a subject in a medium wide

FIGURE 10.9
A broad lighting setup, with the key on the same side of the subject as the camera, illuminating the background as well as the subject. Used commonly in high-key lighting designs.

shot (MWS), our eyes focus on the figure's movement and posture against the background. We do not concentrate on facial gestures. In such a shot, we might set a 4:1 ratio, which will sculpt the figure against the background, emphasizing the three-dimensionality of the subject by making the variation of light and shade quite prominent. However, when we cut to a close-up, our eyes seek detail in the face and the same lighting ratio will look quite harsh. To make the transition look smooth and natural to the eye, we reduce the contrast to a 2:1 ratio. A good rule of thumb is to double the ratio when we go to the wide shot, or cut it in half as we go from wider shots to closer shots.

A principal concern when we are doing broad lighting setups is placing the key light. How high or low and how far to the side should we place the key in relation to the subject? Another concern is the quality of the key light—how hard or soft is it? As mentioned in Chapter 6, these considerations significantly affect the way our lighting renders the portraiture of our subjects.

Cross-Lighting Setups
Extreme wide shots (EWS) present a special problem in creating low-key lighting designs. A narrow lighting setup does not keep light off the background in an EWS because the frame is so wide that, even though the spill light from the key is falling in a direction opposite the angle of the camera's point of view, the light is still visible in the frame.

To create a low key lighting design in extreme wide shots (EWS), another setup we often use is the cross-lighting setup. In this technique, we place a hard key light at some distance to one side of the subject, out of frame. We set up a second hard light on the opposite side of the subject, also out of frame. We scrim the second light, however, reducing the light intensity falling on the subject from this side. Both lights are set up carefully, barndoored and flagged, so no spill falls onto the background visible to the camera. The difference in intensity between the two lights, one light being scrimmed, produces the illusion of a more frontal key with shadow falloff, as shown in Figure 10.10.

An excellent example of this technique is the night exterior scene on the porch in *Who's Afraid of Virginia Woolf?* when Martha (Elizabeth Taylor) comes out to call the "boys" in, interrupting their drunken conversation in the yard near the tree on the swing.

Backlighting

Along with the key light and the fill light, the backlight is the third light used on a subject to create what we commonly call *three-point lighting*. Backlighting creates a rim of light when set behind and above the subject so that it shines along the top and side of the head and shoulder. If we set the backlight lower

FIGURE 10.10
Cross-lighting with two spots, one of which is scrimmed, illuminates the subject with the illusion of key and fill and keeps the background dark in wider shots.

so it toplights the shoulder, usually on the subject's fill side, we call it a *kicker*. If it lights the side edge of the subject's face or body, it is often called a *rimlight*.

The use of backlighting is very important in developing a lighting technique. Film and video are two-dimensional media in which we usually strive to create the illusion of a three-dimensional reality with the photographic techniques of camera angle and composition, lens focal length, and lighting. Backlighting is a basic technique in the creation of our illusion of three-dimensional reality.

Backlights are usually difficult to set up, especially in location shooting with low ceilings. They have to be set high above and behind the subject and often must be set on a crossbeam or attached to the wall or ceiling to avoid including a stand in the background of the shot. Backlighting also restricts subject and camera movement and requires that talent be much more accurate in hitting their positions and tilting their head. A well-placed backlight can create a beautiful rim of light on the head one moment and then suddenly cause the tops of the ears to look white or the tip of the nose to bloom the next if the subject's head moves back slightly. Nevertheless, for all these difficulties, the impact of backlighting cannot be overestimated.

Even in high-key designs in which the background is well lit, a backlight will create separation of subject from background and add a "snap" to the visual rendering, which can be a remarkable improvement over a similar shot without the backlight. (See Figure 10.11.)

FIGURE 10.11
A backlight on a subject adds depth and "snap" to the frame.

The intensity and angle of backlighting can vary, but the general rule is that the backlight should be at least as bright as the key light. If the backlight is especially bright and set to cause a subject's hair to glow, it creates a glamorous or unearthly effect. Carrying this lighting to the extreme by removing most or all of the key and fill light makes the subject into a luminous silhouette, an apparition, against the radiant backlight.

In many daylight interior lighting setups, we use light coming through a window as a source of backlight or rimlight. It etches a subject against the background, even if softly lit.

Eyelights

We mentioned in an earlier chapter that we can set the key light low and to the front so we can see its reflection in the talent's eyes, giving the eyes a twinkle. Because this isn't always a desirable position for the key, we sometimes use a small, separate lighting device called an eyelight, obie light, or inky. We can mount this light either on the camera or near the camera where it will create a "sparkle" in the eyes of the subject. Sometimes a brightly lit white card is held so we can see the reflection of the illuminated card in the eyes of the subject. Whatever specific setup we use, the effect is powerful and, in some scenes, critical. Some lighting designs depend on making the subject look alert, beautiful, romantic, or "starry-eyed." It is amazing how a simple eyelight can make this transformation in a subject.

Set Lighting

Most interior scenes set action against some kind of a background. Spill light from a key in a broad lighting setup illuminates this back wall. To avoid this, we block the action away from the wall and set the lights to achieve the lighting we want, not only on the subject, but also on the background.

If the action is close to walls, key lighting will illuminate the background as brightly as the foreground subjects and distracting shadows will be in the frame. We usually place key lights above eye level, causing the subjects' shadows to be cast downward. Therefore, moving the action away from walls allows key lighting to project down toward the bottom of the frame or below the frame line. In a narrow lighting setup, moving the action can provide enough space that we can direct the spill from the key light completely off-frame. Similarly, keys placed to the side can cast shadows more to the side or beyond the frame line.

Moving the action away from the walls often requires moving the furniture in a room. Sofas in a home, office, or apartment are often placed up against a wall, with a coffee table in front and a chair or two to either side. If we want our characters to have a conversation on the sofa and don't move it, the usual placement of the furniture automatically blocks the action flat against the wall—a nightmare for lighting (and compositions!). Set designers usually dress the set by arranging furniture—sofas, tables, chairs, desks, beds—away from the walls, more in the open spaces of rooms.

In broad lighting setups, key lights also become set lights. A hard key light will spill onto the background, even where there is some distance from subject to background. The falloff from the key causes the background to be less illuminated than the foreground subject, which looks normal. But, unless we scrim or barndoor the key light, the bright, even illumination from top to bottom and side to side of the background still makes the scene look very unnatural.

Lighting falls off toward the ceiling, floors, and corners of most rooms. We see the edges and corners of rooms as a convergence of deepening shadings. This effect is so natural to our eye that if we do not reproduce it in the frame, our lighting designs will look artificial. We accomplish the shading by using barndoors and flags.

Remember that a barndoor creates a feathered shadow. A shot looks much more natural and three-dimensional if we set the barndoors on a key light to cause a subtle shading of light toward the top and side of the frame as it spills on the background. We refer to this simple technique as *capping the light,* and we often use it as a part of our basic lighting strategy. Even in close-up, where the small area of background might not normally show any variation in shading, we usually cap the light with our top barndoor on the key light to cause a subtle shading toward the top of the frame.

Because soft light falls off so quickly, when we use it as a key, we have to place it close to the subject. The exception is when we use an HMI light and bounce it off a reflective surface such as foamcore. Because HMI lighting is so bright, bouncing it off a reflector still creates enough light to softlight large areas, in spite of falloff. Usually, when we use this technique, we also need to add more directional lights on top of the bounced light to create highlights, modeling, and depth.

Lighting for Movement

In motion pictures and video, our subjects often move, of course, and we need to develop techniques that can properly accommodate subject movement within a shot. We usually approach the problem of lighting for movement in one of two ways: *wall lighting* and *pools of light.*

The idea of wall lighting is to do a lighting set up so that, in moving from one space to another, the subject moves through the overlapping light of multiple instruments set to maintain a constant lighting design. For instance, in moving out of the light of one key, the subject moves into the light of another key set to provide a similar effect. We overlap the light from the two or more keys at the edges, maintaining fairly even illumination throughout the space in which the subject moves. Similarly, setting up a wall of several fill lights with overlapping edges maintains a contrast ratio that is more or less uniform.

The second approach to lighting for movement is to create pools of light. This approach sets up two or more areas through which the subject will pass and, usually, pause for actions (dialogue, and so on). We light these areas with key, fill, and backlighting, but we leave unlit the intervening spaces between the areas or only slightly fill them in. Thus, in moving from one area to another, the subject moves from one lit area through a darker, less defined space into another lit area.

This latter approach accommodates a common move made by subjects within the frame—a move from a dark area into an area more brightly lit. Our eyes do not normally see "overexposure," except on occasion when we step from a dark theater or lounge into the bright light of a sunlit day. What we normally see is the brightest area of a scene being "properly exposed" and darker areas in shadow. So, for example, when someone steps from the shadows of a doorway, comes up from a dark cellar, or steps out from the shadow of a tree into sunlight, what we see is the person moving from shadow into normal "exposure." To get this effect in film or video, we light the brighter area into which the subject will move (or out of which if the subject is returning to the shadowy area) and perhaps fill with enough light in the darker area to reveal whatever level of detail we want visible. Then we set the exposure for the more brightly lit area and let the subject move from "underexposure" into normal exposure.

Exterior Lighting

A common remark we often hear on a sunny day is what a fine day it is for photography. Photographers know the truth is usually otherwise. Sunny days create deep shadows. During midday, when the sun is overhead, shadows under the eyebrows on the human face are so dark and "contrasty" that it is impossible for film or video to see detail around the eyes. People look like the Lone Ranger with a mask obscuring the features. Earlier or later in the day, when the sun is more angled, these same deep shadows can cover the side of the face, if a person is not facing the sun, and the camera can lose details of the mouth and eye on the shadow side.

In wide shots, this may not be a problem because the frame includes the entire bright, sunlit scene with the human figure occupying a relatively small portion of the frame. The audience sees the figure cut against the background and notes such details as body posture and clothing, but the subject is too far away, too small in the frame, for the audience to look for facial expression. Medium shots and close-ups are another matter. Because it causes so much contrast, bright sunlight on the face can be intolerable. However, on days when light cloud cover diffuses the sunlight, the contrast between the sunlit side and the shaded side of a person's face is softened considerably. We find that cloudy days provide us with a subdued lighting that is usually much better for portraiture.

A variety of techniques are available to reduce contrasts for portraiture on days that are brightly sunlit. The easiest is to move the talent under the shade of a tree or building. Another solution is to reflect sunlight back into the shadow side of a subject's face with a white or foil-covered board. However, we have to place the reflector quite close to the subject for the intensity of the bounced sunlight to make a noticeable difference, so this technique is usually good only in close shots.

A variation of this technique is to fill and reduce facial shadows with daylight-balanced artificial lighting—either blue-gelled tungsten lights or HMI lights, which have a color temperature similar to daylight. This can be especially effective when we position the subject so that the sun serves as a backlight, brightly illuminating the top of the head and shoulders.

A third technique is to mount a large frame of diffusion material or cheesecloth between two stands over the set to soften the sunlight falling on the subjects. This device, called a *butterfly*, simulates the softened lighting we would get under light cloud cover. Because they are lightweight with large surfaces of fabric, like a sail, butterflies blow down easily and securing them requires sandbags to keep them steady. They cannot be used if there is any appreciable wind.

Another problem on bright, sunny days is the extreme contrast we get when shooting against the sky in low-angle shots. Characters and people we shoot often have actions or are doing things that require them to look down. In exteriors, we may have an angler tying a hook on a line, or a gardener hoeing a row of vegetables, or a detective searching the ground for a clue. If we want to shoot a low-angle shot, looking up at their face, we find that neither film nor video can handle the contrast between the more darkly lit foreground subject and the intensely bright background sky.

Blocking is the simplest way to deal with this problem. Arrange the subject and camera so that the background behind the subject in the shot is not the bright, open sky, but the darker background of a tree or building.

Scene Duplication Exercise

Hollywood films vary enormously in the quality of their scripts, directing, and performances, but they are consistently of high quality in the technical crafts. The craftspeople in Hollywood consistently maintain a standard of excellence in cinematography and lighting regardless of the quality of the script, direction, or performance. This exceptional level of cinemagraphic technique is not a recent achievement but has been developed over more than half a century.

Like painting, the best way to learn is to study the masters. A wonderful heritage of extraordinary work is available to us, and we can spend our time well studying scenes in well-produced films. Videotape and laser disks make it possible for us to view films, scenes, and shots selectively and repetitively, even in slow motion or held on a single frame.

If we wish to study a scene in detail, especially the lighting, it is best to study a film print because video cannot show the range of contrasts that the film medium recorded. Also, video does not have the resolution to show the subtle details revealed by lighting in a film scene. However, with videotape we can conveniently study a comprehensive body of professional work and learn not just the basics, but many refinements of lighting design and technique.

Especially with lighting, the best way to learn is first to study a well-produced scene and then attempt to duplicate the scene and its lighting, photographing the results with a still camera or, better yet, a video camera or film camera.

Naturally, there are multitudes of scenes from which we can choose. Just to illustrate the approach, we are going to examine the lighting design of a scene from Alfred Hitchcock's *Psycho*. In this sequence, Marion Crane (Janet Leigh) has arrived at the Bates Motel on a rainy night and is escorted into the reception room by Norman Bates (Anthony Perkins). She stands at the counter while Norman talks with her, takes her name on the hotel registry, and gives her the key to her room. The scene includes six angles:

1. A profile MWS of the two of them as they enter—Figure 10.12(a)
2. A high-angle three-quarter front MS of Norman from behind Marion's head—Figure 10.12(b)
3. A low-angle three-quarter front MS of Marion from behind Norman's back—Figure 10.12(c)
4. A CU of Marion's hand writing "Marie Samuels" on the motel registry—Figure 10.12(d)
5. A slightly low-angle three-quarter front MCU of Marion as she looks at a newspaper—Figure 10.12(e)
6. A slightly low-angle MCU rear shot of Norman as his back is turned to pick out the key he will give her—Figure 10.12(f)

Shot 1 is a classic example of narrow lighting for two people facing each other in a dialogue. Almost every film has some variation on this kind of setup. Two hard key lights illuminate each character on the side opposite the camera. The sides of the faces toward the camera are in shadow. The key lights are relatively low, near eye level, so that the nose shadows are short and Marion's eyes are illuminated. Both characters have backlighting, with Marion's set almost directly above, causing her hair to glow.

There is a wall lamp in the background between them, acting as a motivating light source. The set lighting in the shot appears to come from this lamp so that the brightest area on the wall is near the lamp. They probably fitted the fixture with a much higher wattage light than we would find in an ordinary wall lamp. The wall falls off into shade toward the edges of the frame. Upward-cast shadows of the mirror frame in the background indicate that the direction of the light on the back wall is coming from the wall lamp. A little additional fill light illuminates the subjects on the shadowed, camera side so that we can see some detail—ears and hairlines.

Shot 2 continues the narrow lighting pattern, but it is interesting that the key light on Norman has been taken farther to the side so that his nose shadow

a b

c d

e f

FIGURE 10.12 Stills from *Psycho*.

Copyright © by Universal City Studios, Inc. Courtesy of MCA Publishing Rights, a Division of MCA Inc.

now closes with his cheek shadow, creating a triangular pattern of light under the eye on the side toward the camera. Increased fill light (reduced contrast ratio) shows more of his ear and hairline, shows more of her ear and hairline, and better illuminates the board of keys behind him. Marion's hair light has been removed from the top of her head, but a kicker added to the side maintains a highlight in her hair. The hairlight on Norman has remained about the same.

In Shot 3 the key light on Marion has been moved slightly to the front and raised a little, more fully illuminating her face and producing a better chin shadow pattern on her neck. As in Shot 2, shadows have been filled more (making a lower contrast ratio) compared to Shot 1. Marion's backlight has moved more overhead, similar to Shot 1, but producing less of an effect because of the angle.

Set lighting appears to be a combination of soft fill plus a harder light illuminating the background near the bottom of the frame. This is not spilling from any key or backlight, but has been set to duplicate the brighter portion of the frame caused by the wall lamp in Shot 1. Flags probably limited how high this brighter light could be seen up the wall. Norman's key has moved around, creating a rim light on his arm and shoulder (acting as a backlight on him in this over-the-shoulder shot).

Shot 4 uses a hard light set above the page to the left of the camera, from the general direction that the light would be coming, giving the appearance that the wall lamp is actually illuminating the page. Contrasts are extreme. Flagging the one light source creates the diagonal shadow at the top of the page in the upper right portion of the frame.

In Shot 5 the key light in this close-up of Marion has been moved even more frontally, and more fill has been added to see detail in the shadows of her chin, neck, ear, and hair. The hair light has been reduced and softened to avoid an artificial look in the MCU. A set light placed high to the right of the camera illuminates the newspaper. Possibly the hard set light used to illuminate the bottom of the wall (also seen in Shot 3) is the same light on the newspaper.

In Shot 6 Norman's back is turned while he picks out a key. The key light, although still narrow, has been moved to illuminate both Norman's hand and the board with the keys on it. Remember, the board was in a much softer set lighting in Shot 2. Barndoors or flags reduce the lighting toward the top and sides of the frame. There is a hairlight above Norman. The effect of the hard key lighting so much of Norman and the board is somewhat glaring and, of course, the action we are watching is the beginning of Norman's plan to murder the woman.

As we've shown with this scene from *Psycho,* a close study of the lighting designs from scenes from well-produced films and television productions is an excellent way to learn lighting strategies. Lighting is an art, and there are as many variations and ingenious techniques as there are DPs and scenes to be lit. We have only provided a summary of basic approaches and techniques here, which hopefully will suggest further elaborations and refinements as the reader gains experience.

Exercise 1

(If shooting film, this exercise can be shot using one roll.) Using the video system or film stock you plan to be using for most of your productions, shoot a latitude test using a gray card and light meter as described in this chapter. Shoot three to five seconds of each shot and label each setup.

With a partner, shoot a contrast test setting up key and fill on their face in 2:1, 4:1, 8:1, 16:1, and 32:1 ratios if you are shooting film or 1½:1, 2:1, 2½:1, 3:1 and 3½:1 and 4:1 if shooting video. If you shoot both, compare the results. Remember to shoot the face shot close enough to see the effects of the contrast change and slate each shot with the contrast ratio used. Shoot five or so seconds of each shot—enough so you can really look at it when you project it or play it back. Try to get a feel for how the lighting appeared to your eye compared to how it looked on the video system or film.

Finally, shoot a wider shot of your partner with an object that has some discernible detail in the background. Alter the lighting ratios in your shots so that the light on the subject stays constant, but the light falling on the background (and the object in it) is one stop darker, then two and three stops darker. When you screen the shots, what is the effect on the subject? How does it compare with how it looked to your eye?

Exercise 2

Shoot and edit one scene that is three to five minutes long. Choose a scene or part of a scene from a theatrical film, preferably one that is accessible in a 16mm or 35mm print. Duplicate the scene as carefully as possible, paying attention to such elements as lighting design, cinematography (focal lengths, framing and angles, camera moves, and so on), editing, and pacing, including split edits and dramatic delivery. Try to duplicate the *mise en scène* as closely as possible.

Notes

1. See Sigfried Kracauer's *Theory of Film: The Redemption of Physical Reality.* London, Oxford, New York: Oxford University Press, 1960.

11

SYMBOLS

In Bergman's *The Seventh Seal,* the Knight (Max von Sydow) plays chess with the cowled figure of death for the lives of his troupe during the plague. The cowled figure is one of the most recognizable symbols in the visual media. (See Figure 11.1.) Film and video producers love symbolism. In Kubrick's *2001: A Space Odyssey,* a mysterious obelisk confounds apemen and spacemen. Buñuel's *Viridiana* is filled with Catholic symbolism. Symbolism can be found in the works of our greatest and most imaginative directors. It's impossible to look at the work of Fellini (for instance, in *8½,* the tower and the mysterious, beautiful woman in white) or of Coppola (the attacking helicopters blaring the "Ride of the Valkyries" in *Apocalypse Now*) without recognizing that there is symbolic value in the images on the screen beyond their function as visual story elements.

FIGURE 11.1
In *Bill and Ted's Bogus Journey,* the lead characters challenge the cowled figure of Death to a series of games in a wonderful send up of Bergman's symbolism in *The Seventh Seal.*

Artwork © Orion Pictures Corporation.

Film as Symbolic Expression

The power of the moving image as a means of symbolic expression—as a form of language—has been a subject of fascination and serious thought for almost as long as films have been made. In his wonderful film history *A Million and One Nights* (1926), Terry Ramsaye devoted an introductory chapter, "The Pre-history of Screen," to the thesis that film is the product of a fundamental characteristic of humankind as a picture and symbol-making animal.

In the late 1920s and throughout the 1930s, the great Russian film director and theorist, Sergei Eisenstein, explored the idea of film as a symbolic language. He pursued a disciplined discussion of it in essays such as "The Cinematographic Principle and the Ideogram" (1929), "Film Language" (1934), and "The Structure of Film" (1939). These essays, along with others, formed the basis of his book, *Film Form—Essays in Film Theory,* a classic in the literature of film theory.

Semiotics

In the years after World War II, a highly sophisticated school of film theory, called *film semiotics,* developed. It grew out of ideas that had evolved both in the study of linguistics and the branch of philosophy called epistemology, which is concerned with how the human mind knows and conceives reality. Semiotics (or semiology, depending on the writer) formally analyzes a film's images for their symbolic meaning. It looks at film as a language composed of signs and symbols.

In *Signs and Meaning in the Cinema* (1969), Peter Wollen helped to explain the sometimes dense arguments put forward by leading theorists, such as Christian Metz,[1] and made the ideas of film semiotics more accessible. André Bazin's writings further contributed to the theoretical foundations and especially to Metz's concepts. Bazin, a founder of the French film periodical, *Cahiers du Cinéma,* was highly influential for the generation of French New Wave filmmakers during the 1960s. As a result, semiotics was a strong influence on the productions of the French New Wave directors, especially Jean-Luc Godard. Other directors as diverse as Makavejev and Kenneth Anger were also strongly influenced by semiotics.

As the preceding cursory summary may suggest, many books of subtle and esoteric thought have been written on the subject of film as symbolic expression. Film semiotics is an intellectual field of study in its own right and can shed interesting light on how a film conveys meaning. The emphasis in semiotics is more purely anthropological, philosophical—even political—however, and is not intended to illuminate film and the filmmaking process so much as to illuminate the workings of the human mind.

Although semiotics has had an impact on the work of some film and video artists, little has actually contributed to the day-to-day creative processes of most media producers. Therefore, with a nod of acknowledgment to this school of media theory and to the interesting, even profound revelations of which it is capable, we will go on. What follows is a discussion of symbolism in film and video with an emphasis that we believe is more directly related to the concerns of the working producer.

Symbolic Communication

The symbols of language, whether written or spoken, are the terms we use to think and to convey meaning. We also use other symbols outside language, such as mathematics, with which to think and communicate. In her landmark book, *Philosophy in a New Key—A Study in the Symbolism of Reason, Rite, and Art* (1948), Susanne Langer discusses how nondiscursive, nonverbal, presentational forms such as art and music are also rational modes of symbolic expression. We feel that exploring this nonverbal, but nonetheless rational, aspect of moving images can be rewarding for the aspiring film or video producer.

Symbolic Expression

Most of us are familiar with the term "visual literacy." The phrase suggests that there is a visual "language" that, once learned, enables us to "read" a film or video message. Yet, as we learn to master the creative techniques of the moving image, we come to realize that this medium of expression "works" very differently from the written word. The visual media are more concrete and specific in their communication and thus must employ less abstract ways in which to convey meaning.

A problem arises when we are treating images like words, attempting to build an argument by juxtaposing various images and intending each image to represent or symbolize some meaning other than itself. Some images may be of recognizable symbols—a cross, a flag, a human form draped in a black cowl—but other images are of subjects that can be more variously interpreted—a door, rippling water, a flying bird. The intention is for the audience to "read" the resulting sequence of images like words on a page—a kind of pictographic writing like a hieroglyph.

When we try to build a visual sequence in which each image is meant to be symbolic, we create a composition in which the symbolic meanings of some images may be recognizable, though cliché (crosses, cowled figures, and so on), whereas other images will remain indecipherable or vague (does the candle flame mean life, love, the soul, or fragile mortality?). At worst, such work makes little or no sense to an audience, despite the rationality and thought that went into its creation. At best, if most images are translatable, the piece may be coherent at an abstract level, but the flow of images will likely seem disjointed (a crouching figure, a hammer hitting a nail, a flower, an eye, an open hand, and so on). The work will seem a dry, rhetorical puzzle—

uncommunicative, unpersuasive, and unmoving—no matter how heartfelt and sincere the intent.

The experience can be very frustrating for those of us who know perfectly well what we mean but discover that no one else does. Sequences of images simply do not convey *didactic* meanings like words on a page. Like words, however, they can invoke worlds, characters, and stories.

Many symbols have evolved especially to denote religious, philosophical, and otherworldly ideas. Sigmond Freud, Carl Jung, Sir James Frazer, Joseph Campbell, and others have brought a new understanding of traditional symbols and have given us some new ones, especially in the area of psychology and more specifically, sexuality. There are graphic symbols of sexual organs or sexually suggestive images such as the train entering the tunnel and large erect monuments; images of youth and vigor exist such as saplings and various animals, many of which become the names of athletic teams or automobiles; images such as clocks, tombstones, and gnarled trees frequently denote age and death. And there is a whole pictographic library of religious symbols: crowns, crosses, fish, water (the sea, rivers, springs, and fountains), stars, triangles, circles, halos and other shining lights, blood, wine, death's head, mythological beasts, various trees, plants, herbs, apples, bread, tea, images of Shiva, the depiction of the Yang and Yin together as Tao, snakes, lambs, lions, goats, calves, and bulls, to mention a few.

In the misty past when these objects and designs took on symbolic significance, they were easily accepted by practitioners as the means to communicate either as code or as preliterate storytelling devices. They were fresh and filled with meaning. Their connotation was clear and relevant. Ultimately, as they were continually used within our cultures over hundreds and even thousands of years, their meanings evolved and expanded, and they became subject to a wider variety of interpretations.

Many of us have grown up knowing these symbols and being generally aware of their meaning. However, some symbols, dating from mythology or even the early days of the Jewish, Moslem, and Christian religions, may no longer carry their original meanings and may have diverse meanings to different individuals and various sectors of the public.

The successful use of objects that have already become universally recognized as having symbolic meaning attached to them is tricky. Symbols based in the recent cultural past have a greater likelihood of having more commonly shared meanings, at least by members within a single culture. The further away in time or in cultural distance we go from the genesis of the symbol, the more likely it is that meanings may be so dispersed that there is little commonality left.

This is not to suggest the use of traditional symbols is ineffective. Films such as Luis Buñuel's *Viridiana* and Ingmar Bergman's *The Seventh Seal* are masterpieces that clearly use religious and psychological imagery to great effect. It is merely to point out that if the audience's understanding of story or character hangs on their responding to the symbolism in some appropriate manner, the result may be disappointing. The communication may not be clear.

Filmmakers experimented with quite bizarre and very personal connotative symbolism mixed with explicit cultural, psychological, and religious symbols in the 1920s and 1930s. Among some stunning artistic creations are films by Luis Buñuel and Salvador Dali (*Un Chien Andalou*). These films reflect trends in the art and experimental theater of the period. In them, the language of symbolism is the overt communication, not a subtle texturing of the more traditional dramatic story line common to the mainstream tradition of film and theater. Visual images and events were strung together to create emotional responses in the audience, convey political or social abstractions, but rarely to tell a story. The world within the frame was surreal, with every form, shape, and object forming a composition that was meant to have meaning at the subconscious level. Today, there are still film and video makers using the media to express intimate personal feelings, attitudes, and visions through surreal imagery.

Symbolic allusions succeed when we embed them within absorbing narratives with distinctive characters. Though there are exceptions in the documentary and experimental genres, film and video are usually most effective when they present sequences of powerful images to create realities inhabited by characters coping with events. Think about some of the more interesting, moving, and meaningful moments you have experienced while watching film and video productions. Memorable scenes and stories involve characters who interact with one another and their environment, have relationships, and do things. Even quality wildlife documentaries are structured in this way. Furthermore, the most memorable scenes are likely to have been created with beautiful or strong visual images.

As we have said, images are not words. They work differently from literary modes in fundamental ways. However, this does not mean that producers should avoid symbolism in their work. In fact, this would be impossible. Symbolism is not simply a technique a producer might choose to employ. It is a phenomenon of human nature that we cannot avoid.

Significant Detail

Beyond the blatant symbols of fire, water, crosses, and hooded apparitions, there are everyday details that carry symbolic communication to us. Manner of dress, articles of clothing, hand and facial gestures, speech patterns, tools, paraphernalia, and decor convey rich implications about a person's background, status, values, and character. Ultimately, every detail in a production can convey meaning. If we, as producers, aggregate significant details into recognizable, coherent patterns or clear, distinct juxtapositions, the audience will sense that their understanding goes beneath the surface of the unfolding action.

If, on the other hand, we do not pay attention to composing patterns of significant details, our work will be superficial, unpersuasive, and arbitrary. Our characters simply will play out their roles without context or motivation.

Denotative and Connotative Symbolism

We are all familiar with the distinction between denotative and connotative meanings in language. Two or more words can have the same explicit, recognized meaning, yet have suggestive implications that are quite different. Whenever we carefully select words or consult a thesaurus to express shades of meaning, we are being sensitive to these implied variations. We can even express simple and concrete references with a subtle nuance.

For example, consider the following synonyms for the word "door": entrance, entry, portal, gate. Or, for the verb "to walk": step, amble, stroll, tread, pace, tramp. Obviously, more complex ideas such as the concept of "knowledge" have many associated words (synonyms), with a broad range of connotations: appreciation, awareness, cognition, comprehension, consciousness, discovery, erudition, experience, familiarity, impression, information, insight, intelligence, judgment, ken, learning, perception, recognition, revelation, understanding, wisdom.

Denotative meanings are explicit and conceptual; connotative meanings are suggestive and felt. Images, as well as words, operate on both levels. When selecting elements for our productions, we must be as sensitive to their connotations as when we select our words.

McCabe's weapon in *McCabe and Mrs. Miller* is a large Swedish weapon. Much is made of it upon his arrival at the town and again later when he straps it on to defend himself. At the denotative level it is merely a gun, but it is far more interesting at the connotative level. It is big, garish, and showy, not unlike its owner. It is not until the end of the film that we discover McCabe has another side to him as well as another gun. And, in the moment of dual revelations, McCabe reveals an aspect of his character we didn't believe possible of him, while at the same time succeeding in killing his assailant, a huge man with a buffalo rifle, with a little derringer and more than a little guile.

In film and video, denotative meanings are those related to the simple realities and explicit, straightforward subject matter of the production. Connotative meanings are the emotional subtext and texture of the production, usually dealing with characterization, mood, atmosphere, theme, and inner conflicts.

Cultural Icons

With use and repetition, denotative symbols accrue more and more connotative meaning. In addition, through some capricious mass psychology, an assortment of media symbols, ads, and events becomes shared experiences that begin to represent the culture of a generation to itself. There are those for whom The Pump, The Clapper, Thigh Master, Ginzu knives, and Colombian coffee's Juan Valdez have become symbols of an age of television advertising just as for a previous generation, the now defunct clothier Robert Hall had seasonal jingles that will probably always return to mind along with the more familiar holiday carols. For the generation before that, L.S.M.F.T. recalls not only Lucky Strike cigarettes but a whole raft of derivations on the initials. For most Americans, a particular jingle will bring back the experiences of a specific time as readily as references to the news of the era or a hit song.

Cultural icons can do more for a production than raise nostalgia for a period. TV comedies and talk show hosts regularly use "product jokes." These relate the use of such products as Maalox, Chia Pets, or Depends for the sake of the joke. Mel Brooks boldly flaunts cultural icons for humorous effect in his productions, especially *Blazing Saddles* and *Space Balls*.

The movie *Aladdin* uses cultural icons brilliantly. This animated film by Disney Studios opens with a reference to Dead Sea Tupperware and a nod to television's ubiquitous Vegematic with a combination hookah and coffee-maker that can also make perfect french fries. The primary purveyor of cultural iconography, however, is the Genie, the voice of Robin Williams, who plays cultural symbols like keys on an organ. There are other cultural symbols besides product advertising, of course. When we first meet the Genie, he transforms his smoky tail into a microphone and becomes a lounge entertainer and then puts on a show by transforming himself into a Scotsman, a Scotty dog, a light bulb, Ed Sullivan, Groucho Marx, a drum majorette, and so on. Throughout the picture, he transforms synchronously with his riff, into a harem girl, slot machine, both waiter, and maître d', a Frenchman, a Roman, a game show host, Jack Nicholson, Arnold Schwarzenegger, Arsenio Hall, Robert De Niro (as Travis Bickle), William F. Buckley, Jr., Walter Brennan, Rodney Dangerfield, Pinocchio, and even Sebastian the Crab. And when not transforming, he continues to invoke the icons of our era by taking a bath with a rubber ducky, wearing a Goofy Disneyland hat and Hawaiian shirt and carrying a bag of golf clubs, and at one point making a camera frame with his fingers and asking Aladdin, "You've just won the heart of the Princess, what are you going to do next?" To which the audience, conditioned by the Disney advertising campaign, responds, if silently, "I'm going to Disneyworld!"

Recognizing the cultural connotations symbols have accrued allows the film or video maker to create layers of texture and meaning, as well as emotional experiences and verisimilitude in the production. This is more than merely an enticing notion. Using words, objects, music, and patterns that have symbolic meaning to the audience allows for another level of treatment and another method of using production elements as threads to weave the thematic tapestry of our communication.

Occasionally, cultural icons are widely known to only a small sector of society and, when using these, we don't want to use them in such a way that the rest of the audience feels left out. It generally defeats the cleverness of the symbol if we have to point it out. In *Jurassic Park,* our party of unsuspecting sight-seers are driven toward a giant gate reminiscent of the huge wooden portals in *King Kong*—an obvious reminder of another story on another island in another movie where giant animals roamed and adventurers encountered harrowing experiences and untimely deaths. But, just in case we miss the point, one character has to say, "What have they got in there, King Kong?" A nice use of a recognizable element transformed into a heavy-handed reference.

Communicating through symbolism is perhaps safer and more universally understandable by using cultural icons that have been directly experienced by a broad spectrum of the audience. Peter Bogdanovich did this brilliantly in his film *The Last Picture Show.* He evoked 1950s small town Texas with cultural icons of the period, including movie marquees, drive-in restaurants, and automobiles. But, he primarily put audiences into a 1950s frame of mind with period rock 'n' roll music, a device that has been used in many film and television productions to evoke a sense of period and place. In these productions, the music, ads, and automobiles do more than properly dress a historical set. He carefully selected them to conjure shared emotional responses in audience members who lived in that period. They express a feeling and recall an emotional context for the production.

The process of identifying which aspects of our culture will speak to an audience symbolically may be based on research into the specific area of the culture being portrayed in the production, but ultimately has to be fairly personal if it is to convey personal concepts and ideas. Writers, directors, and producers have to have a sense of contemporary society in terms of its fads, its icons, its slang, and, specifically, its vision of itself as reflected in the media and in other events shared universally by the culture.

Because the connotative meanings of symbols operate at an impressionistic, gut level of suggestion and insinuation, they can affect the audience quite powerfully and personally. We recognize the symbolism (significance) and respond at a level that is not fully explicit. Meaning ultimately depends to an extent on the audience's subjective experience, reaction, and interpretation. Symbols loaded with connotation are, by their nature, subtle, complex, and at least somewhat open ended.

An example is in *Witness,* when Rachel and her son, Samuel (Lukas Haas), arrive at the train station in Philadelphia. There is a scene where Samuel wanders about the cavernous waiting room, staring at the people in this alien land. At one point, he looks up and sees the huge statue and stares wide-eyed at it as otherworldly music in the sound track soars. (See Figure 11.2.)

The statue is clearly meaningful to the boy and it strikes a responsive chord in us as well, perhaps best described as the awe of entering a new land and discovering it peopled by giants. He confronts something totally beyond his frame of reference. To him it is like the prehistoric apemen confronting the obelisk or Dave (Keir Dullea) confronting the time warp in *2001: A Space Odyssey.* As we empathize with his response, we learn more about the experience of being raised in his community as well as his state of mind.

FIGURE 11.2
In *Witness,* when Samuel arrives at the train station in Philadelphia and sees the huge statues, it is as though he has entered a new land and discovered it peopled by giants.

In *Silence of the Lambs,* Clarice (Jodi Foster) visits the home of one of the victims. While looking about for clues, she discovers a jewelry box. When she opens it, a ballerina figure begins to twirl as a music box plays. It is a touching and emotional moment for both Clarice and us. The box becomes a symbol of the victim as a person with a life, a young woman who was once a little girl with dreams, a future, and a family that loved her. None of this is spelled out, and it may strike different viewers differently, but it is clearly placed in the film for the emotional response it evokes.

External and Internal Symbolism

External symbols are a coded language and they make up a set of common references. They derive from the cultural vocabulary of icons that we all somehow understand as a part of our literary and visual heritage. Internal symbols, on the other hand, are created from features of the story that are developed within and are organic to the drama.

In the vocabulary of external symbols, the symbol of grain stands for nourishment, regeneration, and community. As a symbol in art and design, it is probably as old as agrarian cultures. It establishes the ancient conflict between the hunters and the gatherers, between the killers and the farmers (nurturers of life), between Cain and Abel. In complete compatibility with this mythic theme, grain separates John Book from Rachel in *Witness.*

In the opening of *Witness,* which thematically contrasts the closeness of a community rooted in rural heartlands to the modern, violent world of urban Philadelphia, we fade in on the rolling fields of grain. Then the community of Pennsylvania Dutch farmers crests the hill in front of us visually giving the impression of rising from the ground like the grasses surrounding them. Grain is their strength. (And, in the end, grain is the instrument of retribution!) Immediately following the opening scene, we cut to a low-angled shot of black horse-drawn carriages rolling up and over us. Visually and symbolically, religion dominates their lives. The strong symbols of a community rooted in the land and religion are important in understanding the personality of Rachel as well as the culture in which she lives.

The use of grain in *Witness* is elegant. The symbol is both recognizable as an external symbol and also developed internally as significant within the specific context of the story. It seems natural, not forced or extraneous to the drama. And, if the audience doesn't understand the symbol at the conscious level (as perhaps they shouldn't), it may strike a responsive chord at their subconscious level. If they don't "get it," at least it is not confusing by being intrusive or interrupting the narrative. The story is underway. It does not seem contrived nor does it draw attention to itself.

The title shot for *Thelma & Louise* is a shot of a long highway leading into the mountains. It begins in monochrome and slowly gains color. Clearly, here, the road is externally symbolic of their trip, but internally is symbolic of the growth and changes Thelma and Louise will go through as they venture into a rugged and rocky but more colorful future, forever changing their drab lives.

In film and video productions, we often use external symbols as a shorthand in our storytelling. Perhaps the most obvious is in casting or, more appropriately, typecasting. Heroes look the part. They are generally good looking, virile, and sexy: Clark Gable, John Wayne, Clint Eastwood, Jimmy Stewart, Sean Connery, Judy Garland, June Allison, Denzel Washington, Eddie Murphy, Jimmy Smits, Tom Cruise, Demi Moore, Kevin Costner, and Julia Roberts. Bad people usually look rough or diabolical: Boris Karloff, Bela Lugosi, Jack Elam, Vincent Price, Albert Salmi, Margaret Hamilton, Agnes Moorehead, Lee Van Cleef, Jon Malkovich, and Christopher Walken.

Similarly, as mentioned earlier, many props and wardrobe items have taken on external symbolic value—the good cowboy's white hat, the femme fatale's slouch and makeup, the nice guy's baggy pants, the tycoon's power suspenders, the innocent young woman's cotton floral-print dress, the hard-boiled detective's whiskey straight, the urban gentleman's scotch on the rocks, the intellectual's eyeglasses, and the prissy lady's hair bun. Turn on the television in the middle of almost any production and it is startling how much we can quickly determine by the casting, the mannerisms incorporated into the performance, and the selection of symbols incorporated in costume and the *mise en scène.*

Music in film and video productions usually plays an internally developed, connotative role, creating emotional responses and conjuring passions in the audience in association with specific elements within the story. However, in some productions, most notably animated cartoons and some nature films, the music becomes another voice of the storyteller, using familiar, externally established musical figures, themes, and motifs to create characterization and convey story. Listen to a few minutes of Saturday morning cartoons without looking at the picture. We find ourselves easily able to identify the chase scenes, the scenes on horseback, the dopey guy's music, the bad guy's music. *Jaws* has forever given us the shark-is-coming music. Sound effects have become so associated with fight sounds and gun shots, the sounds of real ones surprise people. A whole range of sound effects is associated with cartoon actions. Some of these extend into live action films, especially in the Three Stooges type of slapstick comedy.

Creating Internal Symbolism

Some of the most effective symbols are those that draw their meaning from the context of the story or production. A marvelous example was the television show *Northern Exposure,* which opened each episode with the moose walking through the town of Cicely, Alaska, symbolic of all that is unconventional and unusual in this make-believe world. That we were willing to believe in the town of Cicely, Alaska, makes the scene no less surreal. The environment in Cicely played a symbolic role in providing atmosphere, characterization, and often the plot lines of the stories. Alaska had drawn to it this cast of characters and participated in the events of their lives.

Obviously, in the case of the moose in *Northern Exposure,* repetition, placement of the object in the frame, and prominence in the opening title shot elevated the animal beyond being a prop or a piece of the scenery to becoming a functioning symbol for the series. When creating the significance of a symbol within a production, we can use the techniques of treatment to establish the object as important. Besides repetition and placement in the frame, such obvious techniques as close-ups, strongly keyed lighting, foreground prominence, arrested or emphatic pacing, and swelling music or sound effects are just part of the arsenal available to highlight objects for special attention.

Of course, many symbolic objects are prominent story elements and their importance can be underscored by dialogue and action. Two obvious examples are the ruby slippers in *The Wizard of Oz* and the falcon statuette in *The Maltese Falcon.* Unveiling the dark denotative truth about the falcon parallels uncovering the darker side of Brigid O'Shaughnessy's (Mary Astor's) character. As developed internally within the story, the ruby slippers are made into symbols at the denotative level simply as shoes that are a mode of transport both along the Yellow Brick Road to Oz and ultimately back to Kansas. At the connotative level, the bejewelled slippers are symbolic of the battle between the good and evil forces in Oz, as well as of that which is of most value to Dorothy—her home and her personal growth.

Perhaps the most famous symbols in movie history are the sled "Rosebud" and the snow globe in *Citizen Kane*. These symbols are important plot devices. Discovering their meaning will be the key to the driving force of Kane's psyche. Welles introduces them at the very opening of the film in a sequence constructed by dissolving through a series of shots showing the exterior of the property, each tilting up, building our expectation that the rising shots will lead us to something important. Eventually, they do. We see the snow globe and then, in an extreme close-up, Kane (Orson Welles) says the film's opening word, "Rosebud," and dies. The association of the cabin in the snow inside the globe is thus made with the whispered word. Associating the visual of the globe with the mysterious utterance is a rather blatant introduction of the symbol. No one can miss the significance. And, although the reason for this connection is not immediately clear, Welles makes it so boldly, we remember it in the final moments of the movie when the sled is finally revealed.

The opening sequence of the film *2001: A Space Odyssey* is also directed at the introduction of that film's symbol, the obelisk rising from the prehistoric African plain. It is in the opening again, but in a sequence illustrating a rivalry between two communities of manlike apes. In the dawn, after a devastating battle between them, one group discovers the obelisk. The scene begins with reaction shots arousing our curiosity, setting up the audience's expectation much the same as the rising camera shots did at the opening of *Citizen Kane*. In addition, there is a powerful swelling of music and when we are finally treated to the shot of the obelisk—a monumental low-angle reveal—the crescendo almost deafens us.

We commonly use symbols to reveal a character's emotional state. Having a character look at a photograph of the person he or she is thinking about will certainly convey what is on the character's mind. Photographs can serve the story, but do little to reveal the emotional state of mind, just that the character is thinking about another character. A more creative solution is to not only associate an object with a character, but also with a state of mind, an emotional framework based on an event or condition the audience has witnessed.

Let us create an internal symbol. A bright young Indian warrior assumes the leadership of his tribe after the old chief dies. Aware of the immense responsibilities that are now his, the stouthearted but unseasoned youth climbs a hill overlooking his tribe's encampment and sits for the night, contemplating his new role and his tribe's future. During the night he notices a Spanish saber cactus nearby, sharp, pointed, hard, and stonelike. A storm erupts, shaking all the vegetation and insects around by the force of the wind and rain, but the cactus, like the watchful brave, is unmoved. The water splashes off of the plant as if from a honed piece of translucent jade. Morning comes and the seemingly inert sculpture comes to life. In a chill so deep that the young man's breath exhales steam, the cactus opens a bright and beautiful flower toward the warming rays of the rising sun.

The youthful chief rises and descends back down toward his village. What follows is a full plot of dangers, disasters, a few victories and gentle moments, and many lost companions. The chief, who has proven an admirable leader throughout these travails and is now much older and wiser, finds his tribe once again encamped at the foot of the hill that he climbed at the beginning of his service. Our mature warrior climbs the hill again and looks around. He and we again find the Spanish saber, now much bigger and very much battered from the intervening years. The cactus is a symbol and has become an outer manifestation of the chief's inner values—strong, enduring, sharp-edged, with great beauty and vitality within a hard reality.

In this way, symbols can serve as a substitute for flashbacks, dream sequences, awkward dialogue, or whatever is going on within the minds of our characters. By associating a meaningful event and set of feelings with an object, we are later able to recall these memories, thoughts, and feelings simply by having the character reencounter the object. This can powerfully suggest to us what the character is thinking and feeling without the intrusive artifice of a flashback or dream sequence.

Spielberg does this to great effect with the touring car in *Empire of the Sun,* shown in Figure 11.3. It becomes a symbol for all that was British, colonial, family, home, and part of the era that comes forever to an end with the arrival of World War II. Spielberg creates the automobile as a symbol very cleverly. In the opening of the film, when Spielberg introduces us to the family, the mother is playing the piano. Later, in the scene preceding the masquerade

FIGURE 11.3
The touring car in *Empire of the Sun* becomes a symbol for all that was British, colonial, family, home, and part of the era that comes forever to an end with the arrival of World War II.

party, the boy (Christian Hale) is left by his mother and drifts off to sleep while staring at his airplane models suspended from the ceiling. In this somewhat dreamy moment, composer John Williams sneaks in the piano theme the mother was playing earlier and we associate the music with home, a mother's tenderness, and his dreamy aspirations of his future.

The next morning, the party sequence is introduced by a trucking shot that puts the car in the foreground with the gardeners working in the yard in the background. The car enters the shot first with its bright, shiny, silver, swan hood ornament passing through center-frame. When they enter the city, we come out of an aerial shot and truck with the car, the camera even with the hood ornament as it moves through the crowded streets. As the scene progresses and becomes more and more surreal, the music takes on an ethereal quality with strings and open notes sung by a boys choir. In the final moments, as we see the clowns and Marie Antoinette faces in the car, Williams repeats the piano melody from the earlier scenes.

Later in the film, as the Japanese are withdrawing from China, the boy marches with hundreds of other prisoners to a large outdoor stadium where the Japanese have stored the spoils of the war. There he encounters a woman playing the same melody on a piano sitting amid the piles of furniture and other belongings of the former diplomatic community. And, in a close shot of the boy, we see he has recognized something important. He moves forward and the camera dollies back with him until he stops. The camera then widens the frame and now we see what had caught his attention: the swan hood ornament from his parents' touring car. We now recognize it and with the music and its associations, we have new emotional insight into the feelings and reactions of the boy.

Note that, in establishing the swan hood ornament as an important object, Spielberg only uses two strong shots of it in the opening of the film. In the first, it is big and bold in the frame, whereas in the second instance, it is the central object in the dolly shot. The two shots are sufficient for us to react strongly to it when we see it a third time in the stadium, near the end of the film.

The Surreal Landscape

The surreal world—the world that exists within the frame where objects and events have symbolic meaning beyond the practical—is an important consideration in mainstream film and television production.

Drama's cause-and-effect relationship between events and the outcome suggests that things happen with purpose and for a reason. Events aren't random, but occur as part of a grand design. Fate manipulates with a heavy hand. Things hold portent. As a result, there is a kind of shamanistic approach to the visualization process.

In their ability to load symbolic meaning on any aspect of physical reality, film and video are truly transcendental media. Transcendentalism was a philosophical and literary movement that was extremely influential in nineteenth-century American culture. Evolving from Protestant Christian belief that every occurrence is the direct expression of the will of God, transcendentalism posited the belief that every object and every event is meaningful beyond the material reality of the senses and fundamentally more significant in the realm of the spiritual. In such a world, everything becomes a symbol, referring to meanings and implications beyond the immediate and obvious, in a multilevel world of metaphor and allegory.

The works of Ralph Waldo Emerson, Walt Whitman, and above all the novels and short stories of the two great American writers, Herman Melville and Nathaniel Hawthorne, all rise from the aesthetics of transcendentalism. In the transcendental world of Melville's *Moby Dick,* the whale becomes much more than simply a whale, and the novel becomes a meditation on the various ways there are to know the whale (or anything else, for that matter) and the multiple levels of reality the whale symbolizes.

In animation, we are quite familiar with elements in the environment taking an active role in the stories. Objects implicit to the story, which can be props, part of sets, and designs of the items necessary to the story, become more than just symbolically communicative to the audience. They become players in the drama. Disney provides us with excellent examples in his *Alice in Wonderland* with the singing flowers, *Legend of Sleepy Hollow* with its ominous trees, and perhaps the most famous examples in *Fantasia.* The most memorable, perhaps, is Mickey Mouse as the sorcerer's apprentice attempting to control the elements through magic and having them turn against him with dreadful vengeance.

In well-crafted, live-action drama, we can make the environment complement the action and resonate the themes of our work. We can approach our productions not simply as stories, characters, and actions. Using the elements of treatment, we can create visions of the world in which our locations, set designs, costuming, lighting, colors, and cinematography present tangible realities that symbolically reflect the unfolding events on the screen.

In *The Unforgiven,* Will Munney (Clint Eastwood) stands on a hill beside a gnarled tree overlooking a village down a dusty road. This naturalistic, location environment is as much a dramatic stage for the action as any well-designed theatrical set. It is a metaphysical landscape. The distance between the hill and the town is open and barren. The hill offers a vantage point, a place to pause and think, removed momentarily from the business in the town. The tree is old and gnarled, like the main character. It is solitary, also like the main character, and the shade and comfort it offers is meager.

In *McCabe and Mrs. Miller,* the warm colors—red, yellow, gold—that we associate with McCabe's and Mrs. Miller's presence as they build their saloon and bring some interior comfort and pleasure to the bleak mountain settlement are in contrast to the cold blue tint of the surrounding outdoor wilderness. This symbolic use of color in the lighting and cinematography, along with the old photographic look that comes from slightly fogging the film to reduce the contrast and mute the colors, creates a distinctive look to the film that reinforces the story. The color and quality of light become symbolic, expressive elements in the drama. Preceding the use of these techniques, the themes of the work first had to be understood by Robert Altman, the director, and his brilliant cinematographer, Vilmos Zsigmond. Then the visual treatment was conceived as a representation of these themes, which then had to be artfully executed.

We can draw examples of treatment used for symbolic purposes from any thoughtfully envisioned work. The somber, underexposed lighting of *The Godfather;* the gritty black-and-white and slow-motion effects of *Raging Bull;* the close distances and confined point of view of *Chinatown;* the hard-edged, dissonant sound effects and Leonard Bernstein's music in *On the Waterfront* are just a few examples of elements of treatment used to symbolize dramatic themes. To repeat a point made near the beginning of this book, technique does not simply serve content, it becomes part of the content.

Of course, as with Spielberg's creation of the hood ornament symbol in *Empire of the Sun,* we can also transform concrete objects such as props, costumes, and settings into symbolic elements in a production. In *Witness,* when John Book tries to disguise himself in Amish homespun, his clothes are ill-fitting and he looks exceedingly awkward and out of place. His inability to fit in to the Amish costume symbolizes his very un-Amish character, which surfaces almost immediately when he decks a bully who taunts his adopted family. It also symbolizes the gulf that will forever exist between him and Rachel, which leads to their inevitable poignant parting at the end of the film.

In television, we also use objects to symbolize dramatic content. Archie's chair in *All in the Family* symbolizes his resistance to change and comfort in the status quo, his belief in the home as his domain, and his territoriality. In *Twin Peaks,* Agent Cooper's love for coffee and pie and his regular audio-recorded reports to Diane back at headquarters symbolize his link with the normal world, while exploring a territory that at first seems simply geographically remote, but we discover to be a truly bizarre and alien world. Laura's diary is symbol of the mysterious fate that befell her, and also a record, a tracing of the evil netherworld that Agent Cooper finds lurking in the Northwest forest.

Our point is not to render a critical analysis of the use of symbolism in films and television, but to refer to the use of these devices in a few productions so that we can understand how we might incorporate similar methods in our own work.

By their nature, through the meaning-laden illusions of reality they portray, film and video are the ultimate transcendental expression. With storytelling and technique, the actual photographic, physical rendition of a rock can be made far more than just a rock, the cactus more than a cactus, the road more than a road, the hood ornament more than a hood ornament, and so on.

Notes

1. Semiology itself was based on the work of linguists such as Ferdinand de Saussure (*Course in General Linguistics* (1915-posthumous)), Roland Barthes (*Elements of Semiology* (1964)), and Charles Sanders Peirce (*Existential Graphs* (1935)). It also is related to a theoretical approach in anthropology, "structuralism," developed by Claude Levi-Strauss.

12

SIGNIFICANCE

Significant Events

Events that arouse passions are significant. In the wake of the Rodney King verdict in the summer of 1992, the streets of Los Angeles erupted with people driven by virulent emotions: rage, lust, greed, vengeance, vigilantism. In a contagious delirium, they coursed through the streets with raw passions controlling their actions. It was true drama. Actors overtaken by emotion performed actions alien to their normal persona. They became, for a while, something most of them were not. They did things, for a while, they normally would never do. Their human inhibitions and restraint evaporated and liberated a new character within them.

Public responses to events such as the Rodney King verdict, or the riots after the assassination of Martin Luther King, or the spontaneous outpouring of national grief after the death of John Kennedy or Abraham Lincoln, or the upwelling of nearly riotous euphoria by fans after a Superbowl or Soccer's World Cup are akin to the way people at rock concerts or in night clubs respond to music. This is the kind of possession of a mass audience's emotions that can be generated, shared, and communicated through significant media production.

When film, video, and television productions are crafted in a way to create believability, we react to the events depicted on the screen with real emotion. We respond at a gut level to these portrayed events almost the same as we would to real events in the world around us.

Gut Reaction

The things we witness on the screen don't just represent events, they become events. They speak to us at that same level of emotional communication as reality. They cause the eruption of passion. They upset the audience. They create vibrations through the viewing public that are personal to each individual. They cause us to feel the emotions of anger, lust, vengeance, sorrow, and irrepressible hilarity.

True, they do not engender actions on the scale of riot or jubilation. On the rational level, adults can distance themselves from the screen portrayals enough not to take action as if the events were real. But, to the extent we believe the events on the screen are real, our beings respond involuntarily to the waves of stimuli before us and transcend the reality of being viewers of the created reality on the screen.

Events That Arouse Passion

Events that make news and events that make drama are very similar. In news or entertainment, we are interested in those events that we perceive to be significant because they activate our emotions. They may also stimulate our intellect, but "the public thinks first of all with its senses."[1] We respond to the events of news and drama intuitively and often in ways that are difficult to translate into language.

In Chapter 6, we referred to one of the most moving moments in Ken Burns's *The Civil War,* the reading of Sullivan Ballou's letter to his wife, just before his death in the Battle of Manassas (Bull Run).[2] What so moved us were not just the words, but the emotions of love and loss behind the words that the music of the production supported so beautifully. The moment touched us. We felt the conflict within the breast of the young soldier caught in the struggle of patriotic duty and love for his wife. For that moment in the production, he was alive yet we could see clearly what he could only speculate, his imminent death. As we listened to his living words, we knew the fate that awaited him and were helpless to prevent it. We, too, were caught in emotional turmoil.

Audience Conflict

The audience sits in comfort trapped by premonitions and trepidations and caught in the trials, tribulations, anguish, pain, and personal embarrassment on the screen. Our conflict is our inability to be physically involved, yet we find ourselves emotionally tangled in the web of the events before us. We are unable to warn, run, withdraw, or suppress any of our instinctive responses that real participation would allow us.

The conflict on the screen and the conflicts we feel are directly related. The stronger the events, the more significant they are to the characters or individuals involved. Participating empathically in the events of characters awakens sympathies in us. As the significance increases for them, it multiplies for the audience as well.

Successful documentary portraits are about people with burning passions, strong convictions, with a mission in life. Productions about events are successful to the extent we can make these events personally relevant to members of the audience.

The events that occur to characters in dramas or the decisions they have to make must strongly affect them. In *Cape Fear,* Sam Bowden (Nick Nolte) decided to withhold information in Max Cady's (Robert De Niro's) trial. This is backstory that is directly revealed to us. His decision, if not very good, is very human, and we sympathize with his reasoning. However, this decision not only puts himself in jeopardy, it endangers his erstwhile girlfriend and ultimately his associates, his wife, and teen-aged daughter. Bowden continues to make reasonable, but bad choices. The threat becomes greater, more personal, and begins to target his family members. The actions he takes are understandable, but they always seem to backfire. He means well, but he screws up, and Cady is waiting for him ahead of every turn. We live these decisions with him. We perceive dangers before he is aware of them; we sense the calamity before it occurs. It becomes a bad dream where we want to cry out and warn him of the implications of his actions. We increasingly participate in his dilemma as it increases in its potential for destruction and violence. For the moments we sit in front of the screen, these events are immediate and significant to our lives yet we are powerless to alter them.

In the opening of *Raiders of the Lost Ark,* as Indiana Jones (Harrison Ford) nears his goal of obtaining the pre-Columbian mask, the dangers multiply and increase in their potential to thwart his efforts. Here, we are no more privy to the consequences of his actions than Indy is, yet like him, we sit in anticipation of the next event that could bring this film to an early ending. And, though *we* might not go where Indy goes, we are compelled to take the journey and powerless to turn back. The film drags us into dangers to which we react as if they threatened us personally, immediately and physically. We are in conflict. By the end of the sequence in the cave, we feel as though we are on a roller coaster with each new danger increasing by quantum levels.

Audiences are not held emotionally captive just through threats of danger. Other situations cause individuals to react and squirm in their seats. Aberrant behavior and human disfigurement can evoke feelings ranging from discomfort to revulsion. Films such as *Hunchback of Notre Dame, Phantom of the Opera, Elephant Man, Mask,* and *My Left Foot* come to mind as examples where the human images on the screen are difficult for the audience. Even *Rosemary's Baby* used the potential of showing the audience a monstrous infant to create strong emotional tensions at the end of the drama.

The rush of adrenalin, the queasy feeling in the pit of the stomach, the euphoria of jubilation, even hysterical laughter cannot be maintained nonstop. If we do not pace events that arouse strong audience reaction, the audience will ultimately withdraw from the drama just to escape its unrelenting barrage. Emotional moments are taxing.

Director Peter Brook's filmed version of *Marat/Sade*[3] exploited this effect by continually putting the audience in a state of discomfort throughout the production. From the blinding white light coming out of nearly totally black titles, the discordant music, and the unsettling confrontation with inmates in an asylum to the final moments with the inmates attacking the screen, banging on their bars, Brook keeps his audience uneasy in their seats. It is an uncomfortable and challenging production. Certainly, and not unexpectedly, it's "sadistic" in its presentation. However, just as neither comedy nor horror can be relentless and be effective, the production gives its audience measured respite from the attacks with some marvelous music and very funny moments.

Knowing how to create discomfort in the audience is as important a skill for a director as knowing how to create suspense, or feelings of loss or sorrow, or a comic moment. Stanley Kubrick proved his mastery of discomfort in *A Clockwork Orange*. When the film was released in 1971, it proved too strong for many viewers with its graphic, if beautifully choreographed, depictions of violence. Many films, from Hitchcock's *Psycho* to Cimino's *The Deer Hunter,* render moments of intense violence to engage the audience in the significance of the events on the screen.

These moments of conflict, however, exist within a dramatic context. The more the production resonates within us, the greater our conflict between being participant and viewer. We respond to the personalities, the characters, the people, and the events in which they become entangled as if they were—at least for the moment—real.

The belief in the reality before us creates involuntary physical reactions: laughter, fear, queasiness, uneasiness, lust, trepidation, the uneasy feeling in the pit of the stomach, or when our flesh crawls and the hair on the back of our neck rises in response to the images on the screen. Draw away from the drama during a good chase scene in a film like *Bullitt* and watch the audience leaning into the curves as if they are passengers in the cars careening across the screen. The reality of the image, especially in a dark theater with a wide screen and a good sound system, transfixes the audience, mesmerizing them. It charms the audience as music does snakes.

Meaning in Events

Significant events are often those associated with pain or struggle. Our normal response is to learn from painful experiences. As Sakini (Marlon Brando) says, in *The Teahouse of the August Moon,* "Pain makes man think. Thought makes man wise and wisdom makes life endurable." Productions gain significance when the audience, like the characters in drama, learns or somehow grows through the experience of the production.

As the events on the screen wrench our emotions, our instincts are to look for implications of relevant importance—to look for patterns, solve puzzles, and resolve riddles. Our own conflicts and our empathic participation produced by the scenes before us induce us to try to understand the cause-and-effect relationships, unmask the structure and logic to the events, and discover their portent.

Portents and Importance

The meaning we look for is beyond character motivation or clues to the resolution of the story. Audiences seek meaning in productions much as the Greeks used drama to provide the connection between the secular and the sacred, to reveal the forces that controlled their lives as manifested in natural events: storms, plague, and death.

We believe in purposefulness. We believe in luck and fate. We believe that independent events are invisibly linked. Gamblers and sports fans regularly attempt to manipulate events, sometimes thousands of miles away, by their actions, clothes, invocations, and appeals. When we see tragedy in our lives— the effects of wars, the devastation following a hurricane, the impact of a lost love, or sudden death—we seek out some reason or impetus to explain the occurrence.

We seek meaning in the events themselves. Powerful and traumatic occurrences speak to us in their own language. We want to understand the powers that control the physical as well as the metaphysical world, the fates that control love, death, friendships, relationships, and personal fortune. These are the significant mysteries of life that are important to us. These are keys with which we can bring significance to our production.

The Mirror of Production

To the extent that we feel these powers control our lives, we believe they manipulate the actions and events of the characters on the screen. The mirror of production gives us clues to understanding the forces that manipulate our lives. A well-wrought production can become for us like the rites of religious ceremonies. Through the process of seeking clues that help make sense of the events of the production, we attempt to discern the machinery that creates the patterns of events that have significance in our lives. We thus believe each element of the production is intentional and could be significant to our understanding of the meaning of the piece *and* its relevance to our comprehending the nature of the human condition.

And so it should be. Productions that emanate from the core of learned experience, the things on which we base *our* perceptions and understanding of reality, touch audiences emotionally. Events that move us emotionally cause us to discover symbolism that in turn gives relevance and greater significance to the events.

Thus events become symbolic battles between good and evil, youth and age, men and women, the id and the ego. The battles on the screen become the conflicts of our lives. Media productions invite us to examine the nexus of our innermost, personal conflicts. But, beyond the intuitive, symbolic communication, there is always the realistic story line for those who prefer, for whatever reasons, to enjoy the production on a purely entertaining level. We don't have to always get it to get it. Significance shouldn't undermine entertainment, but should coexist with it in balance.

Entertainment

All productions that move us emotionally aren't necessarily significant. Clearly there are those who find entertainment in the experience of fear or the fun of farce unbalanced by intellectual content. Some people, and perhaps all of us at some time, enjoy the extremes of horror, the tugging of our heart strings by soap opera, and the uncontrolled release of slapstick. These are escapist productions. The bold manipulation of our emotions removes us from our reality for the moment, giving us respite from our daily lives and worries.

The Dark Side

Often, we respond to the unknown with fear, mistrust, and an exciting rush of adrenalin. Understanding often dispels this fear. But, puzzles yet unsolved threaten us even as they intrigue us. Like motorists who slow to gawk at roadside misfortunes, conjecture and free thought can flow in dark directions.

With hopes for the best, we predict the worse. The myths of our culture reveal a fear of the bogeyman. Western religion is rooted in sacrificial murder and the firm conviction that evil exists as a power. It colors the stories of Western drama. We believe in archfiends and villains, and they people our stories from the Big Bad Wolf, the Wicked Witch, and Joker and Penguin to the characters of Cady in *Cape Fear,* Dr. Hannibal Lecter in *Silence of the Lambs,* or myriad characters representing mindless villainy such as Jason or Freddie Kruger in the horror genre.

There are many significant films of the horror genre, including Tod Browning's *Freaks,* Tobe Hooper's *Poltergeist,* and William Friedkin's *The Exorcist.* However there is also a plethora of productions that give the audience a surprise or "gotcha," but provide no real edifying experience. There is a thrill in the game, a rush of excitement of facing nightmarish fears through a mode in which we are assured of our survival. The theater seat will not open up and swallow us. We are safe in its embrace. This gratuitous, if entertaining, manipulation of the audience's emotions merely for excitement does not necessarily produce a work of significance.

The Lighter Side

There also always seems to be some production being billed as the "feel good film of the year." Soap operas and Movies of the Week regularly build empathy for characters in some manufactured distress or use the elements of *mise en scène,* music, photography, and pacing to build up a big "win" for a character that gives rise to passions, yet reveal nothing of real value or significance about the human spirit. Stories that exalt the good without demonstrating the triumph of the good are flat and empty. They are without action.

Productions that are light, however, don't need to be froth. The most predictable element of drama is that good will triumph. Yet we, as audience, never tire of it. We expect our characters to rise to the occasion, seek out correct solutions, and grow as they succeed. We want Rocky Balboa to overcome his limitations of background, age, habits, and experiences and face Apollo Creed. We want Thelma and Louise to free themselves from the hand life has dealt them. We win as they win, and we enjoy the experience. We experience the up-welling of exuberance as Frank (Al Pacino) dresses down the hierarchy of the elite boy's school in *Scent of a Woman,* and as the students stand on their desks in silent salute of Mr. Keating (Robin Williams) at the end of *Dead Poets Society.* As we see good triumph, we see through lies and hypocrisy and have hope.

Testing the belief that good triumphs over evil is the basis of most drama and many documentaries. Some productions, as with morality plays, physically embody good and evil on the screen. In *It's a Wonderful Life, Raiders of the Lost Ark, The Witches of Eastwick,* and *The Exorcist,* forces of good and evil are visible players in the drama.

So What?

The harshest criticism of any production is "so what?" It reduces all efforts to the point of total insignificance. There are no redeeming moments or shots, the entire piece was a waste of the audience's time.

There can be tremendous fun in slapstick comedy devoid of satirical bite with no pretense or significance. Entertainment *is* a worthy goal of production. However, without significance, one runs the risk of creating something insignificant. Without significance, productions are merely entertainment. After sitting through a television production, a documentary, a feature film or even a music video, the audience should feel that they have experienced something of significance, or they may feel they have just wasted their time.

Audiences appreciate challenge. Productions that represent life's conflicts and difficulties are somehow deemed much more worthy than those that merely depict life's comforts. Sporting contests where the conflict is real and immediate and the stakes are high can have tremendous viewership. Annually, the highest advertising dollar is paid for the Superbowl.

Creative Vision and Coherent Productions

Realizing our vision or executing that of someone else depends on our ability to understand and control the elements of production under our command. Creating productions is like Michelangelo's sculptor discovering the figure in the marble and carving away everything that is not the figure. The process of production is one of refining, editing, and cutting away what doesn't belong. A show is discovered in the elements of production, to greater or lesser success, depending on the clarity of the vision of those who execute it and their abilities to bring the elements together coherently.

A coherent production creates a believable world in which characters and subjects live, whether it is two people talking about how bright the whites are in their laundry, the interior set of a television sitcom, or the fully created world of a fictional story in a feature film.

Coherency means that nothing is extraneous to the production, everything is intentional, relevant, and has meaning. Something that distracts from the flow of the piece arouses the audience's suspicions that the reality before them is not genuine. If they notice a flaw—an unrealistically delivered line, an awkward or unmotivated action, lighting that appears garishly out of place, unmotivated camera movement, or poorly paced edits—we have destroyed the illusion. And, once we have lost an audience's belief in the reality on the screen, it is very difficulty to retrieve it, at least within the same scene.

The Power of Performance

Production values alone cannot make a production significant. There is an adage in the business that one can fix anything by throwing enough money at it, but no amount of money can raise a production to significance. The classic failure of Michael Cimino's *Heaven's Gate* was not that he overspent his budget, but that he spent far too much money on a production that could not be raised beyond the level of its screenplay or the performances of the leading actors Kris Kristofferson, Christopher Walken, Isabelle Huppert. A powerful documentary on an important individual or issue can be killed by a self-conscious or flat performance before the camera. A great screenplay can't survive poor performance. There is a reason actors are the stars in Hollywood: Nothing is more powerful on the screen than a good performance.

Few performers can put on a mask of true feeling successfully. Instead, they must locate those feelings within themselves and let that color their actions, attitudes, and dialogue. This allows them to transmit their emotions in ways we believe are honest and open, thus creating a significant relationship with the audience.

Plastic Reality

In literature, there is the conceit that the world is synchronized to the character. The author, in writing the work, creates an environment coordinated to the character. Environmental elements heighten emotions: the lashing winds, the angry seas, the dark and stormy night.

The illusion of reality in visual media, however, is far stronger than in literature. In literature, the mental image is in the mind of the reader. In film, there is a photograph and we watch the character do things in what appears to be a real world. It is very convincing. We don't read about it, we *see* the environment they are in. As the drama overtakes our senses and we participate in it as if it were our own dream, it becomes almost a virtual reality for us. When we watch a film, it seems so real. Yet it is all contrived.

Responsibility

As the audience responds to the production's apparent reality, we who craft the production need to be constantly sensitive to the fact that it produces significance. We create or show a world where there is a perversity in events. There is no randomness. We direct the acts of fate.

The media have the power to influence the public perception of reality. Ads and programming portray a lifestyle, a code of ethics, dictates of physical beauty, and a definition of normal relationships.

Generally as audiences believe in the reality of the world of a production, they do not think of the production as a creation of technique. In the incident mentioned at the head of the chapter involving Rodney King, what incensed the public was they had seen on television a videotape that depicted a view of the beating of King by the Los Angeles police. They could not accept that there was any other reality than what they had seen. Yet, a court and jury examining evidence not a part of the video found the police officers not guilty. Correct or incorrect, there was clearly more than one perspective to the incident.

Even film, video, and television practitioners, especially those involved in nonentertainment, nonfictional forms of media, can get trapped into believing that technique is inappropriate when presenting "reality." Their job is somehow to merely record the subject directly, without any meddling. This is of no small consequence. It is impossible for a producer *not* to interpret a subject. Furthermore, as we discussed in Chapter 1, most of what we know about the world we have learned through the media.

The controversy arises in films such as *JFK*, which critics feared would color history's memory of the events as they really occurred. If this is true, then what of Shakespeare's histories, Abel Gance's *Napoleon*, Ken Burns's series on the Civil War? How much does the media shape our perceptions of our own past?

When he was Vice President of the United States, Dan Quayle carried on a public debate with Murphy Brown, a fictional television character. What are fictional personalities and what are real personalities? For most of us, we know both only through the media, and the images of both are carefully manufactured and manipulated.

Production as Artifact

Film, video, and television are handcrafted media. The technology serves the creators, but the cameras, machines, and computers do not make the production. People do. Camera direction is pointed, visuals are selected or created, edits are timely. Heroines and heroes triumph. The immature mature. What's wrong is made right. Every word of dialogue, every shot, every sound bite we select, everything is an artifact, a handmade article. In crafting the elements of production, we use forethought and care.

The Role of Dialogue

The kind of production that depends on all the dramatic elements, production elements and elements of *mise en scène* is far richer than one that depends exclusively on dialogue. As discussed in Chapter 7, the elements of *mise en scène* create significant moments. Unlike words, the tool of the actor and orator, the visual media usually evoke significant emotions in us through the visual and aural elements of production rather than primarily through dialogue.

We are sometimes tempted to rely on speech and dialogue to create meaning in productions, forgetting the power of the visual treatment of the frame. We've all heard that a picture is worth a thousand words and there are 24 to 30 of them per second in a media production. That's a lot of "words!" Yet, people have been raised with the belief that thoughts are communicated through speech, reading, and writing. Most schoolwork since kindergarten has focused on these skills, and most homework assignments and serious study has been in the written or verbal language. Most schools relegate visual work to separate art, photography, or video classes and rarely integrate the works of these classes with the work and assignments in the more formal areas of education. Therefore, when we have something important to say, we tend to rely on verbal rather than visual communication.

However, dialogue is linear. We comprehend its meaning one word at a time and generally no faster than it can be spoken. Yet cognition and thought far exceed the pace by which we can read or hear words. We can assimilate the meaning of a painting far faster than we can describe its intricacies. Consequently dialogue is terse. Lengthy passages of prose slow the pace of production and inhibit interaction, making editing difficult and camera shots long and deadly. We hardly find visual artistry in a president's televised speech to the public.

Dialogue is merely *one* of the voices of the production. And even so, often the best dialogue evokes images rather than carrying the action of the drama. Comedy relies heavily on novel or surprising mind pictures created by the choice of words in the dialogue.

We find meaning in events, not in the discussion of an event. We believe what we see far more readily than what we hear. When we think back on a film we've seen, what most often comes to mind is a visual sequence, like a recalled dream. Rarely do we find ourselves quoting a film's dialogue as we do with playwrights and poets except the occasionally significant one-liners: "As God is my witness, I'll never go hungry again," "We're not in Kansas anymore, Toto," "Make my day," "I'm mad as hell and I'm not going to take this anymore," "Hasta la vista, baby." In these examples as well as others that come to mind, it's not so much *what* is said that makes a line memorable, but *how* it was delivered or the visual context in which it was said.

The television or film screen is not a page to be filled with words. It is a space we fill with meaning created by light, shadow, color, form, design, action, camera position and movement, sound and editorial juxtapositions—everything within the boundaries of the frame. Often, we communicate more through silence, facial expression, actions, and reactions than through words. Batman's (Michael Keaton) stony silence responds eloquently to Cat Woman's (Michelle Pfeiffer) challenges in *Batman Returns*. We create visions, not words.

The frame itself often conveys meaning through mood or design as clearly as a hieroglyph. There are thoughts, cognition, ideas, and feelings that are beyond words or for which words and dialogue do a disservice in attempting to communicate or express them. The communication is through the medium itself rather than through any one aspect of the medium.

There are times when we have finished watching a production when all the elements somehow "click." We feel a rush of excitement, and adrenalin seems to course through our veins. We see the faces of people walking out of the theater after seeing an excellent film, and we see a radiance. We leave the theater as high as if there were a narcotic effect, and perhaps it is this effect that brings us back again and again.

Dialogue and narration *have* a role, but it is not a predominant role, merely one of the elements available. Forms, shapes, actions, reaction, the elements of *mise en scène,* the lensing of the image, the angle and movement of the camera, the juxtaposition of images, the pacing and rhythms of the editing, the music all set up a harmonic resonance with the audience and communicate significance on a multitude of levels, creating a thickly textured experience for the viewer. These elements are not merely reflections of the dialogue; they are a language of their own for communicating experience. They can work in unison or can carry their separate and independent communications that can appeal and repel at once.

Coherency

A carefully crafted production shows care and thought in its use and manipulation of the elements of production. Looking at a masterful production such as *Citizen Kane* or *Witness* or *Raging Bull* reveals that nothing is accidental. Every shot and transition is planned.

Creating a production is not the act of discovering something ready-made and ripe for us to use in our production. It is not the act of harvesting. It's the act of conquest. We exercise control. We utilize logic. We create organization and order out of arbitrary randomness. We consider even the smallest detail. We create productions by combining and weaving together the production elements. By our act of choosing and placing them in relation to other production elements, we imbue them with meaning. Even in documentary production, we choose. Ultimately it is the control of all the elements of production that gives our production coherency and raises it above one that has a few good moments.

Once Is Enough

It makes enormous sense that the news isn't syndicated! Once is enough. The birth of an idea is significant as the audience watches it or hears it for the first time. The same gag, the same line, the same gesture, or even the same word repeated in the same paragraph loses its significance. A terrific turn of phrase has only one moment of birth. After that, it is repetitious and soon becomes hackneyed and stale. Like a song after it is a hit, another artist cannot send the same song up the charts again unless their treatment of the tune is unique and makes the song new again.

There is nostalgia value in golden oldies and seeing the great "masterpieces" of film, theater, and opera again. We tend to revere the old masterpieces of film and television. This veneration is pleasant, and we can learn a lot from "the masters." However, at some point, this adoration may encourage us to copy or replicate the experiences they created. We trust in the tried and true and lose touch with our own ideas and feelings. We have no confidence in them.

What *was* or has been "significant" doesn't mean it will always be significant. What we view today as insignificant, perhaps in our snobbishness, may become recognized in the future. Witness now what we call the "golden era" of television. Although enormously popular with the public at the time, shows like *I Love Lucy, Mr. Ed,* and *The Honeymooners* were not taken seriously when they were on prime time. Today it is still in vogue to disparage the programs of the current season. Only 20/20 hindsight will be able to tell how right the public tastes and ratings of today are.

Both wisdom *and* foolishness are associated with age. Works have to speak to our own audiences in our own age. Productions of lasting significance are those things that continue to speak with a fresh voice to contemporary audiences, although the reason may change with time. Significance has a lot to do with relevance to today rather than dealing with the great questions, whatever they may be!

To some extent, much of what we discuss in this book deals with the tried and true: story structure, camera techniques, characterization, editing styles, and so on. All these elements are predicated on experiences media producers have gained in the past. Never avoid experimentation. Without it, we will never create anything new. Clearly the "firsts" are gambles. However, techniques and productions we consider to be significant are usually "firsts." They push the envelope of acceptability. The show *Cop Rock* was a failure. No one wanted musical police drama on television. However, *Twin Peaks* opened the way for *Northern Exposure* and its descendants.

Making Moving Pictures

Ultimately the storyteller has a crucial role to play in society. The stories carry the cultural myths and teach behavior. The lessons of the tribe taught to the young tell of survival, right and wrong, rites of passage, youth and age, romance, and of the metaphysical. As purveyors of the visual media, we should be examining our messages and taking stock of how they are significant to the audience.

Any good subject is a challenge to the film and video producer. Can we rise to the occasion, to the potential of the subject matter? What counts, what is really important usually relates to human experience. Look at the subject and ideas. What is the germ, the kernel of the idea that truly interests us? What won't we give up? Know and trust in their significance. Don't lose sight of it through the long process of production. If we can't see how the subject relates to the human experience, what have we?

Find what is significant. Treat it well.

Notes

1. Artaud, Antonin, *The Theater and Its Double* Trans. Mary Caroline Richards. New York: Grove Press, 1958: 85.

2. This takes place near the end of Chapter 13, Honorable Manhood, in the first program, "Episode One, The Cause—1861."

3. The full title is: *The Persecution and Assassination of Jean-Paul Marat as Performed by the Inmates of the Asylum at Charenton Under the Direction of The Marquis De Sade.*

APPENDIX A

ELECTRICITY

The Formula

The basic formula for electrical current is:

Watts = Volts × Amps

or

$$\text{Amps} = \frac{\text{Watts}}{\text{Volts}}$$

Knowing how to use this formula, especially when lighting on location, can enable us to work efficiently, without suffering embarrassing delays and interruptions caused by blown circuits. It can also save us from causing a catastrophic accident such as starting an electrical fire and destroying property.

Volts

Voltage is a measure of electrical "pressure." In the United States, the electrical outlets into which we plug our clocks, radios, table lamps, and most other electrical devices are on 110-volt circuits. Not all countries are like the United States, and many provide their electricity at 220 volts. We do have 220-volt service in the United States, but it is reserved for clothes dryers, electric ranges, air conditioners, and other large electrical appliances that draw heavy loads of electricity.

So, when we go onto a location—someone's home or apartment or office—and plug our lighting instruments into wall outlets, we are tapping into a 110-volt electrical source. To provide a margin of safety and to accommodate power surges when lamps are turned on, instead of using 110 in the formula, round it down to 100. This also makes calculations easier.

Amps

Amps (amperes) measure a quantity of electricity, and all electrical circuits are rated in amps. If we go to an old-fashioned fuse box or a more modern circuit breaker box, we see that every circuit in a home, apartment, or building can provide a number of amps up to a specific maximum limit.

Sometimes old fuse boxes indicate the amperage of a circuit only by the size of the fuse that is screwed into the receptacle. If the fuse gets blown, people with fuse boxes usually keep spare fuses on hand; otherwise they can be bought at a grocery or hardware store. They are purchased according to the amp size, for example, 15 amp, 20 amp, or 30 amp.[1]

It is very important not to replace a burned-out fuse in a fuse box with a fuse of a higher rating. If a 15-amp fuse blows, do not insert a 20-amp or 30-amp fuse in its place. The wires in a building are rated to carry a certain amperage. Raising the rating on the fuse causes more electricity to go through the wires than they are able to carry, causing the wires to overheat. In older buildings where we still find fuse boxes, the insulation around the hot electrical wire is often covered with cloth and can ignite, setting off a fire within the walls of the building.

More often, we find that the electrical service in a building is provided by a modern circuit breaker box. A circuit breaker box has a row of switches, one for each circuit. When too much electrical load is placed on a circuit, the switch pops off, cutting the power and protecting the wires from overheating. After the overload has been corrected, the circuit breaker switch can just be reset, restoring power to the line.

A circuit breaker switch has its rated amperage embossed on the end of the switch. So, for example, circuit breaker switches serving bedrooms, dining rooms, and hallway ceiling lights often have a "15" embossed at the end of the toggle to indicate that they are rated at 15 amps. Some areas of a house that require more electrical service—kitchens and utility rooms, for example—are more likely to have the numbers 20 or 30 embossed on their circuit breaker switches to indicate their higher amperage rating. It's useful to note that some circuits in these rooms may be dedicated to a single plug for microwaves, refrigerators, dryers, and so on and can be very valuable when we are trying to spread out our amperage usage over several circuits.

Watts

Now we have the information we need to work the formula. Suppose we have a 15-amp circuit serving a bedroom. If we multiply the amps (15) by the volts (rounded down to 100), we get a figure of 1500 watts. That's fine. What's a watt?

Every electrical appliance we buy is rated in watts. Think for a second about buying light bulbs. Our major decision is which wattage to get. Do we buy a soft 40-watt bulb, or a bright 100-watt bulb? How about a switchable 50/100/200-watt bulb for a three-stage table lamp? Or a little 15-watt bulb for the refrigerator?

Take a look at the back of an electric clock, a stereo system, or a coffee-maker. These, too, have wattage ratings. Again, everything we plug in and turn on draws an electrical load measured in watts.

If we have a circuit rated at 15 amps and multiply that by 100 volts to get a figure of 1500 watts, we now know that we can put on any number of electrical devices on that circuit that total no more than 1500 watts of electrical load. Similarly a 20-amp circuit can carry a 2000-watt load, and a 30-amp circuit can carry a 3000-watt load.

Circuits

A circuit is one "branch," or "loop," of electrical wire that feeds from a circuit breaker or fuse box and serves one portion of a house, apartment, or building. Some circuits are reserved for lighting fixtures in the ceilings or on the walls (hallway lights, kitchen lights, entryway lights, and so on). These circuits usually have no outlets. Other circuits serve an area with outlets so we can plug in appliances. Usually there is more than one outlet on one of these circuits. A circuit serving a master bedroom, for example, will have a number of outlets placed around the room for lamps, clocks, radios, and so on. It is important to realize that when we plug lighting instruments into these different outlets, the electric loads from these separate lights are still going onto one circuit.

Occasionally we find circuits distributing electrical power in unexpected ways. For example, we may find a circuit that serves three walls of a living room, then another circuit that serves the outlets on the fourth wall plus all the circuits in the adjacent dining room. How do we find out how the circuits are divided? If the circuit breaker or fuse box is properly labeled, it will show each circuit number, the location each circuit serves (living room, master bedroom west wall, kitchen, and so on), and the amperage rating. Otherwise, we have to take something like a small light and plug it in to an outlet and turn it on. Then we go to the circuit breaker box and switch breakers off and on until the light flashes off and on. Obviously this is easier to do with two people. We can map all the circuits in a building this way, if necessary. Identifying which electrical outlets are on which circuits is a basic step in location scouting, beginning with the obvious—finding the circuit breaker or fuse box in the first place and guaranteeing access to it during a shoot.

Now, suppose we are shooting in a living room served by one 15-amp circuit. It is a night scene and we will have two table lamps turned on as set dressings to motivate the lighting. Each table lamp has a 100-watt bulb in it. Suppose we do our lighting setup with three additional lighting instruments—two 650-watt spots and a 1000-watt softlight (more about these types of lights in a few pages). How do we plug all of these lights in? Here's what we know:

- The 15-amp circuit can carry 1500 watts (15 × 100).
- We cannot combine any 650-watt light with the 1000-watt light—that would total 1650 watts, which would be more than the 1500 watts that the 15-amp circuit can carry.

Here are two connections we know we can make:

- Put the two 650-watts on the 15-amp circuit serving the living room. (That's a total 1300-watt load on a circuit that can handle 1500 watts.)
- Plug in the two 100-watt table lamps on this same circuit for a total 1500-watt load. No problem.

But how are we going to plug in the 1000-watt softlight? We will have to run an *extension cable* and plug it into an outlet in another part of the house where there is another circuit.[2] Even though there still may be unused outlets in the living room, we cannot use them because they are on the same 15-amp circuit.

It takes a minimum of two 15-amp circuits to provide the power we need to do the lighting setup we described. If we had one 30-amp circuit, we could do it on one circuit because the total wattage of our setup is 2500 watts, 500 watts less than the 3000 watts that a 30-amp circuit can handle.

A word about extension cables. We are not talking about thin extension cords designed to carry no more than a few hundred watts for normal household lamps and radios. Extension cords are rated for the amount of current they can carry. In our example, the softlight instrument we plan to plug in carries a big 1000-watt lamp. If we used a thin lamp extension cord, it would quickly overheat and could melt the insulation, posing a very serious electrical and fire hazard. To carry the amount of electricity we need, we must use a heavy-duty extension cable rated to carry at least 1000 watts. Utility cables such as these can be purchased at hardware stores or rented from lighting rental houses.

The Procedure

Lighting on location begins with knowing how to use the basic electrical formula so we can spread our electrical load and avoid overloading circuits. Next, when we scout a location, we locate where the circuit breaker or fuse box is and identify how the circuits distribute power to the various outlets we need to use. Then, when we go on location to shoot, we carry enough heavy electrical cable to gain access to the circuits we will need to do our lighting.

Another way to gain access to large amounts of power on location is by tapping directly into the main lines that feed a building, but this requires special equipment and a certified electrician. It is a dangerous procedure if attempted by someone unqualified, is well beyond the expertise of most of our readers, and is outside the scope of this book.

Notes

1. We should also point out that fuses come with different size screw bases, either a normal screw base or the smaller type S base. If you are replacing a fuse, you need to make sure you purchase one like the one that blew.

2. If the nearest outlet on another circuit is the kitchen or even the dining room wall ad-joining the kitchen, make sure you know what else is drawing current on that circuit. A light may work fine until the compressor in the refrigerator kicks on, overloads the circuit, and blows the fuse or breaker. This invariably occurs in the middle of your best take.

APPENDIX B

MEASURING LIGHT

There are four ways to measure light:

1. Reflected light meter readings, which measure light reflected from a subject towards the camera
2. Reflected light meter readings off of a gray card illuminated by the light falling on the subject in view of the camera
3. Incident light meter readings, which measure the light falling on the subject in view of the camera
4. Foot-candle measurements of the amount of light falling on the subject from various lighting instruments

Reflected Light Reading

Light meters are calibrated to render whatever they are reading as medium gray, that is, half-way between black and white. Consequently, if we take a reflected reading of a subject, we are actually finding out how to register the subject medium gray. This is fine if, indeed, the subject is medium gray but, for example, if we take a reflected light meter reading of a polar bear under direct sunlight, we will be finding out what exposure will render the polar bear medium gray, not white. Our gray polar bear will seem underexposed. Conversely, if we take a reflected light meter reading of a black bear, we will find the exposure that will render the black bear medium gray. We will probably regard the medium gray rendering of the black bear as overexposure.

Reflected Reading from a Gray Card

If we take an object that we know actually to be medium gray such as a photographic gray card and place it in the lighting setup, we can, with a reflected meter reading off the card, find out how to render that gray card as medium gray photographically. This normally would be a correct exposure, hence our second light reading technique in the preceding list.

Incident Light Reading

With incident meter readings, the meter reads off the interior of a photosphere on the lightmeter. The photosphere can be regarded as the meter's own built-in gray card. When the meter reads the light falling on the photosphere, it provides very consistent exposure readings unaffected by variations in the reflectance of objects in the scene. Because one goal in light reading is to provide consistent exposures from shot to shot, this method is usually used as the most reliable in determining proper exposure.

Measuring Contrast by Foot-Candles

Besides proper exposure, we are almost always concerned with determining and adjusting the contrasts in the scene. Contrast ratios (that is, the ratio of key to fill on a subject) can be measured and modified by directly measuring the foot-candles falling on the subject from the key and fill lights. Thus, if we discover that 100 foot-candles are falling on one side of a subject from the key light and 25 foot-candles are falling on the other side of the subject from the fill light, we know our contrast ratio must be 4:1. One complexity we commonly find is that the fill light actually falls both on the fill side *and* on the key side of a subject. In the preceding example, this would mean that the key side of the subject is being illuminated by 100 foot-candles from the key *plus* 25 foot-candles from the fill, making a total of 125 foot-candles. When compared to the 25 foot-candles being delivered by the fill on the shadow side, we find the ratio in this setup is actually 5:1 (125:25).

Measuring Contrast with Reflected Readings

Another, somewhat easier method for measuring contrast ratios is to take reflected light meter readings off the key and fill side of a subject's face. Assuming that the reflectance of a subject's skin is the same on both sides of the face, we can determine the contrast simply by comparing the two readings. For example, if we get a reflected meter reading from the key side of f5.6 and another from the fill side of f4, we then know that there is a one stop difference between the two sides, a contrast ratio of 2:1. This is the ratio regardless of whether the key side is illuminated by the key alone or is illuminated by the key plus the fill. It is important to note that these readings are useful for determining contrast, but not directly for determining proper exposure because reflected readings are calibrated to tell us how to render the subject medium gray.

Lighting ratios (that is, the ratio of light between foreground and background) are normally determined simply by comparing incident light meter readings in different parts of the set.

Latitude

Contrast ratios and lighting ratios are rendered differently by different film stocks and video systems. For example, one film stock will render a 2:1 difference between key and fill as moderately light contrast, whereas another stock will render the same ratio as rather strong contrast. The difference depends on the *latitude* of the filmstock or video system.

Generally speaking, reversal films have little latitude, whereas negative films have much greater latitude. Video has relatively little latitude. Little latitude means that the film stock or video system cannot render large variations in brightness within a scene. For example, if a film is only able to accommodate a range of three f stops (8:1) and a scene has a variation of four f stops (16:1) between the brightest and darkest areas in the frame, the film will not be able to render the entire range. Depending on exposure, some areas that are in shadow but still somewhat illuminated will simply be rendered black, or some areas that are bright but still slightly shaded will simply be rendered white.

Measuring Latitude

The best way to understand how latitude affects the way contrasts within a scene will be rendered is to take a specific example, such as Tri-X Reversal black and white film, and see how it responds in a basic latitude test. Suppose we place a gray card under a light and take a reflected reading from it that indicates an f5.6. We know the reflected light meter reading is calibrated to render a subject medium gray, so we know that an exposure of f5.6 will render our gray card as medium gray in the film. Suppose we also photograph at an exposure at f4, opening up the lens. We would expect this exposure to render the card lighter than medium gray. Suppose we photograph another exposure at f2.8. We know the card will now be rendered lighter still. We can see that, as we continue to open up the lens and make exposures, the medium gray card will become so "overexposed" that it will be rendered white on the film.

Now let's reverse the procedure. Instead of exposing at f5.6, we close down the lens and make an exposure at f8. Naturally we expect this exposure to come out darker than medium gray. Again, we close down and make an exposure at f11. We know the gray card will be rendered darker still. We realize that somewhere along this sequence of "underexposures" the card will be rendered black.

In fact, we do discover that, with Tri-X Reversal black and white film, if we open two stops from the medium gray reading—in this case, from f5.6 to 2.8— the card will be rendered nearly white. We also discover that the card will be rendered nearly black if we close down three stops from the medium gray reading—from f5.6 to f16. Thus we know that the entire range of the film's ability to read variations in light level is five stops—two stops from medium gray to white and three stops from medium gray to black. (See Figure B.1.)

Now, how can we apply this in an actual lighting situation using Tri-X? Suppose we take an incident reading of a scene and determine the proper exposure is f4. Let's take a reflected light reading of the key side of the subject. If it says f5.6, this makes sense because f5.6 in a reflected meter reading tells us how to render the skin medium gray, but we are exposing at f4, not f5.6. This renders the skin one stop brighter than medium gray and about half-way between medium gray to white (remember, with Tri-X, there is a two-stop range from medium gray to white).

Now, let's take a reflected reading of the fill side of the subject. If this reading says f2, we know fairly well how the shadow side will be rendered. The f2 tells us that this is the exposure we would need to render the fill side medium

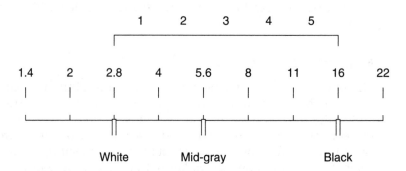

FIGURE B.1   Tri-X B&W Reversal Film
If we take a reflected meter reading off an 18% gray card and get f5.6 and

- We expose at f5.6, we will get medium gray.
- We open up and expose at f2.8, we will get white.
- We close down and expose at f16, we will get black.

Therefore, Tri-X B&W reversal renders the entire range of the gray scale, from white to black, over five stops. Any greater variation in the contrasts of the scene cannot be recorded by the film stock.

gray. We are not exposing at f2, but at f4, two stops closed down. This means that our fill side will be two stops darker than medium gray and we know that, with Tri-X, there is only a three-stop range from medium gray to black. Our fill side will be rendered two-thirds of the way down from medium gray to black— very dark, with only a bit of detail showing. If we want to see more detail in the shadows, we have to add more fill light. If we add enough to get a reflected reading of f2.8, the fill side will still be one stop darker than medium gray. If we add two stops, the fill side will read f4 with a reflected meter reading and, because we are exposing at f4, the shadows will now be rendered medium gray. (See Figure B.2.)

Knowing the latitude of our film stock or video system enables us to light precisely to create the degree of shadow we want in a scene. Shooting latitude tests with film stocks and video systems is standard procedure so that we can set our contrasts in a lighting setup according to the specific latitude of the medium we are using.

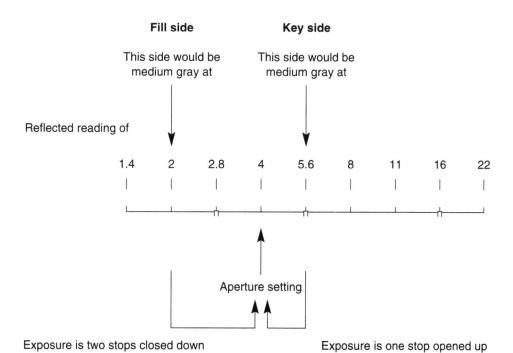

FIGURE B.2   An Aperture Setting of f4, Shooting Tri-X B&W Reversal Film

INDEX